Introduction to the

RESTORATION
IDEAL

by Marshall Leggett

STANDARD PUBLISHING
Cincinnati, Ohio

3175

Unless otherwise noted, all Scripture quotations are from the King James Version.

Scripture quotations marked ASV are from the American Standard Version, ©1901.

Scripture quotations marked NASB are from the New American Standard Bible, ©1960, 1962, 1963, 1971, 1972, 1973, 1975, 1977.

Scripture quotations marked NIV are from the *Holy Bible: New International Version,* ©1973, 1978, 1984 by the International Bible Society. Used by permission of Zondervan Bible Publishers and the International Bible Society.

Sharing the thoughts of his own heart, the author may express views not entirely consistent with those of the publisher.

Library of Congress Cataloging in Publication data:

Leggett, Marshall.
    Introduction to the restoration ideal.

    1. Restoration movement—History. I. Title.
BX7315.L43   1986   286.6'09   86-5844
ISBN 0-87403-067-6

This book is affectionately
dedicated to the two persons
who introduced me to and
taught me to appreciate
the "Restoration Ideal"—

MR. AND MRS. B. FRANK LEGGETT, SR.,
my parents

TABLE OF CONTENTS

PREFACE

Anything worthwhile has a purpose, that which it seeks to accomplish. The purpose for this book has come by way of observation from two perspectives. The first was from a thirty-four-year located preaching ministry; the second, from travel among many congregations as the president of a college. These vantages have shown a need to produce an introduction to the restoration ideal, the ideal that brought into being the Christian church and churches of Christ. That is the purpose of this book.

It is written with the person in the pew in mind. No intention was made for it to be either in-depth or comprehensive. It is an *introduction,* written with the hope that it will whet the reader's appetite to study the subject further. The intention is that it, along with the accompanying workbook, will serve as a guide for small study groups such as prayer meetings, in-home Bible studies, and Sunday-school classes. It is also hoped that it will be put into the hands of new and prospective church members so they can understand some of that which the Lord would have them to become.

The volume is designed to be *historical, doctrinal,* and *practical.* One could never understand the influence of the restoration ideal until he sees it in its historical perspective. The introduction to this dimension is attempted by entering it through the contributions of four early leaders of the restoration movement—Barton Warren Stone, Thomas Campbell, Alexander Campbell, and Walter Scott. A *doctrinal* emphasis follows each biographical chapter: a discussion of the name *Christian* comes after Stone; the Bible after Thomas Campbell; the New Testament church after Alexander Campbell; and several chapters concerning the gospel plan of salvation follow the biographical sketch of Scott. The author felt it important to include a consideration of those groups about which many within the churches wonder: the a cappella churches of Christ, the Disciples of Christ, and the Charismatics.

At some point, the restoration ideal has to enter the *practical* realm in order for it to fulfill its purpose. The heritage and doctrine must be translated into faithful ministry. It is for this reason that the book includes such chapters as "Membership and Ministry," "Evangelism and Discipleship," "Church Polity," "Christian Stewardship," and others.

Underlying all the purposes and designs of the book is the deep conviction on the part of its author that the church is to bring all people into Christ and nurture them to spiritual maturity in Him. This will be accomplished only when all believers unite in this effort. How will this unity come to be? It seems to this writer that the only way to accomplish Christian unity is to return to the church as it was given to the apostles in the New Testament and restore its essential marks. This would enable all believers to be assured that they were participating in the church Christ envisioned and for which He gave His life.

Perhaps every book needs a Scripture text, even as every good sermon must have one. If I were to choose a text for this work, it would be one phrase from Ephesians 4:5—"speaking the truth in love." It seems to me that this is what the movement is all about.

Study the book with an open mind. If this is done, the effort will have been worth it all. May God bless you in His service.

Marshall J. Leggett
Milligan College

8

1

INTRODUCTION TO THE RESTORATION IDEAL

Some time ago, I had the occasion to speak on the same platform with Carl Ketcherside. Brother Ketcherside is a most incisive thinker and precise speaker. "Brethren," he said, "we don't have anything of which to be ashamed. We have something to share."

Many years ago now, the Episcopal rector who ministered across the street from the First Christian Church in Canton, Ohio, crossed that street, visited in the evening service, and responded to the invitation. Upon being immersed by P. H. Welshimer, he said, "Sir, you people have the greatest plea on earth. But you're the stingiest with it."

This is much the way I feel about the movement to restore the New Testament church to its pristine purity. It doesn't have so much of which to be ashamed as it has something to share. It may well have the greatest plea on earth, but it could be that its people are the stingiest with it.

My interest in the restoration movement began in a family deeply dedicated to it. Our home served as a quasi "motel" for itinerant preachers in the area. They would come unannounced, but were always received with a warm welcome. Mother would set the table with her finest dishes and cook a sumptuous meal. Sometimes I would wake up and find a preacher who had arrived after I had gone to sleep.

Conversation among those visitors and my family always concerned the church. They talked about new congregations, camps, conventions, and the Scriptures. Those ministers and my parents believed that God had given a plan for His church in the New Testament, and they wanted their churches to be modeled after it.

From my earliest childhood, I heard such mottoes as, "Where the Scriptures speak, we speak; where the Scriptures are silent, we are silent"; "In essentials, unity; in non-essentials, liberty; and in all things, love"; "Do Bible things in Bible ways, and call Bible things by Bible names." Those preachers back then wanted a "thus saith the Lord" for everything they did in His service.

Time has given me much opportunity to reflect on those conversations around the dinner table of my childhood. I believe now even more deeply that God revealed in the New Testament the plan for His church. It will never be what He wants it to be until the essential marks of that church are restored. The effort to accomplish this is what I have come to call the "restoration ideal." It is my desire to share this ideal every time I have the opportunity. Permit me to share it with you in these next few paragraphs and chapters.

An ideal may be defined as a standard of excellence, an ultimate object of attainment, a model. A young man, for example, may dream of being history's finest surgeon. His mind conceives what that surgeon would be like. That is his ideal, his model. He points his education and dedicates his life to the attainment of that ideal.

The young man may never fully embody all he envisions as the perfect physician. He may fall a little short, as should be expected. However, this should not defeat him. For it is better to set one's goals high, and fall short, than to strive for that which is less worthy. It is the ideal that is good, and the young man will find some virtue just in striving for it.

Surely God must have had in mind the ideal church, one that would perfectly live up to His expectations, whose form and function would be just as He desired. He is a God of order, doing nothing, either in creation or redemption, haphazardly. He envisioned, from the time man sinned, the coming of Christ's "body," the church, which would be the instrument by which He would bring people back to Him. It was this fellowship that Jesus had in mind when He spoke of establishing His church and which Paul foresaw when he said Christ loved the church and gave himself for it. It is the ideal, the standard of excellence, the ultimate object of attainment, the model.

It is also reasonable to assume that God inspired the apostles to lead and shape His church as He would have it. They laid the foundation and built upon it. Jesus promised that the Holy Spirit would guide them into all truth, and they spoke as He gave them utterance. When a congregation made a mistake, they corrected it. They taught, admonished, reproved, rebuked. The church under the apostles' leadership was not perfect, but they continually led toward the ideal. Its essential marks were identified and defined, both in Acts and the epistles, and compose what is referred to as "The New Testament Church." It is the one for which Christ gave himself, which He purchased with His own blood, and which He will bless. It is the ideal.

It may be impossible to restore the church perfectly as Christ conceived it and as the apostles guided it. It might always remain in the realm of the ideal. But virtue will be found in striving for that goal or aiming for it. A congregation may fall short of the mark, just as did the young man who wanted to be the perfect physician. However, if it strives to be the church as Jesus conceived it, it will be strengthened because it can expect His blessing.

Restoration means bringing back to the original condition. It recognizes that the present state is not what it ought to be. For example, a piece of furniture, perhaps a chair, may be found in the attic. It has been abused as it was passed down the family from generation to generation. Its finish is marred, and some of its joints may have loosened. It doesn't look like much, and it fails in its purpose. No one can sit in it because of its weakened condition. Then, continuing our illustration, a connoisseur of antique furniture spots it. He sees in his mind's eye what the chair could be if it were restored to its original state.

He takes it to his workshop and begins to work on it. It is hard because the chair is in bad repair, but he labors patiently, correcting his own mistakes as he makes them. He does not try to change the chair's original form, or alter what it was in the beginning. Instead, he keeps working toward that ideal as he envisions it to have been at its inception. When he finishes, he does not have merely a reproduction, a copy of the original. Instead, he has something much better—the restoration of that which the original builder intended.

Few would deny that the contemporary church fails to fulfill the glorious mission to which God has called it. It is in great disrepair. It finds itself divided into denominations that contradict one another. This is both confusing and wasteful, and has impaired evangelism. The church is not going into all the world to make disciples of every nation with the effectiveness it should have. Cults with false doctrines have arisen in recent time to plaque it. There seems to be a lack of power, even though Christ promised that "the gates of Hell should not prevail against it."

11

The church, like the chair in the attic, seems old, broken, weak, and unable to fulfill its purpose.

Many believe that the church needs more than reformation or repair. That would be superficial. They believe it needs to return to the standard of excellence found in the New Testament church. It contained both the essential marks and the vitality to enable the church to fulfill its mission. A reformation, or repair job, would merely patch up obvious faults, and the church in our age needs more than this. It needs to be restored to what the original Builder intended. The ideal, the standard of excellence, the ultimate object of attainment, the model, can be found in the New Testament church.

It must also be remembered that Jesus said, "I will build my church" (Matthew 16:18). This establishes its ownership. The church belongs to Christ. Paul admonished the elders from Ephesus "to feed the church of God, *which he hath purchased with his own blood"* (Acts 20:28). He went on to explain that the church was to be built upon the foundation of the apostles and prophets (Ephesians 2:20). This means that their teaching shaped the church as Jesus would have it. Then Paul issued a warning. He wrote, "Let every man take heed how he buildeth thereupon" (1 Corinthians 3:10); that is, how he builds on the foundation of Christ and the apostles' teaching. He must be sure that the church of which he is a part is as Christ would have it in life, ordinance, and doctrine. It both belongs to Him and He is its Head.

Those who strive to restore the church to its pristine condition as it was in the New Testament have as their goal what we have called the "restoration ideal."

The restoration ideal is not superficial. It is a serious attempt to accomplish that for which Jesus prayed in John 17. You will remember this important prayer: He said, "Neither pray I for these alone [this refers to the disciples of His day], but for them also which shall believe on me through their word [this includes all Christians, even into the present age]; that they all may be one; as thou, Father, art in me, and I in thee, that they also may be one in us" (John 17:20, 21).

This is Jesus' prayer for Christian unity. He never intended for His church to be divided into denominations with contradictory doctrines. He had already pronounced that "every kingdom divided against itself is brought to desolation; and every city or house divided against itself shall not stand" (Matthew 12:25).

Paul reiterated Jesus' displeasure with division when he chastised the Corinthian church. It had become fragmented into "Paulites, Cephasites, and Apollosites." He asked in dismay, "Is Christ divided?" (1 Corinthians 1:13). He admonished them eloquently, "Now I beseech you, brethren, by the name of our Lord Jesus Christ, that ye all speak the same thing, and that there be no divisions among you; but that ye be perfectly joined together in the same mind and in the same judgment" (1 Corinthians 1:10).

Paul conceived the church to be Christ's body on earth. Jesus, the Head, through the Spirit, would give direction to the members of the body. That is the true hierarchy of the church. There are many members, but they are united and coordinated, and they act in concert with each other. This unity is not realized as long as believers wear divisional names and teach contradictorily. Division among those who love Christ is confusing to unbelievers and wasteful to believers.

However, even Christian unity is not an end in itself, for, like the restoration ideal, it will remain a means to the real end. Notice Jesus' prayer. Why did He want His followers to be one? He said, "that they all may be one . . . *that the world may believe that thou hast sent me*" (John 17:21). The purpose of unity was that the world might believe. It was evangelism. The world will never be won to Christ as long as His people are divided from one another. It will come only when they "all speak the same thing" and are "perfectly joined together in the same mind and in the same judgment."

The New Testament church offers a good example of how God will bless unity. The illustration is found in Acts 6. There arose a murmuring that the Greek-speaking widows were not receiving their fair share of the common fund that had been received to help the destitute within the Jerusalem congregation. This presented the first opportunity for division within the church. The apostles handled the matter delicately and with great skill by having the people choose seven pious men to oversee the fund's disbursement. Each one chosen had a Greek name, which shows the loving, irenic spirit that prevailed. It settled the issue and, once again, closed the ranks.

The seventh verse of Acts 6 describes the result of this renewed unity. It says, "And the word of God increased; and the number of the disciples multiplied in Jerusalem greatly; and a great company of the priests were obedient to the faith." One cannot escape the conclusion that God blessed the church when it possessed the unity He expected it to have.

There is an old story that might even be trite, but it illustrates how the unity of God's people will produce the desired results. It tells of a child who wandered off into the immense wheat fields near his home in Kansas and became lost. Toward evening, his parents began to look for him, but to no avail. Fear seized their hearts, as cold and darkness approached, and there was no sign of him. Neighbors came to help. They each went into different directions to search, often crossing each other's path. However, at dawn the little boy had not been found.

Someone noted the confusion and called a meeting of the searchers. He said, "Let us join hands and form a long line. Then we will sweep the field and not walk in each other's footsteps." Neighbor grasped his neighbor's hand and the long line began to walk across the field. Soon a cry went out that the child had been found. But, alas, according to the story, it was too late. He had died of exposure.

The lesson? If those who believe in Christ would unite as Christians only, as they were in the New Testament church, the lost souls of this world could be saved.

The restoration ideal and Christian unity will remain the means to a greater end—the evangelization of the world. But God's Word makes it crystal clear that the latter one depends upon the former two. Jesus prayed for unity that all men might believe.

A movement began in the early part of the nineteenth century to pursue this restoration ideal. It became known as the "restoration movement" because it embodied that ideal. The movement has been dealt some crippling blows and has suffered deep disappointments, but the ideal has persisted. There have been those, like my parents and the preachers who sat at our table, who remained unwavering. They believed the Lord would bless the church that followed His plan.

A new generation has come on the scene. Those stalwarts who stayed at the "motel" have all gone now. But they left me an ideal in which I believe with all my heart, and one that continues to challenge and motivate me. I have undertaken to write this book. It has not been easy. But I want to pass on to the new generation the opportunity that was given to me. It is my prayer that great numbers of young ministers and Christians will fall in love with the restoration ideal.

14

My feeling about it is much like that of the five soldiers who advanced up Mt. Suribachi on Iwo Jima in World War II. They climbed the mountain with the intent to plant the American flag, the standard of their country, on its summit. In their zeal, they separated themselves from the main body of troops. The commanding officer called up to them saying, "Stop. You move too fast." The answer came back from the soldiers, "We won't stop. We won't slow down. You bring the troops up to the *standard.*" This is the plea to the religious world of those who pursue the restoration ideal: "Let's bring the troops up the the *standard* of the New Testament church."

Or, perhaps, the plea should be seasoned with more humility. Those who are a part of the movement recognize that they have not fully restored the New Testament church. There is much to be learned about what it means to "walk in the Spirit," about Christian stewardship, and about other issues as well. Perhaps they should be more like the old depot manager in the Catskill Mountains of New York state. His depot was run-down, ramshackled, dilapidated. One day, a city slicker happened to stop by. He looked over at the run-down depot and, with syrupy sarcasm, asked, "Is that thing Grand Central Station?"

"Naw," replied the depot manager, "but you're on the right track."

The restoration movement may not have fully restored the New Testament church. But many of us believe with deep sincerity—it's on the *right track.*

What can be more challenging to the young minister than the ideal that calls him to be both Biblical and undenominational in his preaching? Where can a new Christian find more motivation than in the ideal to be a Christian only? Where is there a better model for a church than to seek to restore the essential marks of the church of the New Testament? If you are looking for what will give meaning to your Christian service, let me introduce to you the *restoration ideal.*

2

THE CHURCH FOR WHICH CHRIST GAVE HIMSELF

One cannot have an understanding of the New Testament and not be impressed with the importance of the church to Christ. He loved it, gave himself for it, and purchased it with His own blood. It was to be His body, the agency of salvation whereby people would be reached with His gospel.

Christianity cannot be separated from the church. This is seen in Acts 2:47, which says, "And the Lord added to the church daily such as should be saved." One who accepts Christ is given no option as to membership in His church. He cannot become a Christian and then decide whether he wants to become a church member. To the contrary, he is automatically added to that body of believers, that fellowship that seeks to serve Christ as its Lord. It is his responsibility to become a supportive member of the priesthood of believers in the local congregation of the church.

The importance of the church to Christ may begin to be seen in His gathering of His disciples near Caesarea Philippi in Matthew 16. He wanted very much to know the opinion people held of Him. So He asked the disciples, "Whom do men say that I, the Son of man, am?" They answered that some thought He was John the Baptist, Elijah, Jeremiah, or one of the other prophets. Then He asked who they thought He was, and it was Simon Peter who replied: "Thou art the Christ, the Son of the living God." This statement has become known as the *good confession,* and it obviously delighted Jesus. He said, "Upon this rock I will build my church." The "rock" was the faith revealed in the confession. Christianity became founded upon faith in Jesus as the Christ, which means "the anointed one" or "Messiah," and as the Son of God. The apostle Paul would later say, "For other foundation can no man lay than that is laid, which is Jesus Christ" (1 Corinthians 3:11).

The New Testament goes on to reveal Jesus' love for His church. The apostle Paul made an analogy in Ephesians 5:25, comparing the love of Christ for His church to the love a Christian man should feel for his wife. He said, "Husbands, love your wives, even as Christ also loved the church, and gave himself for it." He admonished the elders from Ephesus to "feed the church of God, which [Christ] hath purchased with his own blood" (Acts 20:28). One cannot fail to appreciate Jesus' affection for the church when the New Testament calls it both His "bride" and His "body."

There can be no doubt about the fact that Jesus loves the church, it belongs to Him, and is essential in His providential plan.

Christ's church began on the Day of Pentecost (see Acts 2) on or about A.D. 30. The Holy Spirit came in power on that day, as Jesus had promised. The gospel was preached for the first time, people responded to it, the means of salvation was defined, and Jesus' church came into being. Three thousand accepted Christ, were baptized, added to the church, and became its charter membership.

The church grew, then multiplied. It became a glorious, powerful church as the inspired apostles guided it according to Christ's plan. This is the reason that in another Scripture the church is said to be "built upon the foundation of the apostles and prophets" (Ephesians 2:20). They brought into being the church as it existed in Jesus' mind. A congregation would get out of line, and they would straighten it out and shape it up according to His plan. The essential marks of the church Jesus loves can be found in the New Testament church as the apostles guided it.

God blessed the church under their leadership. The Scripture says, "The word of God increased; and the number of the disciples multiplied greatly" (Acts 6:7). The apostles . . . and indirectly, the church, carried out the Lord's commission to *go, teach, baptize, and teach all things He had commanded* (Matthew 28:19, 20). It became His *witness* to the uttermost part of the earth. That first generation of Christians saw the gospel spread the length and breadth of the Roman Empire. The church as Christ conceived it became a beautiful fellowship as the disciples loved one another, bore each other's burdens, and shared together. It possessed unity. There was "one body, . . . one Spirit, . . . one hope, . . . one Lord, one faith, one baptism" (Ephesians 4:4, 5). The church within the

18

New Testament reveals the church for which Christ gave himself, and the way He wants it to function.

Then something happened. The church began to lose its purity. The New Testament church penetrated the world, and it seemed that nothing could stop its momentum. No outside force, not even the power of Caesar, could blunt its progress. However, change began to evolve from within. Whereas the New Testament church had penetrated the world, its successors became penetrated by the world. It ceased to be the sect "spoken against" (Acts 28:22) and became in vogue; not just *in* the world, but *of* the world. The church began to leave the plan Jesus had given.

This apostasy gained momentum when Emperor Constantine made Christianity the imperial religion. He came to power at a time when the Roman Empire was coming apart. His mother had been a believer, and this gave him cause to have some affinity for this new, bourgeoning faith. A story says he prepared to go into battle against an enemy named Maxentius, his rival for power. He felt deep anxiety about the outcome. So he decided to inspire his troops. He told them that he had seen in the sky a banner with a cross on it. It said, *"In hoc signo, vinces"* which meant, "In this sign we conquer." He ordered the Greek letters *chi* and *rho,* the first two letters in Christ's name, to be marked on his soldiers' shields. They went into battle under the "sign" and were victorious. It made the emperor a strong supporter of Christianity.

Constantine followed his victory with the "Edict of Toleration," A.D. 313, which made Christianity legal. He proceeded to make it the established faith in 323. However, many believe the emperor's motives to have been more political than religious. There is much evidence that he wanted to use the faith to consolidate his crumbling empire. He exhorted his subjects to embrace Christianity, and many did without faith or conviction. At one time, he promised every "convert" in Rome twenty pieces of gold and a white baptismal robe for becoming a "Christian." Twelve thousand responded.[1] The emperor, although sympathetic toward the church, did not accept baptism himself until just before his death in 337.

More and more, as time passed, Christianity became secularized. One historian says, "The doors of the church were thrown open so wide, that the distinction between Christianity and the world was obliterated."[2] Many Christians protested, but they could not stem the tide of secularism.

Hierarchical structures arose, a departure from Christ's plan. The New Testament church had been composed of autonomous, interdependent congregations. But, as time went on, a monolithic church, with bishops over territories, began to develop, more after the model of the Roman Empire pyramid than after the New Testament model. The Council of Nicea, A.D. 325, gave greater authority to bishops in five cities: Rome, Alexandria, Antioch, Ephesus, and Constantinople. Rome and Constantinople became the great rivals for power within Christendom. The church by this time had gone a long way from simple New Testament Christianity.

Pope Leo I of Rome was the first to claim supreme leadership of all churches (A.D. 440). The Bishop of Constantinople would follow suit and claim the title "Universal Bishop" a hundred years later. However, no man became recognized as "head" of the church until the ninth century when Charles the Great seized great political power.

The Roman church continued to grow even as Constantinople declined. It claimed that Peter was the first bishop of Rome and launched missionary enterprises, often with the sword, into barbarian lands. At the same time, power in the East began to wane because of rivalries among the churches and Muslim invasions.

Papal authority became consolidated when Pope Leo III crowned Charles the Great (Charlemagne) king of the Romans on Christmas day, A.D. 800. This brought into being the Holy Roman Empire, and the church had become married to the world. It contained little resemblance to the New Testament church. New doctrines had developed: papal infallibility, the near-deification of Mary as "Queen of Heaven," prayer to the saints, purgatory, and a system of "salvation by works." The church changed Christian baptism to be the affusion of infants to cleanse them from "original sin." The Lord's Supper was explained by "transubstantiation," where the loaf and fruit of the vine became the very body and blood of Christ. The Roman church demanded conformity, and any deviation amounted to political treason. The New Testament church had been the persecuted; now the medieval church, married to the state, became the persecutor.

Abuses of power became evident. Pope Leo X embarked on an ambitious program to complete St. Peter's Cathedral in Rome, which required large sums of money. He instituted a system called "indulgences" to raise the funds. Indulgences certified that earthly and purgatorial penalties for sin had been remitted. Many wrongly interpreted this as providing the forgiveness of sins before they were committed—an advance payment for pardon. One can imagine what that kind of misunderstanding would do to morality.

Church history reveals that God maintained a faithful "remnant" during this dark age who bore witness to simple New Testament Christianity. However, revolt against papal authority came from within the Roman church.

Martin Luther was a German monk of peasant origin. He became a respected scholar at the University of Wittenberg. His studies led him to the conclusion that the Bible should be in the hands of the people and that the church needed to be reformed. A papal secretary, John Tetzel, came to Germany selling indulgences. He is reported to have promised, "As soon as your cash jingles in the money-box, so quickly will your soul jump into heaven!"

Luther reacted in a forceful way. He wrote his famous "Ninety-five Theses" and nailed them on the door of the Wittenberg Cathedral on October 31, 1517. They issued a challenge to debate the subject of indulgences and called into question the ability of the pope, or any other priest, to grant forgiveness of sins without penitence. He also questioned the pope's wisdom in the extravagance of St. Peter's Cathedral.

The theses led to Luther's trial before the Diet of Worms in 1521. It was before this tribunal that he denied papal infallibility and was told to recant or be excommunicated. He replied, "Here I stand. I can do no other. God help me. Amen!" This statement launched the Protestant reformation. It would emphasize (1) faith, as opposed to a church-defined system of vicarious works, (2) the priesthood of all believers, and (3) the right to private interpretation of Scripture.

Many followed Luther's break from Rome, and they became known as Protestants. Notable leaders among them were John Calvin, John Knox, and Zwingli. The reformation spread across Europe like wildfire. But the leaders of the Protestants could not agree among themselves and the movement fragmented. National churches developed, a system of denominationalism arose, and man-made creeds separated groups.

Sectarianism became the embarrassment of the reformation. There can be no doubt but that the situation displeased Christ.

21

His body was divided, its members warring against one another. He had prayed for unity in His high priestly prayer when he said, "Holy Father, keep through thine own name those whom thou hast given me, that they maybe one, as we are" (John 17:11). The New Testament church sought to "keep the unity of the Spirit in the bond of peace" (Ephesians 4:3). The congregation in Corinth became divided, and Paul wrote to them saying, "Now I beseech you, brethren, by the name of our Lord Jesus Christ, that ye all speak the same thing, and that there be no divisions among you; but that ye be perfectly joined together in the same mind and in the same judgment" (1 Corinthians 1:10). Denominational sectarianism has been called "the scandal of Christianity"!

The twentieth century saw the ecumenical movement come into existence. It was an attempt to bring about union among the various denominations and has done some good. It has created what I call a unity of irenic spirits. This is not the doctrinal unity for which Jesus prayed and Paul pleaded. It has not led all believers to be of the same mind and to speak the same thing. But it has created an atmosphere in which denominations have been able to dialogue. Many barriers to communication have been broken down, and this is healthy. Isolationism can never produce unity. The ecumenical movement has enabled communions that recognize doctrinal differences to respect the integrity of others and rejoice in their good works.

However, many leaders within this movement have sought to create Christian unity by means of organic merger of denominations. The desire is to see a super Protestant church brought into existence by bringing all the existing ones into a whole. Charles Clayton Morrison expressed this in his book, *The Unfinished Reformation*. He wrote:

> In a word, the whole aspiration and purpose of this world-wide movement among Christians is to bring the Church of Christ into an empirical existence so that we can see it, can lay hold of it, and so it can lay hold of us and draw us into itself. The goal of the ecumenical movement cannot be envisaged in any other terms short of the actual embodiment of the now unembodied Church of Christ.[3]

These leaders do not conceive this super church to be a fellowship of autonomous, interdependent congregations. John Knox, a leader of the ecumenical movement, said he could see no real union among denominations without comprehensive organization with an oligarchical head. He said there was no way it could exist without the historic episcopacy.[4] It was to be a super denomination of Protestants replete with a hierarchy.

The ecumenical movement reached its climax in "The Consultation on Church Union" (COCU), which was brought into being by a sermon delivered by Eugene Carson Blake, the United Presbyterian Stated Clerk, in Grace Episcopal Church, San Francisco, on December 4, 1960. This was an historic date. The message proposed unity talks among the United Presbyterian Church, Protestant Episcopal Church, Methodist Church, and the United Church of Christ. "The Blake Proposal," as it became known, called for a union that would be truly catholic, truly reformed, and truly evangelical. In 1962, two other communions, The United Brethren Church and the Disciples of Christ, joined the discussion.

The COCU failed for several reasons. Many objected to the concept of a super Protestant denomination. Bishop Gerald Kennedy of the Methodist Church said:

> Now for one thing we need to consider the problem of deciding what the goal of the ecumenical movement is. Are we committed to one organic union of all Protestantism, or are we aiming at something more limited? . . . I have always said that if I could cast one vote which would make all Christians Methodists I would not cast the vote. Neither the world nor the Methodist Church could stand it. And I have not seen anything in history or in society or in human nature to make it a desirable goal. I have no doubt that churches and denominations can be too small to function effectively in the world. I am just as sure that they can be too big, and I suspect that twenty million members is too big.[5]

Others questioned the idea on doctrinal grounds. The modus operandi of the COCU was to seek institutional union by compromise. It asked, "How much can each denomination give up in order to merge?" Some Protestant leaders saw this as a danger to the faith, particularly with the effort being led by those considered to be most liberal. Clarence E. Macartney, highly respected Presbyterian minister, wrote:

> The mere fact that two denominations or two churches are merged and become one does not necessarily mean that the kingdom of

23

Christ has been strengthened or extended. . . . The great peril in some of the movements today looking toward consolidation of Protestant bodies is the danger of effecting union by ignoring certain fundamental convictions.[6]

Still others joined in with their misgivings. *Time* magazine carried an article on "Ecumenism." It quoted "a prominent Episcopal layman" as saying, "We're in favor of cooperation on all kinds of social levels, but we are not in favor of a monolithic structure."[7]

The Consultation on Christian Union failed, and with its demise came deep disillusionment concerning the attempt to produce church union by merger and compromise. The ecumenical movement has left a climate in which denominations can talk to each other. That is good. But those who seek Christian unity can no longer look with confidence toward that movement to produce it.

However, Christ's prayer remains "that they may be one." The desirability of Christian unity cannot be denied. Christians must seek it to be in the will of their Lord. To whom then can they turn? What can guide them toward that end?

A viable alternative remains.

It is found in a movement that began in the early part of the nineteenth century to seek Christian unity on a Biblical basis. It is the movement of which those ministers who gathered at the "motel" of my boyhood home had become a part. It is called the restoration movement because it embodies the ideal to restore the essential marks of the New Testament church to its pristine purity. It is founded on the premise that the true basis for unity is to return to the church as it was given to, and guided by, the apostles. Its adherents seek to be Christians and to follow the Bible only as they strive to be both Biblical and undenominational in faith, ordinance, and life.

This restoration movement can be introduced in several ways. But perhaps the best is through the central ideas of four of its early leaders. These early leaders of the movement, and the central ideas for which they stood, are

Barton Warren Stone and the Ancient Name,
Thomas Campbell and the Ancient Book,
Alexander Campbell and the Ancient Order, and
Walter Scott and the Ancient Gospel.

NOTES

[1]Albert Newman, *A Manual of Church History* (Philadelphia: American Baptist Publication Society, 1899) Vol. I, p. 307

[2]*Ibid.* p. 313.

[3]J. Marcellus Kik, *Ecumenism and the Evangelical* (Grand Rapids: Baker Book House, 1958), p. 3.

[4]John Knox, *The Early Church and the Coming Great Church* (New York: Abingdon Press, 1955), p. 142

[5]Gerald Kennedy, "How Big Is Too Big?" *Presbyterian Life,* Robert J. Cadigan, ed. (Dayton: Presbyterian Life, Inc., March 18, 1964).

[6]Clarence E. Macartney, *Christianity Today* (Washington: Christianity Today, Inc., Vol. IX, No. 16, June 18, 1964).

[7]Roy Calendar, ed., *Time* (New York: Time, Inc., April 23, 1965), p. 142.

3

BARTON WARREN STONE AND THE ANCIENT NAME

Barton Warren Stone was the only American-born of the four early leaders of the restoration movement. He had deep roots in this country, being a fifth-generation American. He was born on Christmas Eve, 1772, to the Anglican family of John Stone in Port Tobacco, Maryland. His father died in 1775 and his mother took her seven sons and one daughter to Pittsylvania County in the Blue Ridge Mountains of Virginia. He would later call this area, "The Land of Eden."

Stone enrolled in the David Caldwell Academy, near Greensboro, North Carolina, in 1790. He matriculated there to pursue a career in law, but this would change.

Caldwell welcomed the revivalistic evangelists of that day to his school and exposed his students to their preaching. Most were Presbyterians. Among them was David McGready, with whom Stone would later work. McGready was a popular evangelist, but the "hell-fire and brimstone" style of preaching by him and the others only made the young student miserable. He wrote, "For one year I was tossed on the waves of uncertainty—laboring, praying, and striving to obtain saving faith—sometimes desponding, and almost despairing of ever getting it."

It was left to a sermon by William Hodge, a young alumnus of the academy, to move Stone to surrender his life to Christ. He used as his text, "God is love." Stone told about it: "With much animation and with many tears he spoke of the love of God for sinners, and of what that love had done for sinners. My heart warmed with love for that lovely character whom he described, and momentary hope and joy would rise in my troubled breast."

Following the service, Stone took his Bible and entered into the woods alone to pray. He said in his autobiography, "I . . . sunk at his feet a willing subject. I loved him—I adored him—I praised

27

him aloud in the silent night, in the echoing grove around. I confessed to the Lord my sin in disbelieving his word so long and in following so long the devices of men. I now saw that a poor sinner was as much authorized to believe in Jesus at first, as at last—that *NOW* was the accepted time, and the day of salvation."

This experience caused Stone to lose interest in law and propelled him toward the ministry. He taught a year at Succoth Academy, a Methodist school in Georgia, while waiting for his license to preach in the Presbyterian Church. He received his license on April 6, 1796, and began a preaching tour of North Carolina and Virginia, but he met with little success. He migrated to Kentucky and became the regular supply minister of two congregations, Cane Ridge and Concord, about twenty-five miles from Lexington. Eighty persons were added to their membership rolls during the first few months of his ministry with them. This proved to be a great source of encouragement. However, permanent ministries there demanded approval of the Transylvania Presbytery. This concerned Stone because he had misgivings about several articles in the Westminster Confession of Faith of the Presbyterian Church.

However, his approval came without protest. He was asked in a public ceremony, "Do you receive and adopt the Confession of Faith, as containing the system of doctrine taught in the Bible?" He replied, "I do, as far as I see it consistent with the Word of God." This satisfied the examiners, and he was licensed to preach as a Presbyterian. But the answer hinted of Stone's distaste for man-made creeds.

Kentucky lay on the American frontier at that time. Settlers had poured into the region much more rapidly than the churches could keep up with them. The census of 1800 showed that less than one out of twenty persons in Kentucky was a member of any church. This produced a spiritual and moral vacuum. Rushing in to fill that vacuum were what became known as "camp meetings." People would travel many miles in primitive modes of transportation, camp out—sometimes for days—and listen to preaching. These meetings produced what is called the "Great Western Revival."

Stone visited a camp meeting in Logan County, Kentucky, in the spring of 1801. It was led by the same James McGready whom he had met at the David Caldwell Academy. The emotionalism of the meeting mystified Stone, but he became convinced of the genuineness of the meeting's results. The revival spread through Kentucky and Tennessee.

The largest camp meeting on record was destined to be held in early August, 1801, on the grounds of the Cane Ridge Church where Barton Stone ministered. Some historians estimate that 20,000 persons participated in it. The meeting was most emotional. They swooned; they stayed in trances by the hour; history says some of them "yapped" like dogs. Another characteristic of the phenomenon was its interdenominational nature. A Baptist would preach from a rock, a Methodist from a stump, and a Presbyterian from the back of a wagon. But it seemed to the people that God blessed each man's preaching equally.

It should be said in fairness that although Stone rejoiced in the results of the meeting, he maintained great doubt about its emotional content. It was not his preferred method of evangelism. Also, the fervency of the emotionalism diminished on the frontier as people turned to the Word for spiritual guidance.

The Cane Ridge meeting implied that "Christ died for all." This ran contrary to the Calvinistic doctrine of "the elect" held by orthodox Presbyterians and expressed in the Westminster Confession. That creed teaches that God has to act upon the heart of the sinner personally and directly before he can be saved. Those upon whom He chooses to work His "work of irresistible grace" become "the elect." All others remain lost. This is known as the doctrines of election and limited atonement. However, the invitation was thrown open to *all* at Cane Ridge, and this led to conflict.

The Presbyterian Synod brought charges against two revival men, Richard McNemar and John Thompson, on this point. It accused them of deviating from the Westminster Confession. Barton W. Stone came to their defense, along with two other ministers, Robert Marshall and John Dunlavy. They composed a written protest in which they separated themselves from the Synod of Kentucky. They said, "We claim the privilege of interpreting the Scripture by itself." This was their attempt to separate themselves from all human creeds and confessions of faith.

However, the dissidents were reluctant to break all ties with the Presbyterian Church. Instead, they organized an independent association that became known as the Springfield Presbytery. Others began to join it, among them David Purviance, a ministerial candidate whose license to preach had been postponed because he was held doctrinally suspect by orthodox Presbyterians.

Thirteen congregations composed the Springfield Presbytery, which would last but five months. The reformers themselves would dissolve it with a document known as *The Last Will and Testament of the Springfield Presbytery*. It would do much to shape the restoration movement. Stone is given most credit for its composition, although others may have contributed to it. It is dated June 28, 1804, and signed by Marshall, Dunlavy, McNemar, Purviance, Stone, and Thompson. The document's *Imprimis* says, "We will, that this body die, be dissolved, and sink into union with the Body of Christ at large: for there is but one body, and one Spirit, even as we are called in one hope of our calling."

Several items in the *Will* express the desire of the document's signers to be both Biblical and undenominational:

"*Item.* We will, that the people henceforth take the Bible as the only sure guide to heaven. . . ."

"*Item.* We will, that each particular church, as a body, actuated by the same spirit, choose her own preacher, and support him by a freewill offering. . . ."

"*Item.* We will, that our name of distinction, with its Reverend title, be forgotten. . . ."

The group voted to become known as "Christians" only and initiated a plea to unite all believers around that name. It is thought that every Presbyterian Church in southwestern Ohio except two would later become Christian because of this plea. By the end of 1804, just six months after the movement began, there were eight Christian churches in Kentucky and seven in Ohio. In Kentucky alone, the numbers grew to between seventy-two and eight-two by 1827. Its membership there was estimated at 15,000 in 1830.

However, there were defections. McNemar and Dunlavy converted to Shakerism, a celibate and communal cult originated by "Mother Ann Lee" of New York. Stone called this group "worldly-minded, cunning deceivers." Marshall and Thompson rejoined the Presbyterian Church. This left just Purviance and Stone of the six who had signed *The Last Will and Testament*. The latter would become the unquestioned leader of this movement to be "Christians" only. A contemporary would write of him, "Elder Barton W. Stone . . . to whose firmness we may attribute the formation of the Christian Church in the West."[1] Another called him its "guardian" and "only learned champion."

The movement to be "Christians only" spread even as Stone's

popularity and influence increased. Everywhere he went great audiences greeted him. His correspondence was greater than he could handle. This frustration led him to begin to publish *The Christian Messenger,* a journal that gained wide exposure.

Stone was determined to follow the Bible only as a Christian only. This was the foundation upon which he began to build a theology. He rejected total depravity, the Calvinistic doctrine that portrayed a person as helplessly lost until God chose to act upon him with His irresistible grace. Stone felt the Bible taught that man is neither good nor bad in infancy, but human nature possesses a predisposition to sin. He believed that man can and must act in his own behalf to gain salvation. He must hear the gospel, accept the gospel, and be obedient to the terms of the gospel. Stone concluded that Christian baptism was the immersion of a believer "for the remission of sins." He, himself, was immersed and preached that immersion was "ordained by the King."

Alexander Campbell, one of the other early leaders of the movement, visited Kentucky in 1824. He met Stone and a warm friendship developed. Each realized they pursued the same ideal: to be Christians only by following the Bible only. Campbell and his father, Thomas, also had a following, most of which lay north and east of Kentucky. The two groups would later join hands in a formal service in Lexington, Kentucky, over the New Year's holiday of 1832. This was a most dramatic meeting, held at the Christian Church on Hill Street in Lexington. "Raccoon" John Smith, a colorful preacher, spoke first, representing the "Reformers," as those who had been led by Thomas and Alexander Campbell were called. He said:

> God has but one people on earth. He has given them but one Book, and therein exhorts and commands them to be one family. A union, such as we plead for—a union of God's people on that one Book—must, then, be practicable.
>
> Every Christian desires to stand complete in the will of God. The prayer of the Saviour, and the whole tenor of His teaching, clearly show that it is God's will that His children should be united.
>
> Let us, then, my brethren be no longer Campbellites, or Stonites, New Lights, or Old Lights, nor any other kind of *lights,* but let us all come to the Bible, and to the Bible alone, as the only book in the world that can give us the Light we need."[2]

Stone saw in the words of Smith the opportunity for a dream to come true. He climaxed the meeting when he arose and said, "I have not one objection to the ground laid down by him (Smith) as the true scriptural basis of union among the people of God; and I am willing to give him, now and here, my hand."

Stone extended his hand toward Smith, who warmly received it. Others joined in this expression of brotherhood, a song arose, and the meeting was concluded when all participated together in the Lord's Supper. Some believe this meeting launched the restoration movement. Alexander Campbell, who was unable to attend would later say of Stone's constituency, with whom his own had joined: "With all such, I, as an individual, am united. I would rejoice in seeing all immersed disciples of the Son of God called 'Christians.'"[3]

The movement spread. Whole congregations would leave their denominational affiliations to become "Christians only." Stone himself would leave Kentucky and carry the message of New Testament Christianity westward. He moved first to Ohio and served in the state legislature there. Then he moved into Illinois and Missouri. He died in Hannibal, Missouri, November 9, 1844, at the home of Amanda Bowen, one of his eleven children, and was buried near Jacksonville, Illinois. Later, his remains were taken back to Cane Ridge. The marker over his burial place read: "The Church of Christ at Cane Ridge and other generous friends in Kentucky, have caused this monument to be erected as a tribute of affection and gratitude to BARTON W. STONE, Minister of the gospel of Christ and the distinguished reformer of the 19. Century."

Some believe Stone's efforts became overshadowed by those of Alexander Campbell. But Stone possessed "a firmness, a sweetness, and a saintliness in character" which did much to shape the movement to restore Christianity to its original purity.[4] A.G. Comings wrote at His death, "I regarded him as the greatest of the Christian reformers of this century, because he was *great* as a *Christian*.[5] Another called him, "the moderator of the whole reformation."[6]

History credits Stone with being the one who restored the ancient name "Christian" to its proper place. He believed it was the name God had given to His people and the one around which they could unite. He pleaded for all believers to become Christians only.

NOTES

[1]Garrison and DeGroot, *The Disciples of Christ: A History* (St. Louis: Christian Board of Publication, 1948), p. 122.

[2]John Augustus Williams, *Life of Elder John Smith* (Cincinnati: Standard Publishing, no date), p. 95.

[3]James DeForest Murch, *Christians Only* (Cincinnati: Standard Publishing, 1962), p. 95.

[4]Garrison and DeGroot, *op. cit.,* p. 123.

[5]Charles C. Ware, *Barton Warren Stone* (St. Louis: Bethany Press, 1932), p. 332.

[6]Ibid.

4

THE NAME "CHRISTIAN"

What are the most beautiful words in the English language to you? If you are like most people, they would be your name. Your name distinguishes you. It contains and carries all that you are; the sum total of your personality.

Salespersons are taught to learn people's names. Why? It establishes rapport and identifies them with their customers, because they love to hear their names. Industry encourages its executives to do likewise for the same reasons. One's name also represents the sum total of his wealth. A person can sign it to a check and withdraw all his funds from the bank. William Shakespeare asked, "What is in a name?" The answer has to be, "Much! Very much!" One's name distinguishes him from others; it contains all that he is and represents the sum total of his personality.

God takes names seriously. His own name was so holy that He gave it to the Hebrews in a cryptic that could not even be pronounced. It was all consonants, no vowels. Later on it evolved into "Yahweh," and then "Jehovah." The Jews in Jesus' day knew what each of those words meant when they used it. It was the name of their God, who had created the universe and to whom as a people they belonged. God's name distinguished Him from all others and represented the sum total of His personality.

God would often change the names of those whom He called to special service, because names were so important to Him. The new name would have deeper meaning and was given to teach a lesson. Joshua is a good example. The Bible introduces this soldier-statesman as Hoshea, which means "salvation." But, upon assuming leadership of the children of Israel, God changed it to Joshua. This means "Jehovah is salvation." He changed Abram (exalted father) to Abraham (father of a multitude); Jacob (deceiver or supplanter) to Israel (prince of God); Simon (hearing) to

Peter (rock,) and Saul (desired) to Paul (small). God gave His servants special names because names were important to Him.

God would not leave the name of His only begotten Son to Mary and Joseph's choosing. He appeared to Joseph in a dream and said, "... thou shalt call his name Jesus: for he shall save his people from their sins" (Matthew 1:21). Jesus is the Greek form of the name Joshua, "Jehovah is salvation." His name would carry and contain all that Christ is and represent the sum total of His person.

God took seriously the name Jesus' followers would wear. Isaiah prophesied that He would give them "another name" (Isaiah 65:15). It would be a "new name, which the mouth of the Lord shall name" (Isaiah 62:2). He said it would be a "name better than of sons and of daughters ... an everlasting name, that shall not be cut off" (Isaiah 56:5). James, in the Council at Jerusalem in Acts 15, referred to a prediction by the prophet Amos. He had prophesied that, out of the heathen, God would have a people called by His name. (See Amos 9:12 and Acts 15:16-18.) God, who arranges everything in advance, ordained that His chosen of the New Covenant would have a name to distinguish them, to contain and carry all that they were to become. What would that new name be?

The New Testament calls Jesus' followers by several meaningful appellations. They were most often called *brethren*. Over two hundred times, the New Testament refers to them as such. This name denotes relationship. Those who accept Christ become members of the family of God, heirs and joint-heirs with Christ, brothers and sisters. However, there is nothing new about this name. It expresses a beautiful relationship, but it is as old as Cain and Abel. Also, God said the new name would be better than one that just conveys familial relationships.

Those who followed Jesus became known as His *disciples*. This name is most meaningful because it represents learners and followers of Him. At least seventy-three times, the New Testament refers to Jesus' followers as disciples. The term is fraught with meaning. Jesus said the church was to go into all the world and "make *disciples* (disciplined followers and learners) of all the nations" (Matthew 28:19, ASV). However, the name disciple is not new. Socrates had disciples. Nor is it unique to the followers of Jesus. Mahatma Ghandi, and even Karl Marx, had disciplined learners of their doctrines.

Jesus' followers were referred to as *believers* and *saints*. They believed His Word and trusted His promises, and this made them *believers*. They were also set apart for His work, sanctified, which made them *saints*. Every church member was a saint. They were called by other names: *the chosen, the elect, Nazarenes, a people, the way,* and others.

But none of the names for Jesus' followers in the New Testament fulfills Isaiah's prophecy—except one—the name CHRISTIAN. It is a "new name, better than of sons and of daughters, an everlasting name that shall not be cut off" (Isaiah 62:2; 56:5).

Acts 11:26 says, "The disciples were called Christians first in Antioch." Some Bible students contend that this name carried no honor in its beginning, or that it was just a nickname, spoken in derision. But I find nothing in the text to indicate that contention. It seems to imply the opposite. The Greek word used there for "called" is "chrematizo." H. A. Ironside, noted Bible scholar, says of it:

> The Greek word translated "called" really means, "oracularly called," or "divinely called." The evidence bears that out. The disciples were first divinely called Christians at Antioch. This was God's name for them. Now that the work of evangelizing the world had really begun, God said, as it were, "I am going to give you the name by which I want My people known"—and He gave them the name "Christians."[1]

Philip Doddridge translated Acts 11:26, "And the disciples were by divine appointment first named Christians at Antioch." Stone concurred with this interpretation and thought it established forever the providential name for God's people. His biographer said it was one of the few places where he was dogmatic.

Thomas Campbell, another early leader of the restoration movement whom we will meet in the next chapter, agreed with Stone. He favored the use of the name Christian for two reasons: (1) "Christian signified a radical relationship to Christ which comprehends and covers all other appellatives describing the relationship between Christ and his followers," and (2) "its use was consistent with the purpose to restore pure, primitive, apostolic Christianity in letter and spirit."[2]

The apostle Peter added a new dimension to the name Christian not found in Acts. He looked upon it as a badge of honor and an

*CAMPBELL THOUGHT SO.

37

opportunity for praise. He wrote in 1 Peter 4:16, "If any man suffer as a Christian, let him not be ashamed; but let him glorify God in this name" (ASV). It glorifies God to wear the name Christian.

The post-apostolic fathers, Tacitus, Justin Martyr, Tertullian, and others, used this new name as the most distinguished appellation of the followers of Christ. Even the apostate, Emperor Julian, paid it the ultimate compliment. He outlawed the name Christian because the followers of Christ gloried in it. He ordered that they call themselves instead Galileans.

The word etymologically comes from a combination of Greek and Latin, Christianos. It means, "Christ-people, those who belong to Him." The ancient pagans in Antioch and other places would look upon the lives of those early disciples and say, "Those people belong to Christ!" Would that not be a compliment for those who live today? They call us Christians because they know we belong to Christ!

Christian is an appropriate name for the followers of Jesus because of two relationships. First, 2 Corinthians 11:2 and Revelation 21:2 refer to the church as "the bride of Christ." It honors the Bridegroom for the bride to wear His name. Secondly, the New Testament calls the church God's "family" (Ephesians 3:14, 15). He is the Father; Jesus, the elder brother; and church members are brothers and sisters in Him. Christian becomes the family name of those who compose God's church.

The name Christian is both *inclusive* and *exclusive*. It includes all those who believe in Christ and are obedient to His will. Any member of every denomination is proud to wear the name Christian if he loves Jesus. It is the one name around which Christian unity can be wrought. Barton Warren Stone saw this. He said in his *Discourse on Christian Union,* "To be united we must receive the one name given by divine appointment, which is the name Christian. Let all others be castaway and forgotten." (The last sentence refers to denominational distinctions.) He pleaded for all who love Jesus to be Christians only.

Yet, at the same time, the name is *exclusive*. It excludes all those who will not accept Christ and follow in His way. The apostle Paul preached to King Agrippa in Acts 26. The king responded to it by saying, "Almost thou persuadest me to be a Christian" (Acts 26:28). The "almost" excluded him from all the promises of Christ. "For there is none other name under heaven given among men, whereby we must be saved" (Acts 4:12). One who will not become a Christian cannot find salvation in *any other name*.

Christian is the most honorable name a person can wear. It contains and carries all that it means to belong to Christ. It represents those who have become children of God, with all the rights, privileges, and honors appertaining thereto. It is the "new name, out of the mouth of the Lord, a name better than of sons and of daughters ... an everlasting name, that shall not be cut off," of which the prophet Isaiah spoke (Isaiah 62:2; 56:5).

The apostle Peter says, "... glorify God in this name"— CHRISTIAN! Those who pursue the restoration ideal seek to do just that.

NOTES

[1]H. A. Ironside, *Lectures on the Book of Acts* (New Jersey: Loizeaux Brothers, 1943), p. 283.

[2]*Christian Baptist,* Vol. II, p. 12.

5

THOMAS CAMPBELL, MAN OF THE BOOK

The name Thomas Campbell brings to mind a gracious, refined gentleman of deep piety, but staunch in his convictions concerning the Bible. He carried a heavy burden on his heart for the unity of God's people. His biographer credits him with being the creator of the movement to bring them together on the basis of God's Word.[1] He was the first to say, "Where the Scriptures speak, we speak; where the Scriptures are silent, we are silent."

Thomas Campbell was born on February 1, 1763, in County Down, Ireland. He came from Scottish heritage. His father, Archibald, traced his ancestry to the Campbell clan, in western Scotland. His forefathers seem to have emigrated to Ireland as a part of England's program to colonize crown lands on the northern end of that island. Archibald had been reared Roman Catholic but converted to the Church of England when he married. He remained a strict Anglican until his death at eighty-eight. He and his wife had four sons, Thomas, James, Archibald, and Enos; they also had four daughters, all named Mary, each of whom died in infancy, and the subsequent one was give that name.

Young Thomas possessed a deeply religious nature. But the Anglican Church of his father failed to satisfy his pious temperament. He became attracted to the more rigid and devout Presbyterians. He was deeply concerned, like Barton Stone, about his salvation and he, too, sought assurance that he was among God's elect. It was slow in coming. He agonized over his condition until he had an experience that Robert Richardson describes in the *Memoirs of Alexander Campbell:*

> He was one day walking alone in the fields, when, in the midst of his prayerful anxieties and longings, he felt a divine peace suddenly diffuse itself throughout his soul, and the love of God seemed to be

shed abroad in his heart as he had never realized it. His doubts, anxieties and fears were at once dissipated, and as if by enchantment. He was enabled to see and to trust in the merits of a crucified Christ, and to enjoy a divine sense of reconciliation, that filled him with rapture, and seemed to determine his destiny for ever. From this moment he recognized himself as consecrated to God, and thought only how he might best appropriate his time and his abilities to his service.[2]

This experience, similar to that of Barton W. Stone, likewise led Campbell toward the ministry. His father objected because he was Anglican. It may have been because of this that Thomas taught school, first at Connaught in southern Ireland, and later at Sheepbridge near his home. John Kinley, a wealthy man there, took a liking to the young teacher and offered to finance his education for the ministry. At the appropriate time, Campbell set sail for Scotland, with the reluctant blessing of his father. He entered the University of Glasgow in 1783, just before his twentieth birthday.

He graduated from the university in 1786, the theological school in 1791, and returned to Ireland to minister. He applied for license to preach in the Anti-Burgher Old Light Seceder Presbyterian Church. It had denominated itself from all other Presbyterians over who had the right to appoint ministers to local congregations and ramifications emanating from that issue. It was a deplorable fragmentation that Campbell found most distasteful. But he nevertheless began his ministry within this body as he preached and taught school. His kindly and generous spirit made him popular among the churches.

Campbell met and married Jane Corneigle, the daughter of a French Huguenot who had settled in Ireland. They would rear seven children: Alexander, Dorothea, Nancy, Jane, Archibald, Thomas, and Alicia. Their home life is described as deeply religious, with daily Scripture reading and prayer.

Campbell's irenic spirit revealed itself early. He felt the divided state of his church to be deplorable. He called it "an evil of no small magnitude ... hurtful and embarrassing."[3] He hosted a "Committee on Consultation" in October, 1804, at Rich Hill where he ministered. Its purpose was to bring together the Burghers and Anti-Burghers in Ireland. The attempt failed, but it helped prepare the young minister for an even greater mission.

Shortly after the failure of the meeting, Campbell's physician prescribed a sea voyage for his health. His son, Alexander, had already expressed a desire to settle in America when he became of age. It was decided within the family that the father would sail to the new world. The voyage would be beneficial to his health, and, if all went well there, his wife and children would follow. Campbell left Ireland on April 8, 1807, and stepped ashore in Philadelphia on May 13 of that year. He received his license to preach from the Anti-Burgher Synod of North America and was assigned to the Presbytery of Chartiers, where he would minister near Washington, Pennsylvania.

On the American frontier, Campbell came to eschew the denominational structure of Christendom with deeper intensity. His feeling manifested itself in a Communion service. He had been invited to visit some isolated Anti-Burghers near Cannamaugh, Pennsylvania. He presided over the observance of the Lord's Supper and invited other Presbyterians, not of the Anti-Burgher persuasion, to participate. He used the occasion to preach a sermon on Christian unity in which he expressed deep regret at existing divisions.

The incident was reported to the Presbytery of Chartiers by a minister, William Wilson, who had accompanied him to Cannamaugh. The Presbytery censured Campbell on six counts of departure from orthodoxy, and suspended him from all ministerial duties. He appealed to the Synod, a higher clerical court within the Presbyterian Church. It "rebuked and admonished" him, but lifted the suspension, which then allowed him to preach. It seemed to Campbell that the action said, "You have done no wrong. But don't do it again." But, even then, when he returned to Washington, the Presbytery refused to appoint him to any church.

By this time Campbell had determined in his heart to leave the denomination and follow the Bible only. On September 14, 1808, he withdrew from the Associate Synod of North America. He found himself forty-six years old, in a strange country, without family, church affiliation, or ministerial credentials. It was one of the lowest points in his life.

However, Campbell was not without friends. Many shared his dream of following the Bible, and the Bible only. They invited him to preach to them. His messages almost always concerned healing within the divided church on the basis of the Scriptures. His adherents gradually began to form themselves into a fellowship. A meeting was held at the home of one, Abraham Altars, near

Washington, Pennsylvania. A historian refers to it as "the formal and actual commencement of the Reformation." Campbell spoke and defined some of the principles that would shape the restoration movement. A description of the address is given in the *Memoirs of Alexander Campbell:*

> He ... insisted with great earnestness upon a return to the simple teaching of the Scriptures. ... He went on to announce the principle or rule upon which he understood they were then acting. "That rule, my highly respected hearers," said he in conclusion, "is this, that WHERE THE SCRIPTURES SPEAK, WE SPEAK: AND WHERE THE SCRIPTURES ARE SILENT, WE ARE SILENT."

The fellowship organized itself into the Christian Association of Washington on August 17, 1809. One historian says it numbered "not much more" than twenty-one.[4] The Association authorized Campbell to write a statement of purpose. On September 7, 1809, he presented the group with a document known as the *Declaration and Address* which would become the most definitive paper of the restoration movement. It was published as a fifty-six-page pamphlet, the heart of which was a series of thirteen propositions. The principles expressed in them can be summarized as follows:

1. Christ intends for His church to be one, united.
2. Congregations are autonomous, but should feel a sense of interdependence and fellowship.
3. The Bible is the only rule of faith and practice for Christians.
4. Both the Old and New Testaments are the inspired Word of God. But the New Testament is the perfect rule by which to measure the life, worship and government of the church.
5. "Nothing ought to be received into the faith or worship of the church, or be made a term of communion amongst Christians, that is not as old as the New Testament."
6. Inferences and deductions from Scripture may be true, but should not be made binding upon Christians' consciences.
7. Differences over inferences and deductions should not be held as tests of fellowship.
8. Church membership depends solely upon one's realization of his being lost, accepting Christ as his Savior, and being obedient to Him.
9. All those who accept Christ in this way should be looked

upon as brothers and sisters, members of the family of God, the church.

10. "Division among Christians is a horrid evil, fraught with many evils ... antichristian ... antiscriptural ... antinatural."

11. Division has come from two sources: (1) neglect of the revealed will of God; and (2) human opinions which have been made tests of fellowship.

12. The church will be returned to its purity when the New Testament Church is restored to its original life, ordinance, and doctrine.

13. "Expedients" should be looked upon as "expedients," and not as divine commands. They should never divide the church.

Campbell's family arrived in America at the port of New York on September 29, 1809, and continued their journey overland toward western Pennsylvania. Campbell set out to meet them and they met en route. He showed his son Alexander the proof sheets of the *Declaration and Address.* Much to his delight, Alexander confessed that he, too, had come to the same conclusions from his study of Scripture.

Interesting and significant: Three men, Barton W. Stone, Thomas Campbell, and Alexander Campbell, in diverse parts of the world, came to the same conclusion at the same time. They said, "Persons can be Christians only if they would but follow the Bible only."

Thomas Campbell retired, for all practical purposes, in 1843 at his son's home in Bethany. He remained a colorful character with long white hair flowing down over his shoulders, and with his keen sense of humor intact. Both his sight and hearing failed him in later years, and he expressed disappointment at not being able to study and write. However, characteristic of his innate ingenuity, he would have people read the Scripture to him and would sermonize as it was read. By this time, he had become known as "Father Campbell," not spoken in any clerical sense, but out of venerable respect and affection. His deepest satisfaction was the recognition of his son's leadership of the movement he had first envisioned.

Death came on January 4, 1854, less than a month before his ninety-first birthday. His son, Alexander, would say of him, "I never knew a man in all my acquaintance with men, of whom it could be said with more assurance that 'he walked with God.'"

His biography is appropriately entitled, *Thomas Campbell: Man of the Book*. It gives credit to the other leaders of the restoration movement, then it concludes with the observation about his role. It says, "But emphasis of the movement on the importance and authority of the Scriptures in faith and order is the contribution of Thomas Campbell, man of the Book." He believed persons could be Christians only if they would but follow the Bible only.

NOTES

[1]Lester G. McAllister, *Thomas Campbell: Man of the Book* (St. Louis: Bethany Press, 1954), p.11.

[2]Robert Richardson, *Memoirs of Alexander Campbell* (Cincinnati: Standard Publishing, 1868), Vol. I, p. 22.

[3]McAllister, op. cit., p.53.

[4]Winfred E. Garrison and Alfred T. Degroot; *The Disciples of Christ: a History* (St. Louis; Christian Board of Publication, 1948), p. 140.

6

THE BIBLE: GOD'S WORD AND MAN'S GUIDE

Thomas Campbell was called "man of the Book." Adherents to the movement he first envisioned became known as "a people of the Book" because they believed the Bible to be the only rule of faith and practice for Christians. They sought to speak where the Scriptures speak, and to be silent where they are silent.

God solved a dilemma with the Bible. He wanted to reveal those *musterions* hidden in His heart. *Musterion* is the Greek word in the New Testament often translated as "mystery." However, it does not mean a mystery in the sense of a puzzle or riddle. Instead, it refers to that which is hidden from finite understanding, beyond the range of natural apprehension. It would be a truth man's mind could never conceive without Divine help.

Consider some of these "musterions." The greatest would be God's love for man. The human being would never be able to deduce that from logic. He possesses no innate concept of it, nor does nature communicate a clear message of God's love. Nature has been tainted and cursed because Satan is the "prince of this world" (Ephesians 2:2). Other truths lie hidden in God's heart: His grace, forgiveness, justice, hatred of sin, and His plans for the church and future.

The dilemma? How could man ever come to understand these *musterions* in his finite condition?

It is obvious that God himself would have to take the initiative and do for man what he could not do for himself. It would require what is called revelation, which comes from the Latin *revelo*. It means "to uncover; unveil; to make the hidden known."

The classic illustration of revelation comes from ancient Greek art. It tells of the sculptor who would create a statue out of a block of stone. He would want to show it first to his patrons, those who supported him. He would cover the statue with cloths and invite his supporters to come to an unveiling. At the dramatic moment, with everyone assembled, he would snatch the cloths from his work of art. Behold! The statue would be uncovered, unveiled!

In a similar way, God had to remove the veil that lay between the truths hidden in His heart and man's understanding. He chose to accomplish this with His Word.

The rhetorician would call this communication, the ability to express thoughts and feelings to another person. One communicates in many ways: a touch, look, embrace, gesture, gifts. But the most effective means of communication remains words. They become the *vehicles* that carry our thoughts and feelings to others. So, God chose the Word as the medium of His revelation.

It was by the Word that He had created the universe. John says in the prologue to his Gospel, "In the beginning was the Word. . . . all things were made by him; and without him was not any thing made that was made" (John 1:1, 3). He continued this same theme in verse 10, ". . . the world was made by him." This thought is confirmed by the creation account in Genesis. One will remember that it says, "In the beginning God created the heaven and the earth" (Genesis 1:1). Then it explains His *modus operandi,* "And God *said,* Let there be light. . . . God *said,* Let the waters under the heaven be gathered together . . ." (Genesis 1:3, 9) and so on through creation. God spoke, and the Word He spoke was the power that framed the universe.

Others have noted the power of God's Word in creation. The prophet Jeremiah, for one, recognized its power. The Lord asked in Jeremiah 23:29, "Is not my word like as a fire? saith the Lord; and like a hammer that breaketh the rock in pieces?" A recurring theme all the way through the Scripture testifies to the power of the Word of God.

John's gospel goes on to explain that his "Word became flesh, and dwelt among us" in the person of Jesus of Nazareth (John 1:14). He was God's perfect revelation, the unveiling of himself to man. The apostle Philip made a request of Jesus at the Last Supper. He said, "Show us the Father, and it sufficeth us." Jesus replied, "He that hath seen me hath seen the Father. . . . The words that I speak unto you I speak not of myself: but the Father that dwelleth in me, he doeth the works" (John 14:8-10). Colossians calls Jesus both "the image of the invisible God" (Colossians 1:15) and "the fulness of the Godhead bodily"

(Colossians 2:9). Hebrews calls Him "the express image of [God's] person (Hebrews 1:3).

Jesus revealed God perfectly. He can be called the living Word of God. When He spoke, God was speaking, as the writer of Hebrews testifies, "In the past God spoke to our forefathers through the prophets at many times in various ways, but in these last days he has spoken to us by his Son" (Hebrews 1:1, 2 NIV).

But this does not solve the dilemma for man in this present age. Jesus ascended bodily back into Heaven and now sits at God's right hand there. Modern-day man does not have the privilege to converse with Him personally as the ancient disciples did. He cannot hear, see, or experience Jesus in person. So God solved this part of the problem with His *written* Word, the Bible. It is His inspired, authoritative revelation for those who live in this age.

God gave the Bible to man by the process of "inspiration." It says of itself, "All scripture is given by inspiration of God" (2 Timothy 3:16). Inspiration comes from the Greek term, *theopneustos,* which means "God-breathed." It would be like a flute player breathing a melody through his instrument.

God breathed His message through holy men. This does not mean that He took away the unique personalities of these men. To the contrary, they retained their distinctiveness. Amos and David retained a rural flavor to their writings. You can tell that Paul had received rabbinical training and that Isaiah had come from the king's court. God utilized different personalities from different backgrounds. But each, in his own way, was the flute through which God breathed His revelation.

One should realize as he studies the Bible that it is Christ-centered. The purpose of the *written* Word is to reveal the *living* Word. Jesus himself bore witness to this. He referred to the Law of Moses in Matthew 5:17 and said, "Think not that I come to destroy the law, or the prophets: I am not come to destroy, but to fulfil." This suggests that the Old Testament, the written Word for the Hebrews, pointed toward the culmination of God's plan of salvation in the coming of the living Word, Christ. Alexander Campbell referred to the Old Testament as "the schoolmaster" that prepared for His coming. This is an excellent illustration. The Old Testament helped mature the understanding of God's will, like a schoolteacher would, until in the fulness of time mankind would be ready for Jesus' advent into the world.

Most certainly the Gospel writers looked upon their word as

revealing the Word. Luke begins his book with the explanation that "having had perfect understanding," he was writing it so that its readers would "know the certainty" of those things "most surely believed" about Christ (Luke 1:1-4). Acts and the epistles carry on the revelation of Christ's will through His apostles.

The entire Bible is about Christ, as He is the culmination of God's plan to bring men back to Him. But this in no way diminishes the importance of the Scripture. On the contrary, it reinforces its necessity. How could one have knowledge of Christ without the written Word that contains it? How could one know His love and will without "vehicles" that carry that message? It would be like having music without notes and mathematics without numbers.

The Bible says about itself, "*All* scripture is given by inspiration of God" (2 Timothy 3:16). Some parts of it may have more relevance, or even more importance, than other parts. The Beatitudes may mean more to the Christian than the Code of Holiness in the Book of Leviticus, for example. Any student of the Bible knows that much of the Old Testament was written primarily for the needs of the ancient Hebrews. The rite of circumcision and the laws governing tabernacle worship are but two of many examples. Some parts of the Bible may have more relevance for our day than others, but all parts of it are equally inspired, God-breathed. "For no prophecy was ever made by an act of human will, but men moved by the Holy Spirit spoke from God" (2 Peter 1:21, NASB).

"But," someone may ask, "how do we know we have the Bible as God inspired it? Could not the words have been changed as it has been reproduced down through the centuries?" These are legitimate questions. But God took measures to preserve His Word in this way, also. There exist thousands of manuscripts that go back hundreds of years and that can be compared with each other and later texts. Scholars estimate that there are over four thousand ancient Greek New Testament manuscripts and between 15,000 and 30,000 in Latin. They all essentially agree on its text.

It is significant that ancient manuscripts discovered in recent years confirm the authenticity of Scripture. Most important are the *Dead Sea Scrolls* found near Qumran in the Holy Land in 1947. They produced an archaeological sensation. They had been put into caves by the ancient Essenes. Liberals had contended that much of the Old Testament had to be of later origin than traditionally thought. However, these Scrolls proved the liberals wrong. They largely authenticated the Massoretic text from which we derive our English Old Testament. Sir Frederic Kenyon, a noted scholar, says, "The Christian can take the whole Bible in his hand and say without fear or hesitation that he holds in it the true Word of God, handed down without essential loss from generation to generation throughout the centuries."

The Bible is reliable. One can depend on it. As Barton Warren Stone noted, it is the "only sure guide to Heaven."

Skeptics have sought to discredit the Bible. But its indestructibility is impressive evidence of its divine origin. Its persecution began early with Emperor Diocletian of Rome, who ordered that every manuscript of it be destroyed. Those who possessed copies were martyred during his two-year campaign. At the end of it, he erected a column that carried the inscription, *extincto nomine Christianorum*—"Extinct is the name of Christians." That was in A.D. 305. Twenty years later, Emperor Constantine would enthrone the Bible as the infallible judge of truth.

Voltaire was a French skeptic. He boasted, "Fifty years from now the world will hear no more of the Bible." He lived in the eighteenth century. Thomas Paine was an American patriot who lived in that same century. He said, "When I get through, there will not be five Bibles left in America." These predictions could not have been more wrong. *The Living Bible* paraphrase, for example, was published in July, 1971. By February of the next year, it was in its fifth printing and quickly sold 7,175,000 copies. The writings of Voltaire and Paine are no more than novelties. Their boasts mock them, for the Bible remains a perennial bestseller.

William Blake, the poet, composed a verse about the indestructibility of the Scriptures. He wrote:

Mock on, mock on, Voltaire, Rousseau;
Mock on, mock on; tis all in vain!
You throw the dust against the wind,
And the wind blows it back again.

But perhaps Isaiah expressed it best. He said, "The grass withereth, the flower fadeth: but the word of our God shall stand for ever" (Isaiah 40:8). Jesus added, "Heaven and earth shall pass away, but my words shall not pass away" (Matthew 24:35).

It should be noted what the Bible promises to do for Christians.

It says, "All scripture is given by inspiration of God, and is *profit-able* . . ." (2 Timothy 3:16). The same text tells how it profits the Christian. It says the holy Scriptures will make one "wise unto salvation through faith which is in Christ Jesus" (2 Timothy 3:15). It will make the man of God "perfect" (complete) and "thoroughly furnished unto all good works" (2 Timothy 3:17). It is for these reasons that Paul admonishes the preacher Timothy, saying, "Preach the word" (2 Timothy 4:2), and, "Study to show thyself approved unto God, a workman that needeth not to be ashamed, rightly dividing the word of truth" (2 Timothy 2:15).

William Lyon Phelps, a former president of Yale University, believed in the profitability of Scripture. He made this famous statement, "I would rather have a knowledge of the Bible without an education, than to have an education without a knowledge of the Bible."

The early leaders of the restoration movement believed that the Bible was God's inspired Word, His revelation of himself, His will, and His love for man. As Barton Warren Stone said, "We will, that the people henceforth take the Bible as the only sure guide to heaven; and as many as are offended by other books, which stand in competition with it, may cast them into the fire if they choose; for it is better to enter into life having one book, than having many to be cast into hell." Thomas Campbell added, "The Bible is the only rule of faith and practice for Christians." It solves the dilemma of how God would unveil those musterions in His heart.

The restoration movement, early in its history, became known as "a people of the Book." It seeks to do Bible things in Bible ways and call Bible things by Bible names.

7

ALEXANDER CAMPBELL
AND THE ANCIENT ORDER

Alexander Campbell would emerge as *the* leader of the restoration movement. He was the oldest child of Thomas and Jane Campbell, born on September 12, 1788, near Ballymena, Ireland. President James Madison would later call him "the ablest and the most original expounder of the Scriptures" he had ever heard.[1] But his early youth showed little promise of that eminence.

The young Alexander possessed a fine physique and was more given to athletic pursuits than to study. This frustrated his father, who was also his teacher. Robert Richardson relates this anecdote:

> Having gone out on a warm day to con over his French lesson in "The Adventures of Telemachus," under a shade tree, he finally dropped asleep. A cow that was grazing near approached, and seeing the book lying on the grass, seized it, and, before he was sufficiently awake to prevent, actually devoured it. Upon making report of the loss, his father gave him a castigation for his carelessness, and enforced it by telling him that "the cow had got more French in her stomach than he had in his head."[2]

However, his intellectual powers could not be suppressed. Alexander's mind began to thirst for knowledge. His father guided his education with skill and found in his son an apt student. It is reported that upon one occasion, the young man memorized sixty lines of blank verse in fifty-two minutes and could repeat it without missing a word. He likewise memorized Proverbs, Ecclesiastes, and most of Psalms.

His religious consciousness developed. He wrote:

> From the time I could read the Scriptures, I became convinced that Jesus was the Son of God. I was also fully persuaded that I was a sinner, and must obtain pardon through the merits of Christ or be

lost for ever. . . . Finally, after many strugglings, I was enabled to put my trust in the Saviour, and to feel my reliance on him as the only Saviour of sinners. From the moment I was able to feel this reliance on the Lord Jesus Christ, I obtained and enjoyed peace of mind.[3]

This began Alexander's serious study for the ministry. He was to learn so rapidly that his father would be able to turn over the leadership of the Rich Hill School to him when he was only nineteen.

A major contribution to his education occurred, providentially it would seem. Leaving Alexander in charge of both the family and school, Thomas Campbell had gone to America, saying he would prepare for the family to follow if the situation appeared favorable. On October 1, 1808, the family set sail aboard the ship *Hibernia* to join the father in the new world. On the evening of October 7, Alexander dreamed that the ship would be wrecked. He decided to sleep in his clothes and put his shoes where he could reach them easily. The dream proved to be a premonition. A storm cast the *Hibernia* upon the rocks of the Island of Islay, off the coast of Scotland.

The family emerged unharmed and found themselves among those of common ancestry, the Campbells of Argylshire, Scotland. They extended them warm hospitality. But, more importantly, the shipwreck delayed the journey and allowed Alexander to study a year at his father's alma mater, the University of Glasgow. There he came into contact with the religious views of the Haldane brothers, Robert and James. They sought a Biblical Christianity, and that appealed to Campbell's growing disillusionment with denominationalsm.

An incident took place, as he was about to leave Scotland, that illustrates this discontent. The elders of the Seceder Presbyterian Church in Glasgow required him to be examined before issuing a token that would permit him to take Communion. He passed the test. However, when the emblems were passed, Campbell refrained from partaking. Instead, he deposited the token in the plate as it passed. He could no longer recognize the Seceder Church as the church of Christ. The ring of the token in the plate announced his departure from Presbyterianism forever.[4]

The family finally arrived in New York aboard the *Latonia*. It had been delayed almost a year, and much had happened during the interval. The father in America did not know that his son had withdrawn fellowship from Presbyterianism. The son did not know that the father had likewise disjoined himself from it an ocean away. They met and discussed experiences.

Thomas showed Alexander a rough copy of *The Declaration and Address*. The Memoirs of Alexander Campbell tell of his response to it: "To all the propositions and reasonings of this *Address* Alexander Campbell gave at once his hearty approbation, as they expressed most clearly the convictions to which he had himself been brought by his experience and observation in Scotland."[5] He would later express his intention to devote his life to the dissemination of the principles in it. He would build upon the foundation his father had laid.

Becoming active in the Christian Association begun by his father and friends, Alexander became much in demand as a speaker. It was upon such a speaking engagement that he met Margaret Brown, the daughter of a Virginia landowner, John Brown. She is described as being tall and slender, with dark hair and hazel eyes, and noted for her piety, industry, and engaging manner. They were married on March 12, 1811. She would provide him five surviving daughters, a farm that he would make most profitable, and a happy home.

The couple's first child, Jane, was born on March 13, 1812. This confronted Campbell with the question of infant baptism. He had believed it to be an unscriptural practice but had let it slip rather than make an issue of it. The prospect of baptizing his own child forced him to study the whole subject of Christian baptism. He had committed himself to doing Bible things in Bible ways and calling Bible things by Bible names.

He concluded that not only was infant baptism unwarranted in Scripture, but also sprinkling itself. The words rendered baptism and baptize in the English Bible could mean only "immersion" and "immerse." It was at this point that his sister, Dorothea, came to him and expressed her desire to be Scripturally baptized. They took the matter to Thomas Campbell, but he would only say, "You must please yourself," giving no indication that he agreed with them.

They made arrangements with a Baptist minister, Matthias Luce, to be immersed in Buffalo Creek on June 12, 1812. Alexander, Margaret, and Dorothea walked toward the place of baptism. They were joined en route by Thomas. He remarked that Mrs. Campbell had packed a change of clothing for him and her, the first hint that he, too, intended to be immersed. He would later confess that he had no idea that to take the Bible alone, as a rule of faith and practice, would lead to the abandonment of infant baptism.

Their baptisms marked a turning point in the movement. From the moment he concluded to follow the leading of his son to immersion, Thomas conceded to him its leadership. The position of father and son were reversed. "Alexander became the master-spirit, and to him the eyes of all were now directed. He felt that Providence had placed him in the advance."[6] He was not quite thirty years of age.

Alexander Campbell excelled in many ways. His influence was spread widely by his writing. He began to publish *The Christian Baptist* in 1823. Its prospectus defined its purpose:

> The "Christian Baptist" shall espouse the cause of no religious sect, excepting that ancient sect "called Christians first at Antioch." Its sole object shall be the eviction of truth and the exposing of error in doctrine and practice. The editor, acknowledging no standard of religious faith or works other than the Old and New Testament, and the latter as the only standard of the religion of Jesus Christ, will, intentionally at least, oppose nothing which it contains and recommend nothing which it does not enjoin.[7]

He included in this publication a series written by him entitled, "The Restoration of the Ancient Order of Things." It was to set forth the nature and work of the New Testament church. It called for the abandonment of creeds, unscriptural words, and theological theories. It pleaded for the adoption of the original practices of the church: weekly observance of the Lord's Supper, simple order in public worship, and the independence of each church under a plurality of elders and deacons. Campbell's most famous sermon was entitled "Sermon on the Law," and *The Christian Baptist* continued its theme in a series of articles which maintained that the Old Testament was preparatory, "the schoolmaster" for the New. *The Christian Baptist* would be replaced by the monthly *Millenial Harbinger* in 1830. But its aim remained the same: to restore the ancient faith. Campbell's most widely read book, *The Christian System,* continued to plead for this restoration of the New Testament church.

Alexander Campbell became a noted educator. He founded Bethany College in 1840 on land he gave from his estate in what is now the "panhandle" of West Virginia. It would become known as "the mother college" among Christian churches. He expressed its philosophy:

> The formation of moral character, the culture of the heart, is the supreme end of education; or rather is education itself. With me education and the formation of moral character are identical expressions ... We contemplate a scheme in which the formation of the physical and intellectual man shall not be neglected, but which shall always be held in subordination to the moral man. In which, in one word, the formation of moral character, the cultivation of the heart, shall be the alpha and omega.[8]

He said, "Bethany College is the only college known to the civilized world, founded upon the Bible.... [It is] a literary and scientific institution, founded upon the Bible as the basis of all true science and true learning."[9] Campbell served as the school's president and professor of mental philosophy, evidences of Christianity, and moral and political economy. Fifteen hundred persons gathered for its first Commencement on July 4, 1843. It was truly the "mother" to many colleges, Bible schools, and Bible chairs within the movement.

Campbell's fame would become most widespread as a result of the use of debate. He felt more could be accomplished in a week's debate than in a year's preaching. He became most skilled in the art. His first significant debate was with a Presbyterian minister, John Walker. The subject was infant baptism. Walker attempted to show that infant baptism entered the Christian faith through "the door of circumcision." Campbell forcefully demonstrated the error of this position, using the same arguments included in his "Sermon on the Law." It was a rout, and Walker, for all practical purposes, gave up. It enhanced Campbell's stature, particularly among the Baptists. He would later debate a more able opponent on the same subject, W. L. McCalla, also a Presbyterian minister. However, the result was the same—a Campbellian rout. The paedobaptists would make one more attempt to salvage their position, choosing N. L. Rice as their champion. This debate also included other subjects, such as conversion, sanctification, and human creeds. Many were immersed as a result of it.

Another famous debate came when Campbell met Bishop John B. Purcell, of the Roman Catholic Church, who would later become the Archbishop of the Cincinnati diocese. Campbell conducted himself with such honor that his esteem rose high among all Protestants. However, his most famous debate came against an atheist, Robert Owen, who had called Christianity "an opiate of the masses." He had attempted to found utopian, communal societies, the most famous one being at New Harmony, Indiana. Owen sought to show Christianity as a scandal based on ignorance, and he expected Campbell to defend the established churches. However, Campbell rested his case upon the simple revelation of the New Testament. He asked and answered three questions, "What is man? Whence came he? Whither does he go?" Another rout ensued. Owen turned over to Campbell the last part of the time allotted to say what he wished, and Campbell addressed the audience for twelve hours. At the end of it, he asked all those who believed in Christianity to stand. Almost everyone present arose. Then he asked all those who did not believe in the truth of the Christian religion to rise, and only three persons stood. This debate gave Campbell great exposure to and confidence from the religious world. His biographer noted: "No individual was ever known to have been the instrument of converting so many skeptics to the truth of Christianity as Alexander Campbell."

Campbell would continue to lead the restoration movement until his death on March 4, 1866. He would write profusely and speak often to large crowds. His scholarship, self-confidence, and boldness made him unmatched in leadership qualities. Those who wanted to restore the church to its original pristine purity looked to him for guidance as they did none other. One historian called him the movement's "most cherished and capable leader."

No one chapter in a single book could do justice to the life and accomplishment of a man such as Campbell. But perhaps Robert Richardson and Selina Huntington Campbell, Campbell's second wife, best summarize what he wanted to accomplish in their *Memoirs and Reminiscenes*. Richardson wrote, "It may be here briefly remarked in general that it was an effort to heal the divisions of religious society and to escape from all the corruptions of the gospel by a direct return to the faith and practice of the Apostolic Age."

His widow added, "The return to the Bible, and the Bible alone, as the guide and rule of the life of the Christian, apart from the teachings, traditions and doctrines of men, was his motto." She also preserved an acrostic sent to her by one of her husband's admirers after his death that she felt described the purpose of his ministry. It reads:

C arry the warfare on against sin.
A nd bright laurels for "Christian Unity" win.
M usty traditions and doctrines overthrow,
P rove from God's word, that mortals may know,
B y faith and obedience, pardoning love—
E njoy by the same, sweet peace from above.
L ong, long will thy name and thy deeds be known,
L ong as Jehovah sits upon His throne.

NOTES

[1]Dabney Phillips, *Restoration Principles and Personalities* (University, Alabama: Youth in Action, Inc., 1975), p. 37.

[2]Robert Richardson, *The Memoirs of Alexander Campbell* (Cincinnati: Standard Publishing Co., 1868), Vol. I, pp. 31, 32.

[3]Ibid., p. 49.

[4]Ibid., p. 190.

[5]Ibid., pp. 273, 274.

[6]Ibid., pp. 401, 402.

[7]Ibid., Vol. II, 1890, p. 50.

[8]William Kirk Woolery, *The Bethany Years* (Huntington, W. Va.: Standard Printing and Publishing, 1941), p. 20.

[9]Ibid.

8

THE ANCIENT ORDER
OF THINGS

Seeing the evils of sectarian Christianity, the early leaders of the restoration movement eschewed denominationalism. Even before he left Ireland to come to America, Thomas Campbell had called it "an evil of no small magnitude . . . hurtful and embarrassing." Alexander Campbell pointed out that this division among God's people grieves Christ and frustrates His desire to see the world converted. He expressed this thought in a chapter of his *Christian System* entitled, "Foundations of Christian Union," in which he used the high priestly prayer of Jesus from John 17. He italicized the expressions of Christ's desire for unity among His people. Jesus said:

> I pray . . . for those who shall believe on me through their teaching, that *that all may be one;* that as thou, Father, art in me, and I in thee, *they also may be one in us, that the world may believe* that thou hast sent me, and that thou gavest me glory, which I have given them, that *they may be one,* as we are one; I in them, and thou in me, *that their union may be perfected:* and that *the world may know* that thou hast sent me, and that thou lovest them as thou lovest me.[1]

Campbell noted two obvious facts within that prayer. First, division among Christians hurts Christ. He prayed this prayer in the upper room, just before He would be betrayed and crucified. Foremost on His heart, even as He faced the cross, was the unity of Christians. Division fractures the body of Christ and grieves Jesus himself. However, Campbell also pointed to another reason for Christ's desire for oneness among His people: "That the world may believe . . . that the world may know that thou hast sent me." Campbell believed the world would never be won to Christ until all of His people are one, united. It would depend upon their achieving the unity for which Paul pleaded to the Corinthians:

61

"... that ye all may speak the same thing, and that there be no divisions among you; but that ye be perfectly joined together in the same mind and in the same judgment" (1 Corinthians 1:10). Alexander Campbell dedicated his life to the attempt to bring together God's people in this unity for which Christ prayed and Paul pleaded. He would enter into the effort through twin doors opened for him by two other early leaders of the movement.

Barton Warren Stone had found a name that all of Jesus' followers could wear. It was the ancient name, Christian, which God, himself, had given. It was to be the "inclusive" term that would designate His people. Since all members of every denomination are proud to wear the name Christian, Stone suggested that all party names be "castaway and forgotten." He saw a vision of all God's people being Christians only.

Thomas Campbell had emphasized that persons could be Christians only if they would but follow the Bible only. He saw the Scriptures as a door through which they could step into Christian unity. He said that the Bible is the only rule of faith and practice for Christians, "an infallible standard, an all-sufficient basis of union and Christian cooperation." "Therefore," he said, "where the Scriptures speak, we will speak; and where the Scriptures are silent, we will be silent."

Alexander Campbell stepped through those twin doors and added another dimension. He pleaded for the restoration of the essential marks of the New Testament church as it was given to the apostles. He believed that persons could be Christians only if they would but follow the Bible only and do Bible things in Bible ways and call Bible things by Bible names. It was a unique approach to Christian unity.

Campbell greatly admired the Protestant reformers, particularly Martin Luther. He admired Luther's courage, boldness, and intellectual capacity. But he believed the reformers began at the *wrong* end to reform the church. You remember the *modus operandi* of the reformers, do you not? They would find an error in the church and correct it. But that correction would expose a previous error, which they would correct only to expose yet a previous one. The Protestant reformers moved *backward* through the pages of church history in their attempts to purify it.

Luther, for example, first fell out with the selling of "indulgences." This was the opportunity sold to people with a guarantee that it would shorten their time in purgatory and, as we have noted, was interpreted by many as purchasing the forgiveness of sins before they were ever committed. This wreaked havoc with morality and Luther found the practice intolerable. You may remember in his biographical movie, *Martin Luther,* he once came upon a parishioner drunk in an alley. He rebuked the man, who reached inside his cloak and pulled out an indulgence receipt which he interpreted as excusing his drunkenness. This infuriated the young priest, who proceeded to write his Ninety-five Theses that many point to as precipitating the reformation.

However, Luther could not stop there. The correction of that error in his mind exposed the error of the whole system of salvation by vicarious works—the attempt to earn salvation by the perfunctory performance of religious rites without a personal relationship with Christ. The correction of this error exposed still another error, papal infallibility, and, ultimately, the authority of the church over his conscience. It led to his excommunication.

Campbell thought Luther was right in each of these corrections. He did believe, however, that Luther stopped short. He felt he reformed the church only back as far as Augustine (A.D. 354-430), which was not far enough to suit him. Campbell looked upon the sixteenth-century reformers with deep respect and affection, but he was convinced that they began at the wrong end of church history and stopped short.

Campbell's approach was unique. He pled for Christians to jump back over the pages of church history to the church as it was first given—as it was given to the apostles. Let's restore the essential marks of that church, he said, and we will be able to reform it from that end.

He suggested that we should begin with John the Baptist, progress to the life and ministry of Jesus, to the founding of the church in Acts under the direction of the Holy Spirit, and into its life and ministry. The ideal was to restore the essential marks of the New Testament church and then move *forward* to correct the errors that had developed through the centuries.

This restoration ideal was based on the assumption mentioned earlier that God did indeed envision the church as He would have it be. I call it "the church for which Christ gave himself," or, as Paul expressed it to the Ephesians, "the church Christ loved and purchased with His own blood."

Campbell did not believe this church could be found in any age of church history nor in any existing denomination. Instead, he believed God gave this church to the inspired apostles for them to direct and oversee. Restore the essential marks of that church, he thought, and you will have the form and the function of the one God envisioned. Robert Richardson, Campbell's biographer, made an observation about the uniqueness of this ideal:

> Here was an effort not so much for the reformation of the Church, as was that of Luther and of Calvin, and to a certain extent even that of the Haldanes, but for its complete *restoration* at once to its pristine purity and perfection. By coming at once to its primitive model and rejecting all human imitations; by submitting implicitly to the Divine authority as plainly expressed in the Scriptures, and by disregarding all the assumptions and dictations of fallible men, it was proposed to form a union upon a basis to which no valid objection could possibly be offered.[2]

Richardson went on to say that never before had any leader so boldly assumed such a position as this. No one had suggested that all man-made creeds, confessions, and traditions be abandoned. Campbell proposed just that. It was to restore the essence of the New Testament church to its pristine purity.

He began a series of articles in the *Christian Baptist* to promote this ideal. It was entitled, "The Restoration of the Ancient Order of Things," and contained two emphases. First, it urged the abandonment of everything not in use among early Christians which divided believers and constituted "tests of fellowship" among them. Included in these were creeds, confessions of faith, unscriptural words and phrases, and theological theories. Second, it proposed to include in the life of the church everything sanctioned by primitive practice. This included such precedents as the weekly observance of the Lord's Supper, the independence of each church under the leadership of elders and deacons, and a simple order of public worship.

Two tests were to be applied to determine the legitimacy of any article of faith or action within the church. They were *divine command* and *approved precedence.* Campbell insisted upon having a "thus saith the Lord" either in express terms, or approved precedent "for every article of faith, and item of religious practice." He contended for "the original gospel" and "order of things" established by the apostles.[3]

The *divine commands* are fairly obvious. An example is the Great Commission. Jesus said that the church must "go, preach,

64

baptize, and teach all things whatsoever He had commanded" (Matthew 28:19, 20). It is clear from this command that a church after the New Testament order must both evangelize and disciple. It was the application of the *approved precedence* test that would stir up controversy. Campbell could find no New Testament precedent for infant baptism, sprinkling or affusion, or any episcopal form of church government, for example. Instead, he found precedence for the immersion of believers for the remission of sins. He found the New Testament church to be composed of autonomous interdependent congregations. Another precedent included in the life of the church was the weekly observance of the Lord's Supper.

Campbell pleaded for *undenominational* Christianity in the purest sense of that term. He called for denominations to divest themselves of all the divisive elements that men had added to the Lord's church. The New Testament church was the norm, or ideal, to him. The restoration of it in its purity would produce an *undenominational* church. It would be one to which all Christians could belong and would result in Christian unity. He believed that the way to restore the New Testament church was to do Bible things in Bible ways and call Bible things by Bible names. The tests of *divine command* and *approved precedence* were to be applied to determine what the church should both do and teach. The ideal was to be both Biblical and undenominational.

Campbell looked upon those who pursued with him the ideal to restore the New Testament church as being a part of a *movement*. He abhorred the possibility of starting a denomination. He wrote, "I have no idea of adding to the catalog of new sects. I labor to see sectarianism abolished and all Christians of every name united upon the one foundation upon which the apostolic church was founded." He wanted the restoration ideal to be embodied in a *movement* of free Christians, striving to be undenominational as they sought to do Bible things in Bible ways. A denomination would have to adopt sectarian creeds and practices, and form a sectarian organization. A *movement,* on the other hand, could be undenominational by beginning with the confession, "Jesus is the Christ," and proceeding to carry out His will as a fellowship of free, autonomous congregations.

Campbell did not want those who composed the restoration movement to look upon themselves as the *only* Christians. He recognized Christians in the existing denominations. Indeed, he called upon them to join him in returning to the apostolic church. He was asked how he could fellowship with the Baptists and at the same time pursue New Testament Christianity. He replied, "I will unite with any Baptist society in the United States in any act of social worship, such as prayer, praise, or breaking of bread in commemoration of the Lord's death, if they confess the one Lord, the one faith, the one hope and the one baptism; provided always that as far as I can judge, they piously and morally conform to their profession." He did not want the movement to become isolationist. Instead, he sought to have it move within Christianity, calling members of the denominations to return to the ancient order.

The efforts of Alexander Campbell have a peculiar relevance for this present age. Many Christians still feel a deep need for the unity among them for which Jesus prayed. Some embraced the "unity by compromise" approach. It asked denominations to come together and just forget their differences. But many found it diluted the faith "once delivered to the saints." Even the most liberal found that it would cost some revered practices and precious beliefs. The denominations were unable to compromise enough to bring about the union they desired. It was an approach that minimized God's Word and proved unworthy.

The restoration ideal offers an alternative approach to unity. It pleads for Christians to be undenominational. It calls for them to restore the essence of the New Testament church. This can be accomplished if they will be Christians only by following the Bible only and do Bible things in Bible ways and call Bible things by Bible names. The ancient order is the basis for true unity among God's people.

NOTES

[1]Alexander Campbell, *The Christian System* (Cincinnati: The H. S. Bosworth Co., 1866), p. 85.

[2]Robert Richardson, *The Memoirs of Alexander Campbell* (Cincinnati: Standard Publishing Co., 1868), Vol. I, p. 257.

[3]Alexander Campbell, op. cit., pp. x-xii.

9

WALTER SCOTT
AND THE ANCIENT GOSPEL

Barton W. Stone restored the ancient name, Christian; Thomas Campbell restored the ancient book, the Bible; and Alexander Campbell restored the ancient order of the New Testament church. It was left for Walter Scott to restore the ancient gospel. He was called the "Voice of the Golden Oracle" because of his emphasis upon preaching the gospel.

Scott was born October 31, 1796, in Dumfriesshire, Scotland. This made him the youngest of the four early leaders of the restoration movement. He was number six of the ten children of John Scott, a music teacher by trade. His mother Mary, also musical, developed this talent in her son, and he would benefit from it the rest of his life. Scott had an illustrious forefather who could probably have been guessed because of his name. It was Sir Walter Scott, who could have been poet laureate of England if he had not deferred to a friend. The younger Walter would go on to receive a superb education at Edinburgh University in his native Scotland.

Walter Scott came to America soon after his graduation from Edinburgh, at the invitation of an uncle, George Innes, who worked for the Customs Service of the United States. Walter's father had died suddenly on a trip, and his mother, upon receiving the news, died immediately also. It was from this double loss that he accepted his uncle's invitation. He arrived in the port of New York on July 7, 1818, and for a brief time, taught Latin in an academy on Long Island.

However, he was drawn toward the frontier by the stories of opportunity to be found there. He traveled three hundred miles and arrived at Pittsburgh. There he met the man who would do most to shape his early life. He was George Forrester, headmaster of an academy and the minister of an undenominational church that sought to follow only the Bible. It was facetiously called

"The Kissin' Baptist Church." However, it was not a part of the Baptist denomination, though it did immerse and practice the holy kiss. The young Scott and his mentor would sit up long into the night and discuss the Scripture. Scott came to the conclusion that his infant baptism in the Church of Scotland was not Biblical and, therefore, was insufficient. Upon being immersed by Forrester, he exclaimed, "I have now been converted to Christianity."

A tragic accident took away the life of George Forrester. He drowned the next summer in the same Allegheny River in which he had immersed his new friend. This left Scott with the responsibility of both the school and the church to which he had ministered. However, this would occupy just a part of his time; his real interest lay in God's Word. His logical mind began to frame great conclusions. He said, for example, that the Word contained "precepts, duties, ordinances, promises, and blessings, which were meant to follow one upon the other."

It was during this time that he received a tract written by a Henry Errett of New York City. It concerned Christian baptism, about which he had great concern. He decided to visit this congregation. He closed the academy and set out on his journey. He found a congregation there that was dedicated to being Biblical, but it had not evangelistic zeal because it was caught in the quagmire of Calvinism. This depressed Scott, and he left there to visit other independent churches in New Jersey, Baltimore, and Washington. But those, too, lacked a desire to reach the unsaved with the gospel. The condition of these churches caused him deep grief. He said that he was filled with sorrow "at the miserable desolation of the Church of God."

Nathaniel Richardson, a businessman in Pittsburgh, persuaded Scott to come back to that city. He wanted him to tutor his son Robert, who would later write *The Memoirs of Alexander Campbell*. His popularity as a teacher caused many families to want his services. He became the leader of an academy of one hundred forty boys and once again became the minister of the congregation that he had left. It was during this period that Scott discovered "the golden oracle" and would meet both a man and a woman who would have an even greater influence upon his life than Forrester.

Scott had come to the same conclusion as the Campbells: that faith is the result of the evidence and testimony of Scripture. He concluded that the Bible contained a central truth. It was to be found in the great confession of Peter in Matthew 16:16, "Thou art the Christ, the Son of the living God." He said, "The truth of the Christian faith is that *Jesus is the Christ*." He called it the golden oracle, "the sun to which all other Christian truths are planets in a spiritual solar system." This golden oracle would be the heart of his preaching for the rest of his life. It is the reason he would become known as the "Voice of the Golden Oracle."

The Richardson family had become friends with the Thomas Campbell family. Robert had been a student in Campbell's academy. It was in 1821 that the man who would influence Scott's life most would visit the Richardson residence and there make Scott's acquaintance. His name was Alexander Campbell. The meeting deepened into a friendship that would last over forty years.

The men were different in many ways. Campbell was strong of physique, logical of mind, and steady of temperament. Scott, on the other hand, was slight, given more to feeling, and his emotions would often carry him from high hopes to the deepest despair. But the two were kindred spirits. They were bound together in the desire to restore the church to its pristine purity.

In 1823, Scott would meet another person who would greatly affect his life. Her name was Sarah Whitsett. He both converted her to his views of Biblical Christianity and persuaded her to marry him. She became a most beneficial helpmeet. She had been reared in the comfort of a well-to-do home. Her husband would prove himself no manager of money, and his evangelistic forays would leave her alone much of the time. He would testify that her support strengthened his ministry. They moved to Steubenville, Ohio, where Scott opened an academy.

This put him much closer to the Campbells, who had by this time affiliated themselves with the Mahoning Baptist Association. They invited Scott to visit its annual meeting in the summer of 1826. He was invited to address the group. One could predict his subject. He spoke on the golden oracle—Jesus is the Christ. It greatly impressed the hearers. An item on the agenda of that meeting was the selection of an evangelist to work among the churches of the Association. Walter Scott was chosen. This is surprising because he was neither a member of the Mahoning group nor a Baptist.

His first meeting as an evangelist was at Lisbon, Ohio. He used Matthew 16:16 as his text and his subject was, as one would expect, the golden oracle. Upon finishing the message, without premeditation or plan, he offered the same invitation given by the apostle Peter when he concluded the first gospel sermon, which is recorded in Acts 2:38. He said, "Repent, and be baptized every one of you in the name of Jesus Christ for the remission of sins, and ye shall receive the gift of the Holy Ghost." One man responded to the invitation. His name was William Amend. He was not even in the building during the sermon. He listened from outdoors through the window. But he had promised himself years before that he would become a Christian when he heard someone preach like the apostle Peter. He heard that man and responded.

This began an evangelistic ministry without equal within the restoration movement. It is estimated that Scott baptized over 30,000 persons during his ministry. It is said that the Ohio River became a veritable Jordan because of so many immersions. Scott's message centered around the golden oracle, and his invitation would be, "Repent, and be baptized."

However, Scott felt that there was a missing link in his answer to the question, "What must one do to become a Christian?" His logical mind demanded that this link be found. He discovered it in a conversation with a friend, Jacob Osborne. He turned to Scott and asked, "Have you ever thought that baptism in the name of the Lord is for the remission of sins?" That was it! It was the link for which he had searched. One heard the gospel, believed in Christ, repented of his sin, and obedience to Christ in Christian baptism became the culmination of his acceptance of Him.

Scott's logical mind enabled him to develop the "five-finger exercise." He would ride his horse into a village, gather the little children around him, and ask, "Little children, do you know what you must do to become Christians?" Of course, they did not. They had been reared in Calvinism. Scott would raise up his hand for them to see. He would point to each finger, which represented a step in the plan of salvation. He would say, "You must believe in Christ, repent of your sins, be baptized, receive the remission of sins, and the gift of the Holy Ghost." He would say, "Go home. Tell your parents what they must do to become Christians, and tell them that a man will speak on that subject tonight in the schoolhouse." Not only did hundreds respond to this simple, rational explanation of the plan of salvation, but whole congregations would leave their denominational affiliation because of this understanding of the New Testament way to accept Christ.

Scott simplified the gospel in another way. He said, "If man

70

will take three steps, God will give him three promises. If he believes in Christ, repents of his sins, and is baptized into Christ, God will give him the gift of the Holy Spirit, the remission of sins, and the promise of Heaven."

Scott pronounced that these explanations had accomplished the restoration of the ancient gospel. He called it "the gospel restored." Alexander Campbell thought that this might be somewhat pretentious. However, it would seem that Thomas Campbell agreed with Scott. The elder Campbell traveled with him on some of his evangelistic trips. He wrote his son and said of Scott's evangelistic ministry:

> We have spoken and published many things *correctly* concerning the ancient gospel, its simplicity and perfect adaptation to the present state of mankind ... but I must confess that, in respect of the direct exhibition and application of it for that blessed purpose, I am at present, for the first time, upon the ground where the thing has appeared to be practically exhibited to the proper purpose.[1]

Campbell seemed to be saying that he and his son knew the gospel. But it was Scott who had discovered the way to present it so that people could both understand and respond to it.

Walter Scott's health began to fail him. His intemperate evangelistic endeavors may have contributed to this. He moved to Pittsburgh and later to Cincinnati. He would never again be the active evangelist that he had been in the earlier years. However, his influence would increase in other ways. Scott was not just an evangelist, but also an educator, editor, and author. He would become the first president of the first college west of the Appalachian Mountains. It was Bacon College, located at Georgetown, Kentucky, which would later become Transylvania University, Lexington, Kentucky. He would serve upon the Board of Trustees at Miami University, Oxford, Ohio. He would begin an influential journal in 1832, which he called *The Evangelist*. It became widely disseminated. He considered his editorial work as an extension of his pulpit work. Central in the pages of *The Evangelist* were the golden oracle, the gospel restored, and the steps in the plan of salvation.

Scott authored several influential discourses. Among them were "A Discourse on the Holy Spirit"; "The Gospel Restored"; and the one he considered his greatest, "The Messiahship, or Great Demonstration." This last one was a defense of the Christian faith. He said in it, "The Bible is revealed and beyond its sacred pages the true religion does not exist." The thesis of this book, like that of his preaching, rested upon the golden oracle.

The latter years of Scott's life were not happy ones. His beloved Sarah preceded him in death. He would later marry Nannie Allen. She provided him the security he needed. She said, "I would rather be the widow of Walter Scott than to be married to any living man I know." However, she, too, preceded him to the grave. He then married Eliza Sandidge. She was a wealthy widow. She and her new husband would disagree often over money. Eliza was frugal, perhaps to a fault. Walter had shown himself to be spendthrifty. She said of him, "You give more money away than most men make in a lifetime." This led to a more general estrangement. He said that he felt like a forlorn stranger, tolerated but not loved, in her house. Historians say that sometimes he was not even tolerated. A story tells us that upon occasions, when Eliza's rage would reach its highest, he would be driven from the house and locked out. He would be found on the doorstep of a neighbor the next morning. He would say, "I wonder if you would take me in for some breakfast? The little lady isn't feeling well."

It was after one of these expulsions that Scott left the Mayslick, Kentucky home of Eliza. He went to live in Cincinnati. It became the scandal of the movement—one of the leaders separated from his espoused. The elders of the Mayslick church went to Cincinnati and entreated him. They said, "You must return." Scott replied, "Very well. I will go back, but not alone. You must go with me." He returned out of duty and conscience. His biographer says that from this time forward the marriage was at best "a truce."

The Civil War weighed heavily upon Scott. He had *chosen* to become an American. It was 1861. The news of the firing on Fort Sumter reached him. He exclaimed, "O, my country! my country! How I love thee! how I deplore thy present misfortunes!"[2]

Scott died April 23, 1861. The cause of death was diagnosed as typhoid pneumonia. But many people believe that it was at least hastened by a broken heart.

The tragedy of Scott's later life reached the proportions of an insult. In the cemetery at Cane Ridge, Kentucky, there is a large monument to the memory of Barton Warren Stone. It calls him a preacher of the gospel and leader of the nineteenth century reformation. Likewise, in the cemetery at Bethany, West Virginia, there is a stone which calls Alexander Campbell *the* leader of the reformation. They called Thomas Campbell, "Father Campbell," out of venerable affection during his last years. These three early leaders of the movement were honored even in death. However, upon the demise of Walter Scott, they laid him to rest in an unmarked grave. He would lie there thirty-six years until a grand-daughter took the initiative to place upon his grave a modest stone. However, Walter Scott would say that there is a greater monument to his work. It is a living monument. It is those who go forth with the golden oracle and the gospel restored to tell people the steps they must take to become Christians.

Scott was also much appreciated by his friend and co-worker, Alexander Campbell. Upon hearing of his death, Campbell wrote:

> No death in my horizon, out of my own family, came more unex pectedly or more ungratefully to my ears than this of my beloved and highly appreciated brother, Walter Scott. Next to my father, he was the most cordial and indefatigable fellow laborer in the origin and progress of the present Reformation. . . . His whole heart was in his work. I knew him well. I knew him long. I loved him much. . . . By the eye of faith and the eye of hope, me thinks I see him in Abraham's bosom.[2]

NOTES

[1]Robert Richardson, *The Memoirs of Alexander Campbell* (Cincinnati: Standard Publishing Co., 1890), Vol. II, p. 219, 220.

[2]William Baxter, *The Life of Elder Walter Scott* (St. Louis: Bethany Press, 1926).

[2]Dabney Phillips, *Restoration Principles and Personalities* (University, Alabama: Youth in Action, Inc., 1975), pp. 139, 140.

10

SIN

"All have sinned. . ." (Romans 3:23)

Walter Scott believed the plan of salvation to be so simple that even the little children could understand it. He taught that God has revealed it so logically and reasonably that "wayfaring men, though fools, shall not err therein" (Isaiah 35:8). He believed it could be found in God's Word by anyone who sincerely sought it, and he originated what became known as the five-finger exercise" to demonstrate its simplicity.

The plan of salvation, according to Scott, begins when one realizes that he has sinned, is a sinner, and must have God's forgiveness. This realization exposes him to his need for God's grace and moves him toward an acceptance of it. It is the Word of God that convicts people of their sins. This is a purpose of the law in the Bible, and the reason that it is still useful even in this age of grace. The law cannot save anyone, but it does serve to make him aware of his sin—an awareness that is essential to salvation.

Sin is defined several ways in the Bible. The Greek word most often used for it in the New Testament is *hamartia,* meaning "to miss the mark," or "to fall short," and it carries with it a sense of failure. It appears sixty times in Paul's epistles. It would be like the archer who takes up his bow and aims the arrow at the target. He lets the arrow fly, but it falls short and misses the mark. It fails in its intended purpose.

Hamartia denotes the state or condition of a person's life, not just individual sins. The Scripture explains that man was created to walk in perfect fellowship with God. That has remained His divine purpose and one who does not carry out this plan for his life—to walk in fellowship with God—fails, falls short, and misses the mark, even as did the arrow when it fell short of its target. Sin, in this sense, can be defined as the state of condemnation in which one lives who is not in fellowship with God. The great question in the plan of salvation asks: How can one escape this condemnation that comes from his sin?

Some students of the Bible have divided sin into three categories: transgression, omission, and unbelief. It would be profitable to consider each of these.

First is *transgression*. This, the most obvious kind of sin, occurs when one willfully breaks a divine commandment. He lies, cheats, murders, commits adultery. It would also include those sins of the mind like hatred, jealousy, coveteousness, lust, and the like. First John 3:4 speaks explicitly about this category of sin when it says, "Whosoever committeth sin transgresseth also the law: for sin is the transgression of the law."

James 1:14, 15 even tells us how this sin of transgression operates destructively in one's life. It has been called "The LSD Formula." It says, "But every man is tempted, when he is drawn away of his own lust, and enticed. Then when lust hath conceived, it bringeth forth sin; and sin, when it is finished, bringeth forth death." *Lust* leads to *sin* and sin to *death*—LSD.

The second category of sin is *omission*. The Bible says, "Therefore to him that knoweth to do good, and doeth it not, to him it is sin" (James 4:17). This covers all the positive acts of kindness, generosity, faithfulness, and love a person should do, but because of selfishness refuses to do. The priest and Levite in the parable of the good Samaritan are examples of those who sin by omission. This category also covers that which should be done in one's relationship with God but is not done. Faithfulness at the Lord's Supper, witnessing for Christ, and service in His name are but a few of these. It is just as sinful for a person to know what to do and fail to do it as for him to know what he should not do and do it.

People seldom think of *unbelief* itself as sin. But the Bible clearly teaches that to fail to believe God's Word is sin because it makes Him a liar. The apostle John taught this when he wrote, "He that believeth on the Son of God hath the witness in himself: he that believeth not God hath made Him a liar; because he believeth not the record that God gave of His Son" (1 John 5:10). To reject the gospel message requires a great amount of sinful pride. One would have to say, "I am so good I do not need God's grace." That is sin!

Everybody succumbs to temptation at some time. No one escapes it. Sin is not a disease, like the mumps, which some people get and others can avoid. It is instead the universal state of life for humans, even the most moral. The Scripture says, "For all have sinned, and come short of the glory of God" (Romans 3:23); "All we like sheep have gone astray" (Isaiah 53:6); and, "If we say that we have not sinned, we make [God] a liar, and His word is not in us" (1 John 1:10). The plan of salvation begins at this very point for every person who is saved; he realizes that he has sinned, is a sinner, and must have God's forgiveness.

This makes sin the great fact of life with which man must find a way to cope. The human mind can never comprehend the ravages it has caused. Name any heartache, misfortune, or tragedy, and it can be blamed on the entrance of sin into man's realm. God never intended for us humans to hurt or be unhappy. Quite to the contrary, He provided everything man needed for contentment, as is described in Genesis 1 and 2.

These chapters say that God created man in His own image. This enabled Him to have a creature with whom He could fellowship; one whom He could love and by whom He could be loved. He demonstrated His love for man by creating for him *Eden,* a garden, a paradise, in which grew "every tree that is pleasant to the sight, and good for food" (Genesis 2:9). Then God noted man's loneliness, his discontent because he had no one of like kind to love. He said, "It is not good that the man should be alone" (Genesis 2:18). So He created woman, a creature with whom man could share the deepest fellowship and communion in order that he might be complete.

It was a perfect state! Man and woman walked in fellowship with God in a paradise where everything was provided for their needs. Then something happened that changed all of that. Sin entered!

God had placed a tree at the center of the garden. It was called "the tree of the knowledge of good and evil," and He forbade Adam and Eve to partake of its fruit. This command enabled them to demonstrate their love for, appreciation of, and faithfulness to, God. He had provided for their every need, and they were to keep this one simple command.

A new character enters the Genesis narrative—Satan. The Scripture seems to imply that he had been an archangel, called Lucifer, which means "lightbearer." The Bible refers to him also as "that old serpent, called the Devil, and Satan, which deceiveth the whole world" (Revelation 12:9). He may have been the fairest of all Heavenly creatures in the beginning, but he wanted to be God. He rebelled against God's authority and was cast out of Heaven, along with those beings who sided with him.

Satan approached Adam and Eve. It must be remembered that he was a real entity with whom man and woman could converse. The greatest accomplishment of the devil in this contemporary era is to convince modern man that he does not exist; that he is a myth, an antiquated anthropomorphism of evil. The Bible indicates just the opposite of this all the way through the text. He spoke to Adam and Eve in Genesis. Then he confronted Jesus with temptation in the wilderness in Matthew 4 and was very real to Him. Paul called him "the prince of the power of the air, the spirit that now worketh in the children of disobedience" (Ephesians 2:2). Men need not doubt the existence of the devil because the evidence of his work is all about them. The poet asks this question of those who, in this age, dispute the reality of Satan:

"The Devil is voted not to be, and of course, the thing is true;
But who is doing the kind of work the Devil alone can do?"

Satan is real today, just as he has always been. He is still man's adversary, and "as a roaring lion, [he] walketh about, seeking whom he may devour" (1 Peter 5:8).

Satan entered the garden in the beginning and the test came. God had warned Adam and Eve. He said of the tree of the knowledge of good and evil, "Ye shall not eat of it, neither shall ye touch it, lest ye die" (Genesis 3:3). Satan said, "Ye shall not surely die ... in the day you eat thereof, then your eyes shall be opened, and ye shall be as gods, knowing good and evil" (Genesis 3:4, 5). Adam and Eve wanted to be God, to know as much as He knew. This may still be the underlying sin of mankind; people want to be equal with God instead of being subservient and obedient to Him.

Adam and Eve partook of the forbidden fruit. This broke God's command, showed lack of trust in His Word, and revealed the lack of appreciation they had for His love. He expelled them from His garden and no longer provided for their every need. The ground would be cursed with thorns and thistles. Adam would labor and only by the sweat of his brow would he be able to make a living from it. God provided that woman, too, would find sorrow as she suffered pain in childbirth.

The entrance of sin into the world is the most momentous event in history. All mankind in every age has been cursed by it. Sickness, sorrow, heartache, disappointment, and even death are the result of the advent of sin. Paul said it entered into the world by one man, Adam, and death by sin has been passed on to all men because of it (Romans 5:12). He expressed the condemnation that comes from sin when he wrote, "The wages of sin is death" (Romans 6:23).

The Bible describes three "deaths" that are the result of sin. The first is *spiritual death*. It is what Paul meant when he referred to man as being "dead in trespasses and sins" (Ephesians 2:1). Natural man is no longer in God's favor because he does not walk in fellowship with Him and carry out His purposes. It is for these reasons that the world has war, inhumanity, hatred, and the like. Man is out of tune with God's purposes and cannot live at peace with himself.

The early chapters of Genesis reveal the dramatic digression of mankind when it is spiritually dead. Sin entered into man's realm in chapter 3 when Adam and Eve partook of the forbidden fruit. That may seen like an innocuous, harmless act to many because it did not hurt anyone else. But look at what happened in the fourth chapter when sin's depravity took a great stride. This tells of the first murder, as one brother, Cain, killed the other, Abel, probably because of jealousy. By the sixth chapter, the destructive power of sin had gained momentum. The whole earth had become "filled with violence . . . corrupt" and God regretted that He had made human beings because man's mind was continually on evil. The destructive nature of sin had snowballed.

Peace and contentment will never be man's apart from fellowship with God. Augustine saw this in the individual and said, "Your soul can never find peace until it rests in Him." Man was created for fellowship with God, but sin ruptures that fellowship. Peace and contentment can never belong to him until that harmony is reestablished. Natural man remains spiritually dead in his trespasses and sins, lost and condemned.

Physical death is also a result of sin. This occurs when the spirit leaves the body and the process of putrefaction begins in it until it returns to the dust from whence it came. God did not plan for physical death to come to man. He never even intended for people to become sick or debilitated, or to suffer any physical impairment. These have come because of sin as Paul explained: "Death passed upon all men" because of it (Romans 5:12).

Nothing is more certain than physical death. Only two persons in history have escaped it: Enoch, who was translated because he walked in fellowship with God, and Elijah, who was carried away in the whirlwind. Christians who are alive when Jesus returns in the future will also miss it because they will be taken to be with Him in Heaven. However, the vast majority must prepare for the eventuality of physical death. The Bible says, "It is appointed unto men once to die . . ." (Hebrews 9:27). Physical death was not in God's plan, but sin has made it an unavoidable eventuality for most of us.

Those who are *spiritually dead* when they experience *physical death* will ultimately suffer the *second death*. One cannot ignore the Bible's teaching about the second death, which it often refers to as Hell. Walter Scott would call it one of the Scripture's "warnings to be heeded." Even logic demands that there be the punishment of Hell if there is to be the reward of Heaven. The Scripture calls it "outer darkness," "the lake of fire," "the furnace of fire," "everlasting fire," "the unquenchable fire," and so on. It is an eternal place, and once one enters into it, he can never escape from it. Jesus teaches this in His story of the rich man and Lazarus in Luke 16, where He explains that there is a "great gulf" between Hell and "Abraham's bosom."

Hell is essentially separation from God; banishment from all that is good, just, and joyful for eternity. Revelation 20 warns of its prospect in the account of the great white throne Judgment that will come at the end. Every man will be judged there according to his works. Those whose names are not found within the book of life will be cast into the lake of fire, which it calls "the second death." Jesus also warned people about this place called Hell. He said, "And fear not them which kill the body, but are not able to kill the soul: but rather fear him which is able to destroy both soul and body in hell" (Matthew 10:28).

Sin remains man's great problem. It keeps him from peace on earth and can condemn his soul to an eternity of Hell. How can one escape its consequences? Is there no atonement for sin?

The answer to these questions is both yes and no. Of course, the physical ravages sin has wrought upon this world can never be totally avoided. Sickness, suffering, heartache, and physical death are a part of the fabric of this age and will continue to its end. But one can escape from the consequences of spiritual death and the second death. God has made provision whereby fellowship with Him can be re-established. He says, "There is therefore now no condemnation to them which are in Christ Jesus" (Romans 8:1).

William Barclay notes that "there is no book which has so great a sense of the horror and the awfulness of sin as the New Testament has. But equally there is no book which is so sure that the cure and the remedy have been found."[1]

Walter Scott was most concerned about the provision God had made whereby one could enter into Christ and avoid condemnation. He restored the ancient gospel when he identified the steps in the plan of salvation that would re-establish fellowship with God. He discovered that the plan was so clear and simple that even the children, who had reached an age of accountability, could understand what to do to be saved from the consequences of sin. It all begins when one realizes that he has sinned, is a sinner, and must have God's forgiveness.

NOTES

[1]William Barclay, *New Testament Words* (Philadelphia: Westminster, 1976), p. 54.

11

GRACE

By grace ye are saved ... (Ephesians 2:5)

Man's inability to cope with his problem of sin brought into existence one of the most beautiful words in the English language—*grace*. The second most popular hymn in history sings its praises. It says, "Amazing grace, how sweet the sound, that saved a wretch like me." An understanding of the beauty of the word comes with a realization of the nature and consequences of sin.

Walter Scott pointed out that natural man is helplessly lost in sin. It entered the world through Adam, and everybody is condemned by it, for all have sinned and come short of the glory of God. The Bible teaches that one who experiences physical death while he is spiritually dead in his trespasses and sins will receive the second death. The second death is eternal separation from God, apart from all that is good, just, and joyful. The Scriptures call this Hell and warn that it should be avoided at all costs. Jesus said, "And fear not them which kill the body, but are not able to kill the soul: but rather fear him which is able to destroy both soul and body in hell" (Matthew 10:28).

The plan of salvation to save one from Hell, according to Scott, begins when he realizes that he has sinned, is a sinner, and must have God's forgiveness. No one can ever be saved from the consequences of his sin until he accepts this truth.

The sinner must also recognize that he himself can do nothing to earn or merit God's forgiveness. This is where the merely good, moral man misses the mark. He may compare himself to others, even Christians, and look pretty good, but he has sinned. The Scripture says, "All have sinned" (Romans 3:23). The book of James tells us that when a person commits one sin, he is just as much a sinner as if he had broken all the commandments (James 2:10). This truth is seen in the case of Adam and Eve in the garden when their one transgression separated them from fellowship with God.

Man could never save himself; he could never be good enough to go to Heaven. So God had to take the initiative to save man. This initiative is the good news which we call the gospel. God loved man so much that, even though he had rebelled against Him, He would make provision for him to escape condemnation. Paul expressed the good news this way: "But God commendeth his love toward us, in that, while we were yet sinners, Christ died for us" (Romans 5:8).

The good news reaches its climax in God's plan with the advent of Christ. As you will remember, Jesus' coming was first predicted way back in the garden when God cursed the serpent and said that he would crawl upon the earth on his stomach. Then He added, "And I will put enmity between thee and the woman, and between thy seed and her seed; it shall bruise thy head, and thou shalt bruise his heel" (Genesis 3:15). This was a two-fold prophecy: (1) Satan would injure the one who would come from the womb of woman, and (2) this one would destroy the devil's works.

God had His plan of salvation in mind even before Adam sinned. The Bible says He prepared for the coming and the death of Jesus from "the foundation of the world" (Revelation 13:8). Centuries before His advent, the prophets had repeatedly foretold Jesus' coming to take away the condemnation resulting from sin. Isaiah said, "But he was wounded for our transgressions, he was bruised for our iniquities ... the Lord hath laid on him the iniquity of us all" (Isaiah 53:5, 6). The angel told Joseph when he announced Jesus' birth, "Thou shalt call his name Jesus: for he shall save his people from their sins" (Matthew 1:21).

A favorite hymn of Christians exclaims, "Jesus saves! Jesus saves!" This sings of the heart of the gospel message. Jesus came into the world, born of a virgin, to provide man an escape from the condemnation of his sins. He came to seek and save the lost.

God's plan continued as Jesus lived among men and was tempted in all manner as other men are tempted, yet without sin (Hebrews 4:15). It was important that He remain sinless because one could not die for others' sins if he himself were a sinner. It required one as innocent and pure as a perfect *lamb*. Jesus' sinless life would enable the apostle to say, "For he hath made him to be sin for us, who knew no sin" (2 Corinthians 5:21).

God's plan reached its culmination with the cross. Somebody noted that the cross is a stake driven down into God's Word that divides it into two parts. Everything in the Old Testament points toward it and everything in the New Testament emanates from it. It would be the instrument upon which God would provide the way of escape from sin's condemnation.

The cross presents a paradox. It was the Roman method of capital punishment, which inflicted cruel torture upon its victims. Peloubet's *Bible Dictionary* says, "It was unanimously considered the most horrible form of death. . . . A death by crucifixion seems to include all that pain and death can have of the horrible and ghastly."[1] But, on the other hand, the apostle Paul would say of this instrument of torture, "God forbid that I should glory, save in the cross of our Lord Jesus Christ" (Galatians 6:14). Christians in this contemporary age wear replicas of Roman crosses about their necks and on their lapels out of deep affection. They sing:

"In the cross of Christ I glory,
Towering o'er the wrecks of time:
All the light of sacred story,
Gathers round its head sublime."

And the favorite hymn of all time is "The Old Rugged Cross."

The cross means much to Christians for at least three reasons. First, it reveals *God's love* as it could be revealed in no other way. Someone has said that the one picture of *perfect* love is the omnipotent God seated upon His throne in Heaven, with legions of angels at His disposal, but He lifts not one finger to save His only begotten Son from the cross because of His love for unlovely, unlovable sinful man. A story is told about a farmer who had two daughters. He worked hard to provide for them, often pulling rocks from the soil with his own hands to make a living. In so doing, his hands became twisted, gnarled, and calloused. When he died, the one preparing him for the final viewing looked at the gnarled hands and decided it would be in good taste to cover them. He put white gloves on the hands so they would not be seen by those who viewed him. However, this angered the daughters. They ordered the gloves removed, saying, "Those hands may be ugly to you, but they are beautiful to us. Every gnarl, every broken finger, shows just how much our father loved us and how he sacrificed to provide for us."

The nail-scarred hands of Jesus may be ugly to the world. But to those who believe, they are beautiful. They reveal just how much God loves them and how He sacrificed to provide their salvation.

Second, the cross reveals the *seriousness of sin*. Some ask, "How could a God of love punish anyone eternally in Hell?" But think for a moment. He pronounced the wages of sin to be death and said, "The soul that sinneth, it shall die" (Ezekiel 18:4). Habakkuk wrote, "Thou art of purer eyes than to behold evil" (Habakkuk 1:13). God is just, and for Him to overlook or ignore man's sin would be to break His word. Justice demands that sin be punished. The question keeps echoing down through the centuries: "How can man escape eternal death, which is the consequence of his sin?"

This leads to the third reason the cross means so much to Christians. God prepared His own Son to pay the penalty for man's sin on the cross. *He* paid the price. Then he offers escape from condemnation, which we call salvation, as a gift that is free. God never condemns anyone to Hell. One's sins condemn him if he will not accept this free gift God provided on the cross. He has gone the second mile, even turned the other cheek, so to speak, to provide the way of escape.

This brings us to the Biblical word *grace,* which is a beautiful and most meaningful term. It comes from the Greek word, *charis,* which originally meant physical beauty and is still used in that sense. If someone's beauty of person appeals to us, we say he is charming. The word *charm* comes from *charis.* Or, we might say the person is graceful, or, if he really impresses people, we refer to him as possessing charisma. Grace moves in the realm of attractiveness, winsomeness, loveliness, beauty, and charm.

It is a profound word, appearing over 166 times in Scripture. Also, Paul begins and ends every one of his epistles with the word grace. It appears in both the salutation or greeting and benediction of every one of them. William Barclay observes, "Every letter Paul wrote begins by striking the note of grace and ends by leaving the sound of grace ringing in men's ears."[2] He says, "The very essence of and center of Pauline faith and religion can be summed up in one brief sentence: 'All is of grace and grace is for all.'"[3]

The technical definition of grace in the Christian sense says, "It is unmerited favor freely given." It carries the idea of a gift that is completely free and entirely undeserved. No one can earn, merit, or justify grace. It comes from the sheer generosity of the giver's heart and can only be humbly, gratefully, and lovingly received.

The Scripture leaves no doubt but that the Christian's salvation comes from God's grace. Twice the apostle Paul says explicitly, "By grace are ye saved" (Ephesians 2:5, 8). It is the free, undeserved gift of God; free, but not *cheap*. It cost God His Son and was purchased with Christ's blood on the cross.

Paul made a contrast which shows the beauty of the word grace. He wrote: "The wages of sin is death; [if one is paid what he has earned and receives justice, he is lost for eternity]; but the gift of God is eternal life through Jesus Christ our Lord" (Romans 6:23). An acrostic illustrates the meaning of grace:

G od's
R iches
A t
C hrist's
E xpense

God's plan to provide the way of escape through grace presents the Christian with several big, multi-syllable words. But one should not shy away from them because they carry some of the most meaningful, beautiful promises of God's Word. Consider several of them.

ATONEMENT (a-TONE-ment). The atonement involves sacrifice. The Bible says about the forgiveness of sins, "Without shedding of blood is no remission" (Hebrews 9:22). God provided the Hebrews with a system of animal sacrifices, which caused someone to observe that "a scarlet thread" runs through the entire Bible. However, the blood of these sacrifices did not *take away* the sins of the people or absolve the guilt from them. It merely pushed them forward. Every sacrifice would make that accumulated cloud of sin bigger and blacker. The animal sacrifices pointed toward "the Lamb slain from the foundation of the world" (Revelation 13:8), which would be Jesus, who would go to the cross and shed His blood.

John the Baptist looked up, saw Jesus, and exclaimed, "Behold the Lamb of God, which *takethaway* the sin of the world" (John 1:29). The book of Revelation refers to Jesus twenty-nine times as the Lamb of God. But Jesus' sacrifice is different from animal sacrifices in that it does not merely push sins forward. Instead, it eliminates that black cloud. John says, "The blood of Jesus

Christ . . . cleanseth us from all sin" (1 John 1:7). His blood covers up our sin and hides it from the eyes of God.

William Tyndale translated the New Testament from the original language. He sought a word that would convey the renewed fellowship with God one can have in Christ. Unable to find one that suited him, he joined two words . . . "at" and "onement." It was a novel idea that shows how the substitutionary death of Christ on the cross can bring man and God back together. The Christian can enjoy the same fellowship Adam and Eve shared with Him before sin entered. Man's acceptance of the atonement, provided by God's grace, makes him once again "at-onement" with God.

The atonement carries with it the thought that Christ died in our stead. He took our place and His death atoned—paid the price—for our sins.

JUSTIFICATION (JUS-ti-fi-KA-shun). This is an exciting concept discussed extensively by Paul in Romans. It is best understood when put into the scenario of a court of law. The picture is that every person will stand guilty before God in the occasion of judgment, for "all have sinned." Justice demands that he be punished because "the wages of sin is death." But Jesus will step forward and say of the Christian, "I paid the penalty for his sins on the cross. He has accepted my gift of grace." With the penalty paid, God will treat the Christian just as if he had never committed one sin. "There is therefore now no condemnation to them which are in Christ Jesus, who walk not after the flesh, but after the Spirit" (Romans 8:1). This is the promise of God's grace.

Someone has said, "Justification means: just-as-if-I-had-not-sinned." Is that not an exciting concept? "Justified by his blood," it says, "we shall be saved from wrath through him" (Romans 5:9).

REDEMPTION (ree-DEMP-shun). The best picture of redemption is found in the slave market. Man was in bondage to sin; it had become his master. The Law of Moses could not free him. Instead, it condemned him and showed how often he had fallen short. Jesus' death on the cross was the price God paid to buy man back. Mark even calls it a "ransom" (Mark 10:45). The Scripture does not explain how this is effected, but it promises that those who accept Christ are reclaimed by God and are adopted into His family. They become His children, "heirs and joint-heirs with Christ," and can go boldly into His presence, as a child goes to his father. They can call Him, "Abba, Father," the intimate, personal title one gives to his progenitor in the Aramaic language.

There is a story about a little boy who worked long and hard to build a toy sailboat. It was one like he had always wanted. He took it to the pond for its maiden voyage, but a strong wind stirred up a tempest and took the little boat down the drain, into the gutter and sewer. It was lost. Later on, somebody found it, brought it to the toystore in the community, and sold it to the store's owner. One day the little boy, passing by, saw it in the toystore window and went in to claim it because he had made it. However, he learned that he would have to purchase it because it was now the possession of someone else. He went out and worked, sacrificing play time, until he had enough to redeem it When he had paid for the boat, he took it out of the store and said to it, "First, I made you; now I bought you."

This illustrates redemption. God made man who became lost in and possessed by sin. Then God redeemed him, purchased him back, with the death of His Son on the cross.

RECONCILIATION (REC-on-SIL-e-A-shun). This is the biggest of the big words, and perhaps the sweetest. Reconcile means to re-establish friendship. Sin separates one from God and creates a chasm between the two. Isaiah said, "Your iniquities have separated between you and your God, and your sins have hid his face from you" (Isaiah 59:2). There can be no fellowship with God as long as one remains dead in his trespasses and sins. But, once again, God made provision, this time for rapprochement. The apostle Paul said, "It pleased the Father . . . through the blood of his cross, by him to reconcile all things unto himself" (Colossians 1:19, 20). It is as if the cross were laid across that chasm created by sin, even as a bridge, that enables one to pass over it to fellowship with his Heavenly Father.

God made a way to escape the condemnation of sin. He provided the death of Christ on the cross to atone for man's sin, redeem him from its bondage, and reconcile him unto himself, so that he can stand justified before Him in the occasion of judgment. This gift comes from God's grace and begins what Walter Scott called "the ancient gospel," the good news. However, Scott was quick to point out that one must *accept* this gift. Subsequent chapters deal with the steps that lead to its acceptance.

NOTES

[1] F. N. Peloubet, *Peloubet's Bible Dictionary* (Philadelphia: John C. Winston Co., 1925), p. 130.

[2] William Barclay, *The Mind of St. Paul* (New York: Harper and Row, 1958), p. 159.

[3] Ibid., p. 154.

12

FAITH

"By grace are ye saved through faith . . ."
(Ephesians 2:8)

Walter Scott rightfully described natural man as helplessly lost in his trespasses and sin. But God took the initiative to provide him a way of escape from this condemnation. It is in the blood Jesus shed upon the cross. This is the gospel, the good news, which says, "Christ died for our sins," and "There is therefore now no condemnation to them which are in Christ Jesus." This salvation is a gift from God's grace and can never be earned or merited. However, Scott pointed out that it must be accepted, and the question one must ask is, "How can I receive the forgiveness of sins that Jesus procured for me in His death on the cross?"

The first response one must make for the forgiveness of his sins is *faith*. Nothing is more clear in God's Word than that truth. No one can misunderstand the importance of what Jesus meant when he said, "He that believeth and is baptized shall be saved; but he that believeth not shall be damned" (Mark 16:16). The Philippian jailer asked Paul and Silas, "Sirs, What must I do to be saved?" These two missionaries answered without hesitation or equivocation. They said, "Believe on the Lord Jesus Christ, and thou shalt be saved, and thy house." (Acts 16:30, 31). The writer of Hebrews sums up the New Testament emphasis on faith when he says, "But without faith it is impossible to please [God]: for he that cometh to God must believe that he is, and that he is a rewarder of them that diligently seek him" (Hebrews 11:6). The Scriptures show explicitly that faith is essential for one's salvation in Christ; the first step toward no condemnation in Him.

The Bible uses the word faith in several ways. It means, in the first instance, the *substance* or *content* of what a Christian believes. Jude tells us that this substance must be defended. He said, ". . . earnestly contend for the faith which was once delivered unto the saints" (Jude 3).

The faith of which Jude speaks means those truths most certainly believed by the faithful. The center and heart of *the faith* would be what Walter Scott referred to as the golden oracle, and which many today call the good confession. It is the statement of the apostle Peter when he said to Jesus, "Thou art the Christ, the Son of the living God" (Matthew 16:16). That is the essence of *the faith,* and no one becomes a Christian until he accepts that truth. It is the central and essential belief for one who would be in Christ Jesus.

There are other truths that contribute to the faith. Some of them are: the virgin birth, Jesus' sinless life and miracles, His vicarious death on the cross, and the great truth, which Paul uses as the foundation for faith in 1 Corinthians 15, the resurrection. One should include also the fulfillment of prophecy, Jesus' return, Heaven, Hell, and others. The faith refers to all those truths about Christ and the Christian life that God has revealed in Scripture.

Jude makes it clear that *the faith* was "once [and for all] delivered to the saints." It was not progressive and ongoing, but was given *once.* The early leaders of the restoration movement saw this finality. One will remember that Thomas Campbell said, "The Bible is the only rule of faith and practice for Christians;" and, "Nothing ought to be received into the faith and worship of the church . . . that is not as old as the New Testament." Barton W. Stone insisted that people must "take the Bible as the only sure guide to heaven." God revealed "once . . . for all" those truths to be believed by Christians within the pages of the Scriptures, and they became *the faith* for which all believers are to "contend earnestly."

But there is another way in which the Bible more often uses the word faith. It means, in these instances, *to believe in God's Word and trust His promises.*

This usage of faith fits the definition given to it in Hebrews 11:1. The King James Version translates this verse poorly when it calls faith "the substance of things hoped for, the evidence of things not seen." The word *substance* is misleading. It would seem to point to something tangible, such as a book, or pulpit, or house. And faith could not be the "evidence of things not seen." To the contrary, as Alexander Campbell pointed out, it is the *result* of the evidence and testimony of Scripture.

The American Standard Version translates the verse in a way

that gives faith a better definition. It says, "Now faith is assurance of things hoped for, a conviction of things not seen." This is more meaningful. One who believes God's Word and trusts His promises, for example, will have assurance of Heaven, which he hopes for. A Christian will believe his sins are forgiven because God promises it in His Word. Faith also provides a person convictions on such matters as the creation of the universe, which he could never see. He will believe it was "framed by the Word of God" because of the evidence and testimony of Scripture.

The eleventh chapter of Hebrews is sometimes called "God's Hall of Fame" because it contains the stories of those heroes of the Bible who walked by faith. They were great because they believed God's Word and trusted His promises. The chapter gives several interesting examples.

It says, "By faith Noah, being warned of God concerning things not seen as yet, moved with godly fear, prepared an ark to the saving of his house" (Hebrews 11:7, ASV). There was no reason for Noah to believe that a flood would come to inundate the earth, except that God told him to expect it. This warning launched him into one of the greatest engineering projects of history. The size, proportions, and endurance of that ship remain a marvel. It took Noah and his sons over one hundred years to construct it, and it would stay afloat twelve months without sight of land and come to rest on Mount Ararat without breaking up. It would house representatives of all living creatures and preserve their species.

His contemporaries mocked Noah. They laughed at him, made fun of him, but Noah believed God's Word and trusted His promises. He believed God would do exactly what He said He would do. So by faith, Noah built the ark according to God's specifications. His faith convinced him that the flood would come and assured him that the ark would save him, his family, and the human race.

The eleventh chapter of Hebrews makes Abraham the supreme example of one who lived by faith and provides two incidents in his life to illustrate this. The first one concerns his call to leave his home in the Ur of Chaldees when he was seventy-five years old. He was to go to a strange country and be a "sojourner," a nomad, as he would live in tents. It says, "He . . . obeyed; and he went out, not knowing whither he went" (Hebrews 11:8). He undertook this adventure because God promised him that his posterity would be more numerous than the sands of the sea and from it all peoples of the earth would be blessed. Abraham never possessed the Promised Land, except for Machpelah, the cave he purchased in order to bury his wife. But he walked by faith, knowing that God would keep His Word and honor the promise. It says, "For he looked for a city which hath foundations, whose builder and maker is God" (Hebrews 11:10).

Another incident in Abraham's life best illustrates faith as believing God's Word and trusting His promises. God had told Abraham and his wife, Sarah, that He would give them a son from whom would come a blessing to all men. He had reached a hundred years of age and Sarah was ninety, and they had no child. God reassured them when he said of Sarah, "And I will bless her, and give thee a son also of her ... and she shall be a mother of nations: kings of people shall be of her" (Genesis 17:16). God kept His Word and gave Abraham and Sarah a son. They named him Isaac, which means "laughter," because both of them had laughed in disbelief when told of Sarah's impending pregnancy.

When Isaac was twelve, God again tested Abraham's faith. He instructed this father to take his son to Mount Moriah and offer him in sacrifice. The story strikes terror into the hearts of most mothers and fathers because it is a test of one's faith beyond any other imaginable. But notice: Abraham did not hesitate. He made preparation and set out toward the appointed place. He built an altar, put the wood on it, bound Isaac, and laid him upon it. Then this father raised his knife above the breast of his most beloved son ready to deposit it into his heart.

A parent will ask, "How could Abraham do this?" The writer of Hebrews gives us the answer. He says that Abraham knew that God would raise him up from the dead; that, even if he sacrificed Isaac, God would give him back to them (Hebrews 11:19). He had promised; He had given His Word, and Abraham believed and trusted. Of course, God was one step ahead. He halted the father's upheld arm and provided a ram for the sacrifice. But Abraham had passed the test when he demonstrated in a vivid way that he believed God's Word and trusted His promises.

Another lesson should be learned from the lives of these heroes, and one heroine, of the Old Testament listed in Hebrews 11. They show that faith always produces action in one's life. It never lies dormant, idle. Noah's faith caused him to build the ark, which involved much work. Abraham's faith led him to journey into a foreign land and to take Isaac to Mount Moriah. This is the nature of faith—it causes people to do something because they believe God's Word and trust His promises.

The epistle of James substantiates this observation. It says, "Even so, faith, if it hath not works, is dead, being alone" (James 2:17), and goes on to give Abraham as an example. "You see that his faith and his actions were working together, and his faith was made complete by what he did" (James 2:22, NIV), it says. James believed that faith and action go hand-in-glove, and you cannot have one without the other. He points this out by saying, "Ye see then how that by works a man is justified, and not by faith only" (James 2:24).

Faith, in this sense, means to believe God's Word and trust His promises. It moves one to positive action and obedience toward Him because he is confident God will do what He says He will do.

An old-time evangelist would use his child to illustrate faith as trust in God's Word. He would stand up his five-year-old son on a long banquet table and say, "Come, jump into your daddy's arms." The little boy would comply, several times running the length of the table and leaping into his father's waiting arms. Then the father would blindfold him and say, "Come on. You don't have to worry. Your daddy is here to catch you." Without hesitation, the little boy would run headlong off the end of the table without fear. Why? He trusted his father's promise; he believed he would keep his word.

People cannot see far into the future. It is frightful to attempt to walk through life by sight. But Christians face the future confidently. Without hesitation, they enter into it with their Father's promise, "that in all things God works for the good of those who love him, who have been called according to his purpose" (Romans 8:28, NIV). Everybody can be victorious in the Christian life if he will only believe God's Word and trust His promises.

There is still another way in which the Bible uses the word *faith*. It means for one *to trust in Jesus alone to save him,* to depend upon His grace. This kind of faith is the first step one takes to become a Christian in Scott's five finger-exercise. It is the faith Jesus referred to when He said, "He that believeth and is baptized shall be saved" (Mark 16:16). Paul and Silas spoke of this kind of faith when they answered the Philippian jailer's question in Acts 16. They replied, "Believe on the Lord Jesus Christ . . ." (Acts 16:30, 31). They meant that the jailer would have to trust in Jesus *alone* to save him because "By grace ye are saved through faith. . . ."

This step in the plan of salvation was revolutionary to the Jews in New Testament times. Most of them attempted to live up to the law of Moses so their righteousness would make them acceptable to God. The Pharisees and scribes had tried to apply the law to life with such detail as to make it ridiculous. It had become an unbearable burden because no one could live up to its demands. The law's function was to condemn persons because it showed them that they had sinned and were lost. Alexander Campbell, as was mentioned earlier, pointed this out in his famous "Sermon on the Law," in which he called the law of Moses just a "schoolmaster" to prepare mankind for the coming of Christ. No one can be saved by keeping all the Old Testament commands, even if that were possible. He must put his faith in the atoning death of Christ on the cross because there is no other way to escape the condemnation of sin.

Many today try to stand justified before God by keeping rules as they seek to earn His forgiveness. They believe salvation comes from a perfunctory performance of religious rites. Martin Luther quarreled with this concept in the church of his age. He saw people trying to save themselves by performing the requirements laid down by the Roman Church and he knew this was wrong and insufficient. One must have a personal relationship with Christ, Luther said, that comes from trusting in Him alone for salvation. This is faith.

The merely moral person misses the mark the same way. This was mentioned earlier, but it bears repeating. One may compare himself to others and look rather well because he lives a fairly good life. However, he has sinned, a fact common to all mankind. This puts him in the same boat as the rest of the human race. He, too, stands under the condemnation of sin and no number of good works can change that. One is fooled if he thinks he can save himself with good works. Forgiveness comes from God's grace, and the first response to grace is for one to trust in Jesus to save him.

If faith is essential to salvation, a person must certainly ask, "How is it received? Where can it be found so one can appropriate it to his life?" The Bible answers these questions. (You will find the Bible always best interprets itself. Do you have a question about the Bible? Then turn to it and you will most likely find the answer you need.) Paul said in Romans 10:17, "So then faith cometh by hearing, and hearing by the word of God."

There is but one source of faith. A person does not inherit it, nor can it be purchased or borrowed. Faith comes from the teaching, preaching, and reading of God's Word. It contains the law, which convicts people of their sins; the gospel, the good news of salvation in Christ; the steps in the plan of salvation; and how to grow up in Christ and live the Christian life. God's Word alone brings one to the place where he believes and trusts in Jesus and grows in His grace and knowledge.

Both Noah and Abraham, who walked by faith, illustrated its source. Noah built the ark. Why? Because he reasoned that it would be a nice thing to do in his spare time? Or, because Mrs. Noah and the boys wanted a yacht? No! He constructed the ark because God's Word told him to. God's Word was the source of his faith and action. Abraham sojourned in a strange land. A vacation? A sight-seeing trip? Ridiculous! God's Word instructed him to become a nomad in Canaan and gave him the promise of a son. He went to Mount Moriah—to offer Isaac as a perfunctory performance of religious rites? Certainly not! Abraham believed God's Word. This was the source that produced faith and motivated his action.

Faith is essential to salvation because the Scripture says, "He that cometh to God must believe that He is, and that He is a rewarder of them that diligently seek him" (Hebrews 11:6). It is the first step to receiving God's grace. One must trust in Jesus' atoning death on the cross to save him. He must believe God's Word and trust His promises revealed in the teaching and preaching of the faith once delivered unto the saints, which he finds in the Bible. As the early leaders of the restoration movement said, "Faith is the result of the evidence and testimony of Scripture" and leads one to be in Christ, where there is no condemnation.

13

REPENTANCE

"God . . . now commandeth all men every where to repent" (Acts 17:30)

Man remained lost in his trespasses and sins, but God took the initiative and provided a way of escape through the blood Christ shed upon the cross. Faith is the first step in responding to God's grace. It means to trust in Jesus to save us, "For," as the Scripture says, "there is none other name under heaven given among men, whereby we must be saved" (Acts 4:12). One may live a good moral life, filled with virtue, but he remains lost until he accepts Christ as his Savior.

Walter Scott identified *repentance* as the second step in the plan of salvation. It may well be the most difficult step for the unsaved person to take and also the most neglected in contemporary preaching. There can be no doubt about its being essential to salvation. Peter made that clear on the Day of Pentecost in Acts 2, when he preached the first gospel sermon. A gospel sermon is one that portrays Jesus as Savior, the way of escape from the consequences of sin. Peter showed the people how God had prepared Jesus to come into the world. He used both prophecy and His miracles to sustain this point. Then he drove home the accusation of their sin as he said, "Him . . . ye have taken, and by wicked hands have crucified and slain: whom God hath raised up, having loosed the pangs of death: because it was not possible that he should be holden of it" (Acts 2:23, 24). Peter's sermon accomplished its purpose. It convicted the people of their sins, for the Scripture says, "They were pricked in their heart." They asked, "What shall we do?" How could they be forgiven and enter into a right relationship with God? Peter, under the inspiration of the Holy Spirit, answered, "Repent, and be baptized every one of you in the name of Jesus Christ for the remission of sins, and ye shall receive the gift of the Holy Spirit" (Acts 2:37, 38).

Peter's sermon had made believers out of the listeners. That is an obvious inference because they would not have asked what to do if they had not believed. The next step they had to take, according to the apostle, was repentance.

The apostle Paul reiterates Peter's emphasis upon repentance. He preached to the Athenians in Acts 17 using an altar "to the unknown god" as a beginning point. He chastised them for their idolatry, gods made of silver, gold, and wood. He said, "And the times of this ignorance God winked at; but now commandeth all men every where to repent: because he hath appointed a day, in the which he will judge the world in righteousness ..." (Acts 17:30, 31). Paul uses redundancy—"all men every where"—to establish the necessity of repentance for salvation.

There can be no doubt but what repentance is a step in the plan of salvation. However, its necessity was proclaimed long before the Christian gospel was known. Jonah preached repentance to the Ninevites back in the Old Testament, and it says they turned to God as a result of it and were saved. Ezekiel, another prophet, said, "Repent, and turn yourselves from all your transgressions; so iniquity shall not be your ruin" (Ezekiel 18:30). John the Baptist came with a message of repentance, exclaiming, "Repent ye: for the kingdom of heaven is at hand" (Matthew 3:2).

Jesus emphasized repentance. His disciples were concerned about why misfortune comes both to the righteous and unrighteous. They asked Him why the Tower of Siloam fell and killed so many; was it because of the victims' sins, or the sins of their forefathers? Jesus replied, "Nay: but, except ye repent, ye shall all likewise perish" (Luke 13:3). Jesus' lesson was clear. Misfortune comes to everyone, the good and the bad. No one escapes it because it is a part of the fabric of life. But those who fail to repent will remain lost in their trespasses and sins and will perish in the end.

Some of Jesus' loveliest parables deal with repentance. He told the story of the Good Shepherd in Luke 15; how He came to seek and save the lost. At the end, He added, "Joy shall be in heaven over one sinner that repenteth, more than over ninety and nine just persons, which need no repentance" (Luke 15:7). And some people believe the parable of the prodigal son (Luke 15:11-32), best illustrates repentance. The boy wasted his substance in riotous living, found himself in need, confessed his sin, and returned to his forgiving father.

The etymology of the word repentance presents an interesting study. It is translated in the New Testament from the Greek word, *metanoia*. It originally meant "to perceive afterwards," or as "an afterthought," but came to mean "a change in one's mind or purpose." The word is found often in Scripture: nine times in Luke, five times in Acts, and Revelation uses it twelve times. It always refers to a change for the better, never the worse; an inward change that produces outward results for a person's betterment.

John W. McGarvey, one of the later leaders of the restoration movement, defined repentance as a *change of will*. He let the Scripture interpret itself. Many erroneously define repentance as "godly sorrow for one's sins." They believe that, if a person feels badly enough about his lack of obedience to God's will, he has repented. This is a most common misunderstanding. It is true that there can be no repentance without godly sorrow, but it is also true that one can possess godly sorrow and remain unrepentant. McGarvey points out this truth correctly from one verse of Scripture, 2 Corinthians 7:10. The apostle Paul had written a previous letter to the congregation at Corinth and had rebuked many members of the church there. There were numerous problems within that church, some of a most serious nature, and it is obvious that his strong words had hurt the feelings of many. So the apostle wrote this explanation, "Though I made you sorry with my epistle, I do not regret it: though I did regret it . . . for ye were made sorry after a godly sort. . . . *For godly sorrow worketh repentance unto salvation, a repentace which brigneth no regret*" (2 Corinthians 7:8-10, ASV).

The point is this: the godly sorrow produced by the earlier epistle was not repentance itself, but was the cause of it. One preceded the other—godly sorrow was the cause; repentance, the result. The two could not be the same.

Other people make the mistake of equating repentance with a *reformation of life*. However, McGarvey used the teaching of John the Baptist to point out this error. John preached a baptism of repentance, and some came to him to be baptized who were not sincere, namely the Pharisees and Sadducees. So John refused to baptize them, saying, "Bring forth fruits worthy of repentance." This evoked questions from others present. They asked, "What shall we do then?" or, "What are the fruits of repentance?" John replied, "He that hath two coats, let him impart to him that hath none; and he that hath meat, let him do likewise." Their repentance would bring forth the fruits of generosity and kindness. He told the publicans, tax-collectors, that the fruit of their repentance would be to "exact no more than that which is appointed" them. Repentance would make them honest. Soldiers were present who asked, "What shall we do?" John replied, "Do violence to no man" (Luke 3:8-14).

In each case, the fruit of repentance was a reformed life. The cause and effect were the opposite from godly sorrow and repentance. Godly sorrow caused repentance and, here, repentance was the cause and a reformed life was the result.

It is obvious from this analogy that repentance lies somewhere between godly sorrow, on the one hand, and a reformed life on the other hand. It is the *link* connecting the two. What is this link? What bridges the gap between them? McGarvey had no difficulty in identifying it. He said, "It is a change of that stubborn will which is the seat of all rebellion and all sin against God." *Repentance, then, is a change of will in regard to sin.*

A person can test this definition in his own experience. He is rebellious toward God, lost in his trespasses and sins, unwilling to become a Christian and be led by the Holy Spirit. He may even want Jesus to be his Savior, but he has not accepted Christ. Then the Word of God convicts him of his sin, and he becomes sorrowful. This causes him to change his *will*. He becomes willing to leave his sin, become a Christian, and follow the leading of the Holy Spirit. This, in turn, creates within him different attitudes and a reformed life.

This change of will in regard to sin is obviously essential to salvation. So, the next question would be: how is one brought to the godly sorrow that causes repentance? It is easy to identify the conveyance. It is the Word of God.

The early leaders of the restoration movement clearly identified the Scriptures as the power that brought about this change of will within a person. Calvinism was the prevailing doctrine of the American frontier of their day. It teaches that God has to act directly and personally upon one before he can be called, or saved. Those whom God chooses to give His "irresistible grace," as it was called, are the *chosen*. All others are lost, unable to help themselves; doomed and damned. Barton W. Stone disagreed with this doctrine and it contributed to his leaving the denomination of which he was a part. He emphasized that "Christ died for *all*"— not just the elect.

Alexander Campbell expressed his agreement with Stone. He said, "It is an overwhelming fact that God does nothing in creation or redemption without His Word. . . . There was *through the Word* an almighty power put forth, and still there is both in conversion and sanctification. God works mightily in the human heart by His Word."[1]

Jesus taught that it is the Word of God that brings people to repentance through His story of the rich man and Lazarus in Luke 16. Lazarus was a beggar who ate the crumbs that fell from the table of the rich man. Both died, and Lazarus went to "Abraham's bosom," but the rich man went to "Hades," a place of torment. The rich man asked Abraham to send Lazarus that he might dip his finger in water and cool his tongue. But that was impossible because a great gulf existed between the two. Then the rich man thought of his five brothers who remained on earth. He pleaded with Abraham to send Lazarus to warn them of the "wages" of their sins. But Abraham rejected the request, and his answer shows Jesus' understanding of what produces repentance. The rich man had said, "If one went unto them from the dead, they will repent." Abraham replied, saying, "If they hear not Moses and the prophets, neither will they be persuaded, though one rose from the dead" (Luke 16:31).

The law of Moses and the teaching of the prophets composed the Scriptures of that day. Jesus was teaching that it is the Word of God that brings people to repentance, and one who will not be brought to godly sorrow and a change of will in regard to sin by the Word is lost. Even a messenger from the dead would have little effect upon him.

Consider how the Word of God leads one to repentance. First, *it exposes the reality of sin.* One might possess an innate sense of ethical right and wrong as Paul seems to imply when he speaks of those who "do by nature the things contained in the law" (Romans 2:14, 15). However, it would be slight and unreliable. But God provided a sure definition of the rules of life in the law and the prophets, and then refined these in the New Testament. The searchlight of Scripture shows the presence of sin in a person's heart; even the best people see themselves as sinners by it. Peter said, "I am a sinful man" (Luke 5:8), and Paul called himself "the chief of sinners."

Second, the Word of God *warns of the consequences of sin.* Walter Scott divided the gospel into several parts. He said it is composed of facts to be believed, commands to be obeyed, promises to be received, and warnings to be heeded. The consequences of sin would be its most ominous warning. Some in this contemporary age would eliminate Hell and its eternal punishment on cultural grounds because they feel it offends sophisticated people, and, of course, it is not the primary emphasis of Scripture. However, to eliminate punishment for sin altogether truncates the gospel. A teacher or preacher who fails to warn of the consequences of sin is unfaithful both to his hearers and to the Word of God. The Bible's warning of the consequences of sin is a powerful force to turn people from sin that they may walk in righteousness.

But there is a stronger power in the Word that will bring people to repentance. *It is love of God as revealed in Christ.* This was demonstrated in the life of Barton W. Stone. Remember? The "hellfire and brimstone" preaching of the revivalists of his day failed to reach him. Then he heard a sermon by William Hodge entitled, "The Love of God," preached with tears. It brought him to godly sorrow for his sins, which led him to be willing to give himself to Christ, and launched him into a fruitful ministry.

Paul used both the love of God and a warning of the consequences of sin to bring the Romans to repentance. He wrote, "Do you think you will escape God's judgment? Or do you show contempt for the riches of his kindness, tolerance and patience, not realizing that God's kindness leads you towards repentance? But because of your stubbornness and your unrepentant heart, you are storing up wrath against yourself for the day of God's wrath, when his righteous judgment will be revealed" (Romans 2:3-5, NIV). According to the apostle, both God's judgment and His kindness lead people to repentance.

Repentance presents the most difficult step in the plan of salvation to induce. Most people believe that God exists and "is a rewarder of them that diligently seek him" (Hebrews 11:6). McGarvey observed that it is not difficult to plant faith within the souls of people. Neither does it require great effort to persuade penitent believers to receive Christian baptism. Most of them are anxious for it. The difficulty in bringing one into Christ lies in the *stubborn will.* The lost remain so, in most instances, because of their unwillingness to turn from sin to walk in righteousness. This is the reason for joy in Heaven when a person repents; it represents a great victory. One who can persuade people to repent will be the most effective evangelist. This is where the difficulty most often lies.

Consider a lesson on repentance from the lives of Peter and Judas. The contrast is most dramatic, for both were apostles and walked with Jesus for three years, and both sinned. Judas betrayed Christ to the authorities while Peter denied Him three times, once with cursing and swearing. However, Peter would later be honored. He would go on to preach the first gospel sermon and would use "the keys to the kingdom" (Matthew 16:19) to open the door of salvation to all who would accept it. Christians remember Peter with respect and affection as the "big fisherman." Judas, on the other hand, is remembered only for his villiany. What made the difference? *Repentance!* Peter wept bitterly, changed his will toward Christ, and came back to Him. Judas went out and hanged himself. The forgiveness of God awaited him just as it did his compatriot. The gospel assures that. The difference? One repented and was honored; the other failed to do so and goes down in history with infamy.

Jesus' words are just as relevant today as when He spoke them: "Except ye repent, ye shall likewise perish." Repentance is not salvation itself. Some make the mistake of thinking it is because of the relief felt when they change their will toward Christ. It brings joy. However, repentance is just a step toward salvation— one accepts Christ as his Savior, which is faith, the first step; then he becomes willing to become a Christian, to give his life to Christ, which is repentance, the second step. But Walter Scott was careful to point out that repentance does not achieve salvation, but is a step toward being "in Christ," where there is no condemnation.

NOTES

[1]*A Compend of Alexander Campbell's Theology,* Royal Humbert, ed. (St. Louis: Bethany Press, 1961), p. 113.

14

THE GOOD CONFESSION

"Whosoever shall confess me before men, him will I confess also before my Father which is in heaven."
(Matthew 10:32)

Put yourself in the position of one who realizes he has sinned, is a sinner, and must have God's forgiveness. The gospel speaks to his need. It says, "Christ died for our sins" and "There is therefore now no condemnation to them which are in Christ Jesus." This leads him to want Jesus to become his Savior and to receive the grace He provided on the cross. This could be called a change of mind, or heart. He accepts the evidence and testimony of Scripture and trusts in Jesus alone to save him—which is *faith*.

Then this person must decide to become a Christian. He must be willing to turn from sin to walk in righteousness. The Bible calls this repentance—which is a change of will. One who has not been willing to become a Christian and be guided by the Holy Spirit changes his will and becomes *willing* to surrender himself to God's plan for his life.

The next step in the plan of salvation might be called a change of identity. A person changes his mind or heart toward Christ by faith; he changes his will toward Him in repentance; and by means of the good confession he changes his identity.

Walter Scott, who restored the ancient gospel, identified the good confession. He found it in Matthew 16:16, called it "The Golden Oracle," and it became the heart of his preaching. He referred to it when he said, "The Holy Book contains one truth which is the sun to which all other Christian truths are planets in a spiritual solar system. [It] is the creed of the Christian, the bond of Christian union, and the way of salvation."[1]

The background of the good confession may be found in the ninth chapter of John. There Jesus healed a blind man on the Sabbath, and the Pharisees condemned Him saying, "This man is not of God, because he keepeth not the sabbath day" (John 9:16). Then they made an agreement among themselves, saying, "... if any man did confess that [Jesus] was Christ, he should be put out of the synagogue" (John 9:22). His enemies rejected the miracles that attested to Jesus' deity and drew a line: anybody who confessed Jesus as the Christ, the Son of the Living God, would be expelled from the synagogue's membership.

It may have been within this context that Jesus met with His disciples in Matthew 16 on the coasts of Caesarea Philippi. He asked them, "Whom do men say that I the Son of man am?" They responded politely, "Some say that thou art John the Baptist; some, Elijah; and others, Jeremiah, or one of the prophets." Then Jesus turned the question and aimed it at them: "But whom say ye that I am?" Their answer would determine on which side of the line they stood. The Scripture seems to indicate that the apostle Peter almost blurted out the answer, "Thou art the Christ, the Son of the living God." One can feel Jesus' delight with this reply. Knowing it was a divine statement, given by God, He pronounced Peter "blessed" and gave him "the keys of the kingdom of heaven" (Matthew 16:13-19).

The faith expressed in this confession would serve as the foundation upon which Jesus would build His church. Every Christian must accept Him as "the Christ, the Son of the living God." It is the essence of faith, the truth upon which Christianity rests, the sun of the spiritual solar system. The early leaders of the restoration movement came to call it the *good* confession.

An analysis of the statement reveals *why* it is good. First of all, it asserts that Jesus is the *Christ*. Many people make the mistake of believing that Jesus Christ was the Lord's given name, as George Washington was that given to the father of our country. This is inaccurate, or, at least, it is half wrong. Jesus was His given name, prescribed by God Himself, even before the child was born. His angel said to Joseph, "And [Mary] shall bring forth a son, and thou shalt call his name Jesus: for he shall save his people from their sins" (Matthew 1:21).

Jesus was an often used name for boys in New Testament times. It was the Greek version of the Hebrew, *Joshua*. Everyone will remember another famous Bible hero with that name—the military leader who took the children of Israel into the promised land. His name had been Hoshea, the son of Nun. The name meant "salvation," but Moses changed it to Joshua when he sent him with the twelve spies into Canaan in Numbers 13. In Hebrew the new name meant "Jehovah is salvation" or "Jehovah saves." It is significant that God gave His Son the Greek name *Jesus,* because it was His purpose to save people from their sins.

However, the word *Christ* is not a name at all. Instead, it is a title. In comparison to the father of our country, it would be more nearly *President* Washington or *General* Washington, which denotes an office or position. The word comes from the Greek, *Christos* which is the equivalent to the Hebrew word translated, Messiah, and means "the anointed; the one appointed by God whom the Jews anticipated." Three offices in the Old Testament required the anointing of God: king, priest, and prophet. One who makes the good confession acknowledges that Jesus is each of these in a unique way.

First of all, the *Christ* means that Jesus is *King.* There can be no doubt but what He thought of himself as such. A central theme in His message was the kingdom, and how can there be a kingdom without a king? Pilate asked Jesus, "Art thou the King of the Jews?" His reply is interesting, "Thou sayest" (Matthew 27:11). William Barclay says of this answer, "It is as if Jesus said that it was verbally correct to call him a king, but that at the same time neither Pilate nor the Jews had even begun to understand what that kingship meant."[2] Modern language translations have Jesus answering more positively. J.B. Phillips, for example, translates His reply as, "Yes, I am."

Others recognized Jesus' royalty. The Magi came asking, "Where is he that is born King of the Jews?" (Matthew 2:2). The angel said to Mary, "The Lord God shall give unto him the throne of his father David: and he shall reign over the house of Jacob forever; and of his kingdom there shall be no end" (Luke 1:32, 33). The apostles looked upon Jesus as king. Nathaniel addressed Him saying "Rabbi, thou art the Son of God; thou art the King of Israel" (John 1:49). James and John asked to sit on either His right or left when He came into His kingdom. Even Pilate may have sensed His kingly nature, for one will remember the inscription he placed on the cross in three languages, "Jesus of Nazareth the King of the Jews." The chief priests sought to have him change this to read, "He said, I am King of the Jews," but Pilate refused (John 19:19-22).

However, the greatest affirmation of His Kingship is found in the book of Revelation. Twice it proclaims Him as "King of kings," and Lord of lords" (Revelation 17:14; 19:16). It says, "The kingdoms of this world are become the kingdoms of our lord, and of his Christ; and he shall reign forever and ever" (Revelation 11:15).

A quality of a king is that he rules. One who makes the good confession accepts this and becomes Jesus' subject within His kingdom. Paul often spoke of Christians as being servants of Christ. He would most often use the Greek word, *doulos,* which carries the implication of "one who belongs to another, even as a slave is owned by his master." The price of redemption from the slavery of sin was paid by Christ in His death on the cross. The apostle points this out when he says, "Know ye not that . . . ye are not your own? For ye are bought with a price: therefore glorify God in your body, and in your spirit, which are God's" (1 Corinthians 6:19, 20). One who wants Jesus to be his Savior must, at the same time, accept Him as his Lord, in voluntary servitude.

However, this servitude is the only way to abundant life. For Christ's kingdom is not of this world; it is within the heart. He rules not by force but by love, and what a glorious thing it is to have the kingdom of heaven within one's heart!

A person who makes the good confession also recognizes Jesus as his great *High Priest.* The high priest occupied a peculiar position in the life of the ancient Hebrews. He was the only person who could enter into the Holy of Holies in the Temple, the place that represented the presence of God in the midst of His people. He could enter it just one time each year on the Day of Atonement. The purpose of this entrance into God's presence was to sprinkle the blood of the sacrificial lamb on the Ark of the Covenant. This pushed forward the sins of the people, gained God's forgiveness temporarily, and enabled them to remain His people. This act had to be repeated year after year.

The theme of the book of Hebrews shows that Jesus is the Christian's great high priest, superior to His Old Testament type, forerunner, or shadow. Jesus, the High Priest, serves the Christian in two ways. First, He makes intercession in his behalf before God, even as only the Jewish high priest could plead the case of his people before Him.

This role of Jesus for the Christian is most comforting. Twice the book of Hebrews says that He makes intercession before God for Christians (Hebrews 7:25; 9:24). The apostle John expressed it this way, "And if any man sin, we have an advocate with the Father, Jesus Christ the righteous" (1 John 2:1). An advocate is one who pleads another's case, or represents him, a supporter, a defender. Is that not a comfort? The Christian sins, but he knows that Jesus stands at the right hand of the throne of God pleading his case and making intercession for him.

This work of Jesus as high priest may demonstrate the necessity of one's making the good confession. It will be remembered that Jesus said, "Whosoever therefore shall confess me before men, him will I confess also before my Father which is in heaven. But whosoever shall deny me before men, him will I also deny before my Father which is in heaven" (Matthew 10:32, 33). It is obvious from this statement that one who has not confessed Jesus as "the Christ, the Son of the living God," will not have Him as his advocate before the Father.

But Jesus is not only the Christian's advocate before God. He is also, in the second place, the way through whom one can enter into the presence of God. The Latin word for priest is *pontifex,* which means "bridge-builder." This is what Jesus accomplished in His death on the cross. He built a *bridge* whereby those who accept Him can enter boldly into the presence of God even as His children. Jesus said, "I am the way . . . no man cometh unto the Father, but by me" (John 14:6). Christians need no human priest or saint to intercede for them because, in Christ, they can enter into the presence of God even as children would approach a loving Father. Jesus is their *pontifex,* their bridge-builder, their priest, who has provided the way for them to enter into the heart of God.

In the good confession, the statement, "Jesus is the Christ," also implies that He should be seen as a *Prophet.* Kings and priests had to be anointed, and so did prophets.

There is no doubt but what many people in Jesus's day looked upon Him as a prophet. He asked the apostles on the coasts of Caesarea Philippi, "Whom do men say that I, the Son of man, am?" One will remember their reply, "One of the prophets" (Matthew 16:13, 14). When He healed the widow of Nain's son, this miracle produced a reaction from the people who exclaimed, "A great prophet is risen among us" (Luke 7:16). The multitude extolled Him as a prophet when He entered Jerusalem on His triumphal entry, saying, "This is Jesus the prophet of Nazareth of Galilee" (Matthew 21:11).

Jesus also referred to himself as a prophet. In the thirteenth chapter of Luke, Herod had threatened to kill Him, and His friends begged Him to leave Jerusalem because of the danger, but

He refused, saying, "For it cannot be that a prophet perish out of Jerusalem" (Luke 13:33). Upon another occasion, His townspeople expelled Him from Nazareth. He lamented the act, saying, "Verily I say unto you, No prophet is accepted in his own country" (Luke 4:24).

However, the Jews made the mistake of thinking of Jesus as just *a* prophet, along with all the others, which was an inaccurate conception. Jesus was *the* prophet that had been anticipated for centuries. Peter referred to this expectation when he said, "For Moses truly said unto the fathers, A Prophet shall the Lord your God raise up unto you of your brethren, like unto me; him shall ye hear in all things whatsoever he shall say unto you" (Acts 3:22). The book of Hebrews shows Jesus to be the prophet above all prophets. It begins with this statement, "God, who at sundry times and in divers manners spake in time past unto the fathers by the prophets, hath in these last days spoken unto us by his Son ..." (Hebrews 1:1, 2).

Jesus did fulfill the role as *the* Prophet. A prophet was one sent by God to forth-tell His Word and to call men back to Him. This Jesus did in a unique way. He was the Word—the Living Word, God's ultimate revelation of himself. He not only called people back to God, but also provided them the way back to Him.

So, when one makes the good confession, he says he believes that "Jesus is the Christ." This implies that he accepts Him as (1) the King to reign over his life; (2) the High Priest who will make intercession for him before God, and (3) the Prophet who came to reveal God's will in an ultimate way.

But, the good confession contains a second part. Jesus is also "the Son of the living God." Just as He was *the* Prophet, He is also *the* Son of God, not just *a* son. He was the one born of a virgin who lived a perfect life because He was fully God. When one knows Jesus, he knows God because Jesus was God in the flesh. This is the central truth of the Christian faith to which the Scripture gives testimony over and over.

The apostle Philip made a request of Jesus at the Last Supper. He said, "Show us the Father, and it sufficeth us." Jesus rebuked him and replied, "He that hath seen me hath seen the Father" (John 14:8, 9). Twice in the little book of Colossians, Paul proclaims this truth: "For in Christ all the fulness of the Deity lives in bodily form" (Colossians 2:9; cf 1:19, NIV). He says He is "the image of the invisible God" (Colossians 1:15), to which Hebrews adds, "the *express* [or very] image of his person" (Hebrews 1:3). Paul goes on to explain that Jesus, being in the form of God and equal with God, "took upon him the form of a servant, and was made in the likeness of men" (Philippians 2:6, 7). Jesus was God who lived in the flesh. When people saw Him, they saw God because He *was* God. That truth bears repeating because it is so important. A believer testifies to that when he says, "Thou art . . . the Son of the living God."

The New Testament also points out that the good confession is a link between faith and Christian baptism. Romans 10:9 and 10 says, "If thou shalt confess with thy mouth the Lord Jesus, and shalt believe in thine heart that God hath raised him from the dead, thou shalt be saved. For with the heart man believeth unto righteousness; and with the mouth confession is made unto salvation." It is logical progression: one believes in Christ as his Lord and Savior and it is natural for him to express it in the good confession. Acts 8:26-39 records an incident which reveals that the confession must precede Christian baptism.

Philip the evangelist had preached Jesus to an Ethiopian while riding in his chariot on the road to Gaza, and the man believed. He accepted the evidence and testimony presented by the preacher and said, "See, here is water; what doth hinder me to be baptized?" Philip told him that he had to believe with all his heart and the Ethiopian responded with the good confession. He said, "I believe that Jesus Christ is the Son of God." The good confession was the link that connected the man's faith and desire to be baptized into Christ.

The most beautiful and profound words ever spoken are, "Thou art the Christ, the Son of the Living God." They identify an individual's faith in Christ, and upon them Jesus founded His church. The good confession is truly "the sun to which all other Christian truths are planets in a spiritual solar system."

NOTES

[1]Dwight Stevenson, *Walter Scott: The Voice of the Golden Oracle* (St. Louis: Christian Board of Publication, 1946), p. 54.

[2]William Barclay, *Jesus As the Disciples Saw Him* (New York: Harper and Row, 1962), p. 241.

15

THE MEANING OF CHRISTIAN BAPTISM

". . . even baptism doth also now save us . . ."
(1 Peter 3:21)

Our consideration of responding to God's grace now brings us to one of life's most beautiful experiences, Christian baptism, the climax of one's acceptance of Christ.

Faith, as has been noted, might be called a change of *mind* or *heart;* one accepts the evidence and testimony of Scripture and trusts in Jesus to save him. Repentance is a change of *will;* one is unwilling to become a Christian; then he changes his will and becomes willing to leave sin and walk in righteousness. The good confession could be called a change of *identity* because it makes known one's faith and desire to accept Christ as his Lord and Savior. Christian baptism marks a change of *state* or *relationship with God.* It is the sign, seal, climax, and culmination of one's acceptance of Christ in faith and marks his becoming a Christian. Walter Scott considered it the "missing link" in his "Gospel Restored" when he discovered it was associated with salvation in the New Testament.

Christian baptism must be taken seriously because Jesus commanded it. He gave the apostles the Great Commission, which became the marching orders of the church. He said, "Go ye therefore, and teach all nations, baptizing them in the name of the Father, and of the Son, and of the Holy Ghost: teaching them to observe all things whatsoever I have commanded you: and, lo, I am with you alway, even unto the end of the world" (Matthew 28:19, 20). The commandment of Jesus to the church was that it should *go, teach, baptize and teach*—which makes Christian baptism essential to the mission of the church. It must never be considered lightly because Jesus commanded it, and He said, "If ye love me, keep my commandments" (John 14:15).

The importance of Christian baptism is also seen in the book of Acts, which contains six accounts of conversion. Faith,

115

repentance, and the good confession are implied in each of them but are not always explicitly mentioned. However, the Holy Spirit was careful to specifically mention Christian baptism in each account.

The first conversion was on the Day of Pentecost in Acts 2, after Peter had preached the gospel on that occasion for the first time. The people responded with the question, "What shall we do?" This query implies faith, for it is obvious they believed the evidence and testimony of the apostle's sermon or they would not have asked the question. Peter told them to "Repent, and be baptized . . ." (Acts 2:38). It says, "Then they that gladly received his word were baptized . . . about three thousand souls" (Acts 2:41). This account implies the good confession, for how else could be people make known their faith and their desire to become Christians? Faith and confession are only implicit in this conversion, while repentance and baptism are explicit.

The conversion of the Ethiopian treasurer is found in the eighth chapter of Acts. It will be remembered that he wanted to be baptized and said, "See, here is water; what doth hinder me to be baptized?" However, it was necessary for him to confess his faith before he could receive Christian baptism. He said, "I believe that Jesus Christ is the Son of God" (Acts 8:37). Repentance is not mentioned explicitly in this conversion. Neither will that word be found in the case of the first Gentile convert, Cornelius, in the tenth chapter of Acts. The apostle Peter preached to him and his household. They believed, and Peter "commanded them to be baptized in the name of the Lord" (Acts 10:48). Repentance is only implied in each of these accounts, but, once again, Christian baptism is explicit, clearly required of those accepting Christ.

Acts carries the conversion of Saul of Tarsus in chapter nine. Once again, faith, repentance, and the good confession are not mentioned explicitly, but it says, "He . . . arose, and was baptized" (Act 9:18). The Philippian jailer and Lydia accepted Christ in chapter 16. Only baptism is mentioned specifically in Lydia's conversion. No reference is made to repentance or the good confession in the jailer's case, but he was told to "believe on the Lord Jesus Christ . . ." (Acts 16:31), and he "was baptized, he and all his, straightway" (Acts 16:33).

Christian baptism must be taken seriously by one who wants to be saved by Christ. Jesus commanded it, and every person who accepted Him as his Savior in the book of Acts was baptized.

Much of the rest of the New Testament associates Christian

baptism with salvation. This also cannot be ignored because so many Scriptures allude to this truth. Jesus said, "He that believeth and is baptized shall be saved . . ." (Mark 16:16), which associates it with salvation in plain language, so that "wayfaring men, though fools, shall not err therin" (Isaiah 35:8). But there are many other Scriptures that corroborate this association.

The apostle Peter, in the third chapter of his first epistle, spoke of how Noah's family was saved from the flood and compared that experience to Christian baptism. He said, "The like figure whereunto even baptism doth also now save us, (not the putting away of the filth of the flesh, but the answer of a good conscience toward God,) by the resurrection of Jesus Christ" (1 Peter 3:21). Once again, this is plain language, "baptism doth also now save us." One will remember that Peter included Christian baptism when he told the people on the Day of Pentecost what they had to do to be saved. He said, "Repent, and be baptized every one of you in the name of Jesus Christ for the remission of sins, and ye shall receive the gift of the Holy Ghost" (Acts 2:38). The construction of that sentence should be studied. Note: *Repent* is an imperative clause separated from the rest of the sentence by a comma: *and be baptized every one of you in the name of Jesus Christ for the remission of sins,* is another clause set apart in between commas. This grammatical construction most certainly associates Christian baptism with the remission of sins.

It would appear that Jesus associated baptism with salvation in His interview with Nicodemus in John 3. He told the Pharisee that he must be "born again." Nicodemus replied, "How can these things be?" Jesus answered, "Except a man be born of water and of the Spirit, he cannot enter into the kingdom of God" (John 3:5). The water would seem to refer to Christian baptism. Some interpret this water to be that which breaks just before a mother gives birth to her child and believe it refers to physical birth. However, remembering all the other Scriptures which associate Christian baptism with salvation, it would seem reasonable to assume that Jesus was pointing Nicodemus toward it, too.

B. W. Johnson, in his commentary, says Jesus spoke to Nicodemus' understanding of what being "born of the water" meant:

> We are to understand Christ as he expected his auditor to understand him. The Jewish proselyte, as a sign that he had put off his old faiths, was baptized on entering the Jewish church. John the Baptist

baptized both Jew and Gentile as a sign of purification by repentance from past sins. Nicodemus would certainly have understood by the expression, *born of the water, a reference to the rite of baptism.* [1]

John W. McGarvey and Philip Y. Pendleton concur with Johnson and add that the Greek and Latin fathers, who followed the apostles in leadership of the church, interpret with unanimity that "except a man be born of the water" refers to Christian baptism. [2]

But the clearest association of Christian baptism with salvation is found in the testimony of Saul of Tarsus in the twenty-second chapter of Acts. The Holy Spirit considered his conversion so important that He had Luke include it three times in that book, in chapters nine, twenty-two and twenty-six. One will remember that Saul had been a vile persecutor of Christians; he had imprisoned many and, as in the case of Stephen, had been party to the martyrdom of some. He was on the way to Damascus, in Syria, to persecute the Christians there when he was struck down by a bright light from Heaven. Jesus spoke to him through that light. He said, "Saul, Saul, why persecutest thou me?" and identified himself, "I am Jesus of Nazareth, whom thou persecutest." (Acts 22:7, 8). There can be no doubt but what Saul believed at that moment. He had, in all likelihood, been pricked in his conscience by Stephen's sermon back in Acts 7. He asked, "What shall I do, Lord?"—a question which would seem to constitute a confession of faith. Jesus told him to go into Damascus and he would be told what he must do. He was in that city three days before he would receive his instruction. We are told that he repented with such intensity and fervor that he did not eat a morsel of food or drink a drop of water.

At this point, God sent a man named Ananias to Saul in order that he might know what he must do. Ananias laid his hands on Saul and he received his sight, for he had been blind from the time Jesus had spoken to him. Then Ananias said to Saul, "And now why tarriest thou? arise, and be baptized, and wash away thy sins, calling on the name of the Lord" (Acts 22:16).

Notice: Saul had believed in Christ three days earlier on the road to Damascus and had repented with intensity and fervor. He may have even made a confession of faith in his question, "What shall I do, Lord?" But his relationship to God had not changed; he was still lost in his trespasses and sins. That cloud of guilt he had accumulated over the years still stood as evidence of his disobedience to God. He was not in Christ, where there is no condemnation, until he arose, was obedient to Christ's command, and his sins were washed away.

There is another association of Christian baptism with salvation that deserves consideration. It is found in the sixth chapter of Romans, where Paul says, "Know ye not, that so many of us as were baptized into Jesus Christ were baptized into his death?" (Romans 6:3). The significance here is in the observation that Christians have been baptized into Jesus' *death*. This is important because the Scripture emphasizes that one must come into contact with the blood of Christ in order to be cleansed of his sin. It says, for example, "Much more then, being now justified by his blood, we shall be saved from wrath through him" (Romans 5:9), and "Unto him that loved us, and washed us from our sins by his own blood" (Revelation 1:5), and, again, "In whom we have redemption through his blood" (Ephesians 1:7).

There can be no doubt but what God's forgiveness depends upon one's coming under the blood of Christ. The question is: at what point in the plan of salvation does one come into contact with His blood? Some believe it is when one is baptized into Jesus' death," for it was in His *death* that He shed his blood. This is inferential, but it does merit consideration.

There is another important association of Christian baptism with salvation. Galatians 3:27 says, "For as many of you as have been baptized into Christ have put on Christ." One should be reminded that the purpose of the plan of salvation is to lead one *into Christ,* because it says, "There is therefore now no condemnation to them which are in Christ Jesus . . ." (Romans 8:1). And Galatians tells us that a person is "baptized into Christ." Consider the word *into.* It is a preposition, which denotes going from one place to another or one state to another. Let me illustrate. One cannot say, "I am going into the kitchen," if he is already in the kitchen, can he? If he is in the room, he cannot go *into* it because he is already in it. That is obvious. Then one would have to infer that a person is outside of Christ until he is baptized *into* Him.

There is another blessing that accompanies Christian baptism, in addition to the remission of sins. It is the gift of the Holy Spirit. Peter promised this gift in his admonition on the Day of Pentecost when he said, "Repent, and be baptized . . . , and ye shall receive the gift of the Holy Ghost." He went on to say to his hearers, "For the promise is unto you, and to your children, and to all that are afar off, even as many as the Lord our God shall call (Acts 2:38, 39). This promise was both general and perpetual. Christians are to be filled with the Spirit and walk in the Spirit. The Holy Spirit guides and protects them as they live the Christian life. This gift is a precious promise to those believers who repent and are baptized.

The Scripture associates Christian baptism with salvation. One who would turn to the Bible only in search of the plan of salvation will see this relationship. However, this does not mean what some people call "water regeneration." Nobody, with any knowledge of God's Word, would teach that a person is saved by baptism *only*. It is merely a step in the plan of salvation that requires prerequisites. Baptism would have no meaning to a person without the prerequisite of faith—who does not trust in Jesus to save him. This is one reason that infant baptism is inappropriate, for a baby is not aware of sin in his life and, therefore, cannot trust in Jesus to save him. (This subject will be discussed at some length in the next chapter.) However, when one wants Jesus to be his Savior and Lord, Christian baptism becomes the mark of his acceptance of Christ in faith.

Indeed, it is impossible to separate faith from Christian baptism in the plan of salvation. They are two links in the same chain. James said, "Even so faith, if it hath not works, is dead, being alone" (James 2:17). He goes on to say, "Ye see then how that by works a man is justified, and not by faith only" (James 2:24). Now Christian baptism is not a work because it requires no labor on the part of a person, and in no way should be thought of as an attempt to earn God's forgiveness. Instead, it is obedience to a command of Christ and carries with it precious promises when prompted by faith in God's Word. But the point is: faith without obedience is just as dead as faith without works.

Consider how faith leads to obedience as illustrated in those examples given in Hebrews 11. Do you remember? Noah and Abraham, for example, walked by faith, but their faith was shown in the obedience to God's command. Noah built the ark because he believed God's Word; Abraham sojourned as a stranger in a foreign land because he trusted God's promises. Their faith necessitated obedience. These two Old Testament heroes could not have said they believed if they had failed to obey, because the two are linked together. Faith alone is dead, James says, and, likewise, baptism alone accomplishes nothing. They cannot be separated. Consequently, one who refuses to receive Christian baptism will have difficulty convincing others that he truly believes in Christ.

Baptism without repentance is also meaningless. What would it accomplish for one to be immersed if he did not want to be a Christian? If he wanted to remain lost in his sins? Early leaders of the restoration movement expressed this contradiction in an interesting way. They would say, "An unrepentant person enters the baptistry a dry sinner and emerges nothing more than a wet sinner." They knew that baptism without repentance accomplishes nothing.

However, the baptism of a penitent believer carries great meaning and delivers precious promises. Walter Scott identified four blessings that would result from this faith and obedience. First, the person's sins are "remitted" (washed away) and he is "in Christ," where there is no condemnation. Then, he receives the "gift of the Holy Ghost" to guide and protect him as he lives the Christian life. He is also born into the family of God, the church, and becomes a child of God, with all the privileges and responsibilities appertaining thereto; heir and joint-heir with Christ himself. The fourth blessing that comes, according to Scott, is the promise of Heaven.

Consider the alternatives to associating Christian baptism with salvation. This is a negative approach, but the alternatives must be addressed.

First of all, a popular alternative is to use baptism as an *initiation into a denomination*. It says, "One is saved, and then, perhaps months or even years later, he is baptized into the church." This position is both unscriptural and unreasonable because there were no defined denominations in New Testament times for one to be baptized into. And no one *joins* the church. Instead, the Scripture says the Lord adds persons to the church when they become Christians (Acts 2:47). Church membership is automatic, not optional, for one who accepts Christ, and to use baptism as the initiation rite into a denomination or church falls short of its meaning.

Another popular alternative is expressed this way: "Christian baptism is an *outward expression of an inward conversion.*" However, that term is never found in the Bible, and it presents a grave danger. Repentance is the most difficult step in the plan of salvation to achieve. It involves, as McGarvey said, the stubborn will.

Many wrestle with the necessity of turning from sin, and it is often a great struggle. Finally, when the victory is won, there is a release and one feels good about it. But this presents a danger because the person may equate that feeling with salvation. He may say, "I *feel* saved; therefore, I *am* saved, with my sins remitted." However, the Bible teaches that one must walk by faith, not by feeling. Our feelings and emotions may fool us, while faith comes from the sure promises of God's Word. One's sins are not remitted, and he is not in Christ because he feels inwardly that he is converted. He can know he has received the gospel's promises only when he has followed the plan God's Word prescribes whereby he can come into Christ.

Still another attempt to disassociate Christian baptism from salvation says, "One is saved by putting his faith in Christ, and then he ought to be baptized." Those who hold to this position may sometimes receive a confession of faith and will not baptize the person for months, separating this act of obedience from coming into Christ. But if one is saved without baptism, why be baptized at all? What is its purpose and meaning? The word *ought* implies that Christian baptism is optional and ignores Jesus' statement, "He that believeth and is baptized shall be saved," and many other Scriptures. The apostles never told anyone they *ought* to be baptized; they never hinted at its being optional. In answer to the question, "What shall we do?" they replied, "Be baptized for the remission of sins," or to "wash away your sin."

But the consideration of these alternatives is negative, and this chapter should conclude on a positive note. Christian baptism is one of the most beautiful and meaningful acts to which a person can submit himself. It dramatizes the central facts of the gospel message: Christ's death, burial, and resurrection. It depicts one's dying to his past life and rising to walk in newness of life as a child of God. One's obedience to this command of Christ should produce great rejoicing among all of those who believe.

Is it not beautiful and meaningful to say to a penitent believer, "Upon the confession of your faith in Jesus Christ, and in loving obedience to His command, I now baptize you in the name of the Father, and of the Son, and of the Holy Ghost, for the remission of your sins and the gift of the Holy Ghost"? This baptismal formula, as it is sometimes called, contains the beautiful, meaningful promises of the gospel. Those who come to Christ in faith will receive Christian baptism with anticipation and joy.

NOTES

[1]B. W. Johnson, *The People's New Testament* (Delight, Arkansas: Gospel Light Publishing Co., 1889), Vol . I, p. 333.

[2]J. W. McGarvey and Philip Y. Pendleton, *The Fourfold Gospel* (Cincinnati: Standard Publishing, no date), p. 127.

16

THE MODE AND SUBJECTS OF CHRISTIAN BAPTISM

"Therefore we are buried with him by baptism . . ."
(Romans 6:4)

Christian baptism is the climax of one's acceptance of Christ in faith and marks his becoming a Christian. The person wants Jesus to save him because he believes His word and trusts His promises. That is faith. He turns from sin to walk in the way of righteousness. That is repentance. He confesses that "Jesus is the Christ, the Son of the living God," and is baptized. This culminates his response to God's free gift of salvation. He receives the promise of the remission of sins and the gift of the Holy Spirit.

Christian baptism is one of the most beautiful, meaningful experiences to which one can submit himself. Jesus commanded it and the apostles were dutiful in their administration of it. Even Jesus, himself, gives an example of the importance of one's compliance with it. He came to John the Baptist in Matthew 3 to be baptized of him. John's baptism was not Christian baptism because the blood of Christ had not been shed at that time and no promise of the gift of the Holy Spirit accompanied it. But it was important because it was a baptism unto repentance. Multitudes were baptized by John "confessing their sins." Jesus came to be baptized, and John protested. He said, "I have need to be baptized of thee, and comest thou to me?" Jesus answered, "Suffer it to be so now: for thus it becometh us to fulfil all righteousness" (Matthew 3:14, 15). Even John's baptism was an act of righteousness to which Jesus, the sinless one, felt the necessity of compliance. Christian baptism is even more important because of its precious promises. It cannot be ignored and should not be belittled by those who love Christ.

Therefore, it is necessary to know what baptism is, its mode, and how it is administered. Alexander Campbell had to face up to the question of the mode of Christian baptism when his first child was born. He and his father had committed themselves to do

Bible things in Bible ways, which precluded in his own mind the sprinkling of infants. The reader will remember that it was Dorothea, Campbell's sister, who came to him with the conviction that she believed Biblical baptism to be something other than sprinkling.

Once again, the Scripture best interprets itself and unveils how God would have Christian baptism administered. It reveals that, in the New Testament, it was the immersion of a repentant believer into Christ.

The word immersion means "to submerge, to put under, or to place beneath." A person says he is immersed in his work. He means that he is absorbed in it, all wrapped up in it. This is what immersion means. Baptism in the New Testament was the immersion of one in water, which marked the burial of a past life and the resurrection into a new life.

It may have had its symbolic root in proselyte baptism used by the Jews. This practice will not be found in the Old Testament because it developed during the Inter-Testamental period. But it was rich in symbolic meaning in that the act climaxed a Gentile's becoming a Jew by faith. He believed God's Word in the Old Testament and wanted to receive His promises. The Jews would subject him to intensive instruction in the faith. He would renounce his Gentile heritage and would confess his faith in Jehovah. He would then be immersed, which symbolized the burial of his past life. He was dead as a Gentile, was buried in a watery tomb, and arose a new creation spiritually, a Jewish proselyte. The rupture with his past life was so complete that he renounced his Gentile parentage and lineage. It was proselyte's baptism, a burial in water, that marked his transition into new life. Some scholars believe Jesus may have referred to it in His conversation with Nicodemus when he said, "You must be born of the water." Then He emphasized that in addition to it, one would have to be born of the Spirit, a new dimension to the rebirth, in order to become a Christian.

There is much internal evidence within the New Testament that baptism is immersion. John said to Jesus when He came to him, "I baptize with water." This established the element used; people were baptized with water. It says, "And Jesus, when he was baptized, went up straightway out of the water" (Matthew 3:16). This leaves the implication that Jesus had been down in the water in order for Him to come up "out of" it. Mark's gospel corroborates

Matthew's narrative, for it, too, speaks of Jesus "straightway coming up out of the water" (Mark 1:10).

The conversion of the Ethiopian treasurer in Acts 8 adds another dimension to the deductive evidence that baptism is immersion. One will remember that he wanted to be baptized after Philip the evangelist preached Jesus to him. It says, "And he commanded the chariot to stand still: and they went down both into the water, both Philip and the eunuch; and he baptized him. And when they were come up out of the water, the Spirit of the Lord caught away Philip, that the eunuch saw him no more: and he went on his way rejoicing" (Acts 8:38, 39). This reveals that both the candidate and the one to administer Christian baptism went down into the water and came up out of it.

Another strong evidence that John the Baptist immersed is found in John 3. It says, "And John also was baptizing in Aenon near to Salim, because there was much water there: and they came, and were baptized" (John 3:23). Sprinkling water, or pouring it upon a candidate, would not require *much* water. John had chosen a place to preach, not because of its proximity to the people, or its acoustical value. He chose it because he needed a place where there was much water in order to immerse people.

The apostle Paul helps to answer the question, "What is Christian baptism?" Some people in the church at Rome reasoned that if God's grace was sufficient to cover all sin, why not sin and let God's grace abound? It was unthinkable to Paul that one in Christ would want to continue in sin. He exclaimed, "God forbid." He goes on in the sixth chapter of his epistle to the Romans to show that those who are in Christ no more want to sin, or, as he expressed it, "are dead to sin." He said, "Know ye not, that so many of us as were baptized into Jesus Christ were baptized into his death?" (Romans 6:3). Then he painted a word picture of the beautiful drama portrayed in Christian baptism. It reads, "Therefore we are buried with him by baptism into death: that like as Christ was raised up from the dead by the glory of the Father, even so we also should walk in newness of life" (Romans 6:4). Christian baptism carries with it two dramatic truths mentioned here by the apostle that can only be portrayed by immersion.

First, it dramatically reenacts the central fact of the gospel message: the death, burial, and resurrection of Christ. Paul said of baptism that it is "like as Christ was raised up from the dead." He rests the validity of the Christian message upon this resurrection in 1 Corinthians 15. He said, "If Christ be not risen, then is our preaching vain, and your faith is also vain" (1 Corinthians 15:14). Christian faith rests upon the fact that Jesus arose from the dead on the third day. Baptism portrays this truth. The person baptized confesses his faith in Christ with his lips. Then, in Christian baptism, he confesses his faith in a way that involves his entire being. He is baptized in the likeness of Jesus' death, burial, and resurrection. Only immersion carries this drama.

Secondly, Paul's description of baptism dramatizes regeneration or rebirth. He said that the person baptized "should walk in newness of life." The old man of sin is dead; that cloud of guilt is washed away, and he is born anew, a child of God. It is significant that the Greek word used for baptism in the New Testament is always feminine. Could it be that the Holy Spirit is portraying it as the womb from which comes the new babe in Christ? Of course, only immersion could fulfill that meaning.

There is more evidence. Paul says, "We have been planted together in the likeness of his death . . ."(Romans 6:5). When something is planted, it is placed under or within. A seed, for example, must be placed beneath the earth, or within it, for new life to come. Likewise, the person baptized is "planted" with Christ and rises to walk in newness of life. Immersion alone carries with it the beautiful symbolism and dramatic message that the Lord put within Christian baptism.

It should also be mentioned that the apostle Paul spoke of baptism as a burial in another place. In Colossians 2:12, he said, "Buried with him in baptism, wherein also ye are risen with him through the faith of the operation of God, who hath raised him from the dead." One who reads the New Testament would conclude from the internal evidence therein that Christian baptism in the beginning was an immersion in water.

However, conclusive evidence comes from the etymology of the word itself. Baptism is not a translation from the Greek to the English language. Instead, it is a *transliteration*. A translation occurs when a person takes a word in one language and finds the corresponding word in another language. For example, *amor* in Latin becomes *love* in English. A transliteration differs. It takes the letters in a word from one language, transfers them to the other, and coins an entirely new word.

This is what happened in the case of baptism. The letters were taken from the Greek word *baptidzo,* or the noun *baptisma,* replaced by the corresponding English letters, and a new word was born. Both Greek words came from the same root word, *bapto*. It means "to immerse, dip, or plunge beneath."

The word is used in the New Testament to refer to occasions of immersion other than Christian baptism. Jesus said at the Last Supper, "It is one of the twelve, that *dippeth* with me in the dish" (Mark 14:20). And the rich man cried up to Abraham in Luke 16:24, saying, "Send Lazarus, that he may *dip* the tip of his finger in the water, and cool my tongue." The same word, *baptidzo,* is used in both examples. Alexander Carson, from his exhaustive study of the subject of Christian baptism, says, "My position is, that it always signifies to dip."[1]

Other Greek words existed that New Testament writers could have used for sprinkling, or pouring (affusion). *Raino* meant "to sprinkle"; *cheo* was "to pour"; and, if one wanted to use water regardless of the manner, he would use *hudraino.* None of these are ever used with reference to Christian baptism. They would not fit. How could one "be buried with Christ" in Christian *sprinkling?* Or "planted in him" with *pouring?* However, a person can substitute the word immersion every time baptism is mentioned in the New Testament and it will fit perfectly.

Alexander Campbell did this when he translated the New Testament in a version called, *The Living Oracles.* Every time the word *baptized* was found, he used *immersed,* and *baptism* was translated *immersion.* In every instance, it fit and carried with it the meaning the author desired. For example, "And they went down both into the water, both Philip and the eunuch; and he *immersed* him" (Acts 8:38); and, "Therefore we are buried with him by *immersion* into death" (Romans 6:4).

Some who testify to immersion as the true mode of baptism are surprising. Martin Luther said, "'Baptism' is a Greek word, and may be translated 'immerse.' I would have those who are to be baptized to be altogether dipped." John Calvin was the progenitor of the Reformed Churches, including the Presbyterian. He wrote, "The word 'baptize' signifies to immerse. It is certain that immersion was the practice of the primitive church." John Wesley referred to it this way: "'Buried with him by baptism' . . . [alludes] to the ancient manner of baptizing by immersion.

It would seem that the departure from the New Testament norm of immersion came gradually. P. H. Welshimer, in his book, *Concerning the Disciples,* traces its evolution. He wrote:

The first case of affusion, so far as history records, was in A.D. 251, when Novotion desired to be baptized while on a sick bed. Being unable to be taken to water, they poured water around him until his body was covered. Note, that was in the third century.

The first law of sprinkling was obtained in 753, from Pope Stephen II, who permitted pouring and sprinkling in cases of necessity.

In 1311, the Legislature, in the Council at Ravenna, declared immersion or sprinkling to be indifferent.

At the Council of Constans, about 1356, a decree was made legalizing all such cases of clinic sickly baptism already past or that might come in the future.

The Anglican Church, which sprang from the Roman Catholic, began in 1534; the Presbyterian, an offshoot of the Anglican, began in 1541; and the Congregational soon after. It is an historic fact that for a hundred years these churches practiced immersion. The Westminister Assembly was called together by the Parliament of England in 1643, and voted to substitute sprinkling for immersion. It was a tie vote, which led Dr. Lightfoot, the president of the Assembly, to cast the deciding vote, which favored the substitution.

In 1664, the parliament of England repealed that part of the old law which enforced immersion, and passed a new law, enforcing sprinkling in its stead. The change came long after the Scriptures were written.[2]

All the evidence points to the conclusion that Christian baptism is to be the immersion of a penitent believer in the likeness of Jesus' death, burial, and resurrection. It carries with it God's promise of new life with the remission of sins and the gift of the Holy Spirit.

The New Testament also informs the earnest seeker about the proper persons, or candidates, to receive Christian baptism. Remember the rule? *The Bible best interprets itself.* It answers the question, "Who should be baptized?"

One will recall that Jesus said in the Great Commission, "Go . . . teach . . . baptize . . . and teach." A person must be teachable in order to receive Christian baptism because that is a prerequisite for it. Jesus also said, "He that believeth and is baptized shall be saved." Therefore, the proper candidate must have the Word of God taught to him so he can believe in Christ and trust His promises. The apostle Peter told the people on the Day of Pentecost that they must "repent, and be baptized." They could not receive Christian baptism until they had resolved in

their hearts to be willing to turn from sin and walk in righteousness. The Ethiopian treasurer illustrates another quality required
for baptism. He said, "See, here is water; what doth hinder me to
be baptized?" Philip's answer was most specific: "If thou be-
lievest with all thine heart, thou mayest." The Ethiopian answered
with the good confession, "I believe that Jesus Christ is the Son of
God." His baptism was contingent upon his faith in Christ as
expressed in the confession.

It is obvious from these prerequisites that an infant is an im-
proper subject for Christian baptism. He cannot comprehend the
truths of the gospel that must be taught; nor can he accept the
evidence and testimony of Scripture that produce faith. And it is
absurd to expect him to repent. Baptism is for the remission of
sins, and it would be both cruel and unfair to hold an innocent
babe responsible for his actions. Also, Christian baptism is the
"answer of a good conscience toward God" (1 Peter 3:21), and an
infant of a few days has no conscience.

Accepting the gift of salvation begins when one realizes that he
has sinned, is a sinner, and must have God's forgiveness. A baby
has no sense of sin and cannot understand God's laws. Jesus
recognized the innocence of infants when the little children were
brought to Him in Matthew 19. The disciples sought to protect
His privacy. But Jesus said, "Suffer little children, and forbid
them not, to come unto me; for of such is the kingdom of
heaven" (Matthew 19:14). A child is not accountable to God until
he reaches the place when he understands that he has sinned.
Some call this "the age of accountability." It is when a person
knows enough to be accountable to God for his actions. This age
varies from person to person, depending upon the teaching to
which he has been exposed. But a child should never receive
Christian baptism until he knows the meaning of the good confession.

Infant baptism came into being because of a false doctrine that
said that people inherit the guilt of their parents' or forefathers'
sins. It states that the whole human race stands under the condemnation of sin. Therefore, even the baby is condemned because he
is human. Augustine said, "There are babes in hell not a span
long." A span was the distance between the tip of a man's thumb
to the tip of his little finger on his outstretched hand (or half the
distance from his finger to his elbow). Few believe that any-
more; even the Roman Catholic Church provides "Limbo" for

unbaptized infants. Limbo is not Hell, but a place of shadows, where there is neither light, nor darkness, happiness or sadness. Of course, the Bible makes no mention of such a place. it is merely an attempt to soften what Augustine would call "total depravity."

Most classical Protestant churches use infant sprinkling as a dedication. They no longer believe that a baby would die and go to Hell. They merely use the child's sprinkling as a dedication to God. However, this is a great departure from the Biblical meaning of Christian baptism. There is not one shred of evidence in the New Testament that an infant is to be baptized; neither is there precedence for the practice. The danger is that the child will grow up thinking he has been baptized and miss out on this most meaningful command of Christ.

God's plan of salvation is beautiful in its simplicity, even wayfaring persons can understand it. One realizes that he is a sinner and must have God's forgiveness. The gospel, the good news, says, "Christ died for our sins." Faith means to trust in Jesus alone to save; to believe His word and trust His promises. When one wants Jesus to be his Saviour, he must be willing to turn from sin and walk in righteousness. This is called repentance, and the person's desire to become a Christian is made known in the good confession. Christian baptism is the beautiful climax of one's acceptance of Christ. It marks his becoming a Christian, and with it comes the promise of the remission of sins and gift of the Holy Spirit.

Just think! Try to comprehend it! If everyone who loves Christ were to go into all the world, united with this simple explanation of the plan of salvation, would this not answer Jesus' prayer in John 17? There is reason to believe that then the "whole world would believe." The rivers around the globe would become veritable Jordans with people accepting Christ, even as was the Ohio River in Walter Scott's day.

NOTES

[1]Alexander Carson, *Baptism: Its Mode and Subjects* (Grand Rapids: Kregel Publications, 1853), p. 55.

[2]P. H. Welshimer, *Concerning the Disciples* (Cincinnati: Standard Publishing, 1935), pp. 111, 112.

17

THE HOLY SPIRIT

"... Be filled with the Spirit" (Ephesians 5:18)

No one could move to restore the essential marks of the New Testament church without including the Holy Spirit. Indeed, John W. McGarvey believed that the fifth book of the New Testament should not be named "Acts of the Apostles." According to him, much is included in it that did not involve them. He suggested that it be called "The Acts of the Holy Spirit." The book began with the anticipation and coming of the Holy Spirit, who guided the early Christians in the paths God would have them go. The Holy Spirit, through the apostles, shaped the New Testament church.

The early leaders of the restoration movement were much concerned about the Holy Spirit. One of Walter Scott's most famous discourses was entitled, "The Holy Spirit." He composed another discourse that he called, "The Gospel Restored," in which he said, "Read, obey the gospel; enter by faith and immersion his kingdom on earth and you shall receive the Holy Spirit; and when you do so, walk in the Spirit; cherish and reverence his blessed presence in your soul...."[1]

All the early leaders of the movement faced up to the unscriptural Calvinistic doctrine of "election." It teaches that no one can become a Christian until God works in him "His irresistible act of grace." The Holy Spirit has to act personally and directly on a person before he can be saved, according to this teaching. Those upon whom God chooses to act are called "the elect"; all others are lost for eternity. Barton W. Stone took issue with this doctrine just after the Cane Ridge meeting. He said that Christ died for *all,* not just for the elect and his ministry would go on to emphasize "whosoever will may come." Alexander Campbell knew that the Holy Spirit used the written Word of God that He inspired to convict people of their sin and lead them to Christ. He wrote: "God now speaks to us only by his word. By his Son in the New

Testament, he has fully revealed himself and his will. This is the only revelation of his Spirit which we are to regard. . . . It is an overwhelming fact, that God does nothing in creation or redemption without His word."[2]

Some have said that the Holy Spirit is a neglected subject within the restoration movement. This may be an accurate observation concerning its subsequent generations. However, it is not true concerning its early leaders. The issues may have been somewhat different in their era, but the Holy Spirit was prominent both in their concern and teaching.

The Holy Spirit should never be referred to either as "it" or as just a power. The Holy Spirit is a person, along with and equal to God the Father and Jesus. The Great Commission says that repentant believers should be baptized in the name of the Father, Son, and Holy Spirit. The early church fathers called these the "Trinity," although the term is not found in the Bible. It represents God, who has revealed himself in three persons.

The classic illustration of this understanding of God comes from ancient Greek drama. It was a low-budget production, so one actor would often play three parts. He might be the hero, the heroine, and the villain in the same drama. When he spoke the lines of the hero, he would hold a mask up to his face. He would hold another mask up to his face when he was the heroine, and still a third as the villain. They called each role he played a "persona." It was one actor who played three parts, or "persona." Ancient Christians took this understanding and said that there is one God who has revealed himself in three persons ("persona") . . . God the Father, Jesus the Son, and the Holy Spirit.

Most people refer to them in that order. The Holy Spirit is usually last in the listing, but this does not imply His inferiority in any way to the other two because the Bible always portrays them as equal. Chronology may be a reason for the order. Someone has observed that the work of the Father is emphasized in the Old Testament; the work of the Son in the Gospels, and the Holy Spirit in Acts. Also, Christ died for us back then but it is the Holy Spirit who lives in us now.

All three persons can be found in the beginning. God said, "Let *us* make man in *our* image, after *our* likeness . . ."(Genesis 1:26). The Hebrew word translated God in that verse is *Elohim*. Matthew Henry says it signifies "the plurality of persons in the Godhead, Father, Son and Holy Ghost. . . ." The three persons are seen even more clearly in the New Testament. Paul's familiar benediction reads, "The grace of the Lord Jesus Christ, and the love of God, and the communion of the Holy Ghost, be with you all. Amen." (2 Corinthians 13:14).

The Holy Spirit is a person equal to the Father and Jesus. He can be grieved (Ephesians 4:30); lied to, as in the case of Ananias and Sapphira (Acts 5:3, 4); insulted (Hebrews 10:29); and blasphemed (Matthew 12:31, 32). He is omnipotent (all-powerful, Luke 1:35); omnipresent (everywhere present, Psalm 139:7); and omniscient (all-knowing, 1 Corinthians 2:10, 11).

The Holy Spirit's coming on the Day of Pentecost in A.D. 30 marked the beginning of a new era characterized by God's grace. It enabled Peter to preach the first gospel sermon and to tell those who believed it what to do to be saved. Those who obeyed received the remission of their sins and the gift of the Holy Spirit. God added them to His church, and they continued steadfastly in the apostles' doctrine, fellowship, the breaking of bread, and prayers. This age in which Christians are God's people may well be called the Holy Spirit era because of His influence upon it. His importance to the church should not be underestimated.

The great act of God on the Day of Pentecost in Acts 2 was not the miracles, signs, and wonders performed by the apostles. These were merely temporary and performed by a few. The great divine act was the promise of *the gift of the Holy Spirit to Christians*. This should not be confused with the gifts of the Holy Spirit which will be discussed at some length in a subsequent chapter. The *gifts* will differ from Christian to Christian. But the *gift* of the Holy Spirit is the same promise given to all Christians.

One will remember that Peter had preached the gospel on the Day of Pentecost. He concluded by saying, "God hath made that same Jesus, whom ye have crucified, both Lord and Christ." His sermon had convinced many in his audience; so they cried out, "What shall we do?" Peter, under the inspiration of the Holy Spirit, told them, "Repent, and be baptized every one of you in the name of Jesus Christ for the remission of sins, and ye shall receive the gift of the Holy Ghost" (Acts 2:36-38). The promise of the "gift of the Holy Ghost" was to all who would accept Christ, not just to the Twelve or the hundred and twenty who were meeting together in Acts 1. Three thousand responded, were baptized, and received the promise that very day. Peter said, "For the promise is unto you, and to your children, and to all that are afar off, even as many as the Lord our God shall call" (Acts 2:39). This made the gift of the Holy Spirit both universal and perpetual ... "to your children, and to all them that are afar off."

The gift of the Holy Spirit belongs to every Christian. This should never be doubted. It is wrong to believe that one has to agonize for it after he is baptized or that it is a second act of God's grace. It is promised to every person who accepts Christ and becomes a Christian.

Then what is this precious gift? The Scripture teaches that the gift of the Holy Spirit is the indwelling presence of Christ in a person's life. The Holy Spirit in one's heart and Christ living in his heart may be looked upon as synonymous. Paul said, "God hath sent forth the *Spirit* of his *Son* into your hearts, crying, Abba, Father" (Galatians 4:6). And again, "But ye are not in the flesh, but in the Spirit, if so be that the *Spirit of God* dwell in you. Now if any man have not the *Spirit of Christ,* he is none of his" (Romans 8:9). The gift of the Holy Spirit is the presence of the Spirit of God, or Spirit of Christ, who comes to live in the life of a person. This He will not do until one accepts Christ and becomes a Christian.

However, when he accepts Christ, the Christian's body then becomes "the temple of the Holy Spirit"; the sanctuary in which He lives on earth. The Christian continues the ministry on earth that Christ began insofar as he lets His Spirit guide him. John R. W. Stott summarizes well the work of the gift of the Holy Spirit:

> Once he has come to us and taken up his residence within us, making our body his temple (1 Corinthians 6:19, 20), his work of sanctification begins. In brief, his ministry is both to reveal Christ to us and to form Christ in us, so that we grow steadily in our knowledge of Christ and in our likeness to Christ (see e.g. Ephesians 1:17; Galatians 4:19; 2 Corinthians 3:18). It is by the power of the indwelling spirit that the evil desires of our fallen nature are restrained and the good fruit of Christian character is produced (Galatians 5:16-25). Nor is he kind of a private possession, ministering only to the individual Christian; he also united us to the body of Christ, the church, so that Christian fellowship is 'the fellowship of the Holy Spirit' and Christian worship is worship in or by the Holy Spirit (e.g., Philippians 2:1; 3:3). It is he, too, who reaches through us to others, prompting us to witness to Christ and equipping us with the gifts for the service to which he summons us.[3]

Paul gives two admonitions to those who have received the gift of the Holy Spirit. They are to be *filled* with the Spirit and *walk* in the Spirit. He said, "And be not drunk with wine, wherein is excess; but be filled with the Spirit" (Ephesians 5:18). The grammatical construction of this command in the Greek language reveals much of what the apostle meant. He put it in the imperative present tense and mood. This indicates that it is repetitious or continuing action; something that should occur again and again, or a process that continues on and on. The gift of the Holy Spirit is that which a person receives *once,* when he is baptized into Christ. But he must be filled with the Spirit time and again, a recurring experience.

Perhaps the action can be best illustrated this way. A Christian receives the gift of the Holy Spirit but proceeds to put it in the back closet of the temple of his life. He does not use it; keeps it locked up; fails to let the Spirit have His way with him. This makes him carnal. He fails to grow in Christ, becomes defeated, and even cynical. Sin and worldliness keep the Holy Spirit from growing His fruit in his life. Then the carnal Christian repents, confesses his sins (1 John 1:8, 9), and releases the Holy Spirit from the back closet so He can lead him. He removes the sin and worldliness in order for the Holy Spirit to *fill* him. Paul's admonition indicates that the Christian must repeat this action often in his life to remain "filled with the Spirit."

Also, Paul said, "Walk in the Spirit" (Galatians 5:16). This refers to the guidance given as He leads the Christian in "the way, the truth, and the life" (John 14:6). He does this primarily through the written Word of God, the Bible, which He inspired. One should be most cautious about ascribing intuitive impulses to the guidance of the Holy Spirit. Other spirits can speak to him intuitively that are not the Holy Spirit and make his witness look absurd. John MacArthur tells about people who claim washing machines to have been healed, empty gas tanks supernaturally filled, and one lady who reported being given a new "belly button."[4]

The Bible says to test the spirits (1 John 4:1); prove them; be sure they are of God. The best way to accomplish this is to be sure that they are in harmony with the written Word, which the Holy Spirit inspired. He has given it for a "lamp unto [our] feet and a light unto [our] path (Psalm 119:105) and has called it "the sword of the Spirit, which is the word of God" (Ephesians 6:17).

Christians must be careful not to *grieve* the Holy Spirit. This is a part of His nature in that He can be hurt and be made sorrowful. Paul said, "Grieve not the Holy Spirit of God . . ." (Ephesians 4:30). The context of this admonition reveals what makes the Holy Spirit sorrowful. Read Ephesians 4:20-32. It refers to those attitudes and actions that grieve Him: lying, anger, letting the devil have his way, stealing, corrupt life-style, bitterness, wrath, clamor, evil speaking, and malice. A Christian who manifests these traits of character grieves the Holy Spirit. Paul added one more: unkindness. He said, "And be ye kind one to another, tenderhearted, forgiving one another, even as God for Christ's sake hath forgiven you." Sin in the life of a Christian brings sorrow to the Holy Spirit.

Christians are also warned not to *quench* the Spirit. Paul put it rather bluntly in 1 Thessalonians 5:19 when he said, "Quench not the Spirit." The Holy Spirit is sometimes represented by fire in the Scriptures, even as the Word is compared to light. Fire can be quenched or put out in two ways. Deny it fuel and it goes out. Our family spent a week at the lake one summer and it turned unexpectedly cold. We tried to light the oil stove but to no avail. The reason? The valve had been turned off. God has provided many kinds of fuel to enable the Spirit to burn brightly in the Christian's life: preaching, teaching, fellowship, prayer, worship, singing, and study. However, turn off the valve, deny a Christian these fuels, and the Spirit is quenched in his life.

Fire can also be put out by dousing it with water. Likewise the influence of the Holy Spirit in one's life can be extinguished by unbelief. Let a person douse the leading of the Holy spirit with unbelief often enough and the fire goes out. It is within this context that "the sin against the Holy Spirit" should be considered. It is called sometimes "the unpardonable sin." Jesus spoke of this sin in Matthew 12. He said, "All manner of sin and blasphemy shall be forgiven unto men: but the blasphemy against the Holy Ghost shall not be forgiven unto men. And whosoever speaketh a word against the Son of man, it shall be forgiven him: but whosoever speaketh against the Holy Ghost, it shall not be forgiven him, neither in this world, neither in the world to come" (Matthew 12:31, 32).

The context of this Scripture reveals how unbelief can quench the Spirit until it leads to the "unpardonable sin." Jesus had been performing miracles, which attested to both His deity and the validity of His message. He healed a dumb and blind man in the first verses of the chapter. The people were amazed, but the Pharisees attributed the miracle to Beelzebub, the demon of the barnyard. Their unbelief had hardened their hearts. They refused to accept Christ, even though the evidence of His deity was obviously before them. They resisted the leading of the Holy Spirit concerning Jesus until their unbelief hardened their hearts.

A purpose of the Holy Spirit is to guide people into all truth concerning Christ (John 16:13). Unbelief is like dousing the fire with water. It puts it out. Continued refusal to accept the Holy Spirit's testimony concerning Christ will cause one to be cut off, or insensitive to His witness. God warned the people in Noah's day saying, "My Spirit will not always strive with man" (Genesis 6:3). However, it should be said to allay fear that if the possibility of committing the "unpardonable sin" concerns a person, he has not yet committed it. The Pharisees had rejected Jesus so long that they were impervious to the witness of the Holy Spirit. Their hearts had become so hard that they had no concern for His testimony. That is the blasphemy against the Holy Spirit for which there is no forgiveness, "neither in this world, neither in the world to come."

What happens to the person who receives the *gift* of the Holy Spirit, who is *filled* with the Spirit, and who *walks* in the Spirit? The apostle Paul answers that question. He says one will grow spiritual fruit in his life. This fruit is described in Galatians 5:22, 23. Someone has said that when a person reads this list of graces in the "fruit of the Spirit," he has described Jesus. This is true because they are the graces He exemplified. If a person perfectly embodied them, he would be just like Christ because the Holy Spirit is the Spirit of Christ and will grow the same fruit in the Christian's life.

LOVE. This is the supreme grace and rightfully comes first. Christian love is best defined as unselfish concern for the other person. It is the kind of love God manifested when He gave His Son to go to the cross. It was exemplified by the willingness of Christ himself to die for the sins of others. It means to give unselfishly for the good of another. The greatest commandment of them all is to love God, and the second is to love your neighbor (Mark 12:29-31). Jesus said to His followers, "By this shall all men know that ye are my disciples, if ye have love one to another" (John 13:35). One who is filled with the Spirit grows the grace of love in his life.

JOY. This word and its derivatives are often used in the New Testament to describe Christians. Jesus said to the disciples, "These things have I spoken unto you, that my joy might remain in you, and that your joy might be full" (John 15:11). This is not a glib, superficial kind of Pollyanna attitude. Instead, it is a deep peace that comes from the knowledge that one is in God's plan and enables him to give thanks for all things (Ephesians 5:20).

PEACE. It is kin to joy. Paul said, "Now the God of hope fill you with all joy and peace in believing, that ye may abound in hope, in the power of the Holy Spirit" (Romans 15:13, ASV). This peace that passes understanding comes to the Christian when he yields his life to the filling and leading of the Spirit and is no longer torn and fragmented.

LONG-SUFFERING (patience). This means for one to remain steadfast when provoked; to refrain from retribution and vengeance. Jesus described patience when He said, "Bless them that curse you, do good to them that hate you, and pray for them which despitefully use you, and persecute you" (Matthew 5:44). Patience is the virtue that enables the Christian to endure all hardships gracefully.

GENTLENESS. This is sometimes translated kindness. Is it not significant that Jesus, the Word powerful enough to create the universe, could be so gentle with sinners? Unkindness ruins the Christian's witness. Paul said to Timothy, "The servant of the Lord must not strive; but be gentle unto all men" (2 Timothy 2:24). The B.Y.K.O.T.A. formula for living says, "Be ye kind one to another" (Ephesians 4:32).

GOODNESS. The Greek word for goodness, agathosune, carries with it the implication of being like God. One who is filled with His Spirit will be like Him. Barnabas is a good example. It says of him in Acts, "For he was a good man, and full of the Holy Ghost and of faith" (Acts 11:24). Being filled with the Holy Spirit made him a "good man."

FAITH. This virtue means faithfulness, in contrast to the faith that leads to salvation, which comes from the evidence and testimony of Scripture. The gift of the Holy Spirit enables one to remain faithful to Christ, and this is essential for one who would be a victorious Christian. Jesus said, "Be thou faithful unto death, and I will give thee a crown of life" (Revelation 2:10). Only those filled with the Spirit will remain "faithful unto death."

MEEKNESS. Nowhere in the Bible does this word mean

140

dispirited timidity. It is rather the kind of humility that enables a person to remain always a servant however exalted his position. This quality enabled Moses to earn the title "a servant of the Lord" even though he was the greatest man in the Old Testament. Jesus was also meek in this sense, was He not? They called Him the "suffering Servant."

TEMPERANCE. This means self-control. The gift of the Holy Spirit enables one to control his life. It protects him from those evil forces and habits that would destroy him, such as a quick temper, overindulgence, negativism, and self-centeredness.

Every Christian receives the gift of the Holy Spirit when he accepts Christ. Those who are filled with the Spirit and walk in the Spirit grow the fruit of the Spirit in their lives and become more like Jesus as time passes. This is the ministry of the Holy Spirit.

NOTES

[1]Walter Scott, *The Gospel Restored* (Cincinnati: O. H. Donush, 1836), p. 571.

[2]Alexander Campbell, ed., *The Christian Baptist,* p. 50.

[3]John R. W. Stott, *The Baptism and Fullness of the Spirit* (Downer's Grove, IL: Inter-Varsity Press, 1964), pp. 20, 21.

[4]John W. MacArthur, Jr., *The Charismatics* (Grand Rapids, MI: Zondervan, 1978), p. 11.

18

MEMBERSHIP AND MINISTRY

"The Lord added to the church daily such as should be saved" (Acts 2:47). . . . "For the work of the ministry" (Ephesians 4:12)

The response to God's offer of salvation culminates with one's being baptized into Christ. It is a part of his acceptance of Him in faith and a result of his repentance. He receives two explicit promises: the remission of his sins and the gift of the Holy Spirit.

Also, another precious blessing comes with it: the person becomes a part of the family of God on earth, the church. It is represented as the body of Christ, the bride of Christ, the kingdom, and other metaphors that show just how important it is. The Scripture says, "Christ also loved the church, and gave himself for it" (Ephesians 5:25). This means that Jesus went to the cross in order to die for those who comprise the church. Paul expressed the same sentiment when he called the elders from Ephesus down to Miletus in Acts 20. He admonished them saying, "Take heed therefore unto yourselves, and to all the flock, over which the Holy Ghost hath made you overseers, to feed the church of God, which he hath purchased with his own blood" (Acts 20:28). Nothing on earth is more precious to Christ than His church, which He purchased with the ultimate price.

It is a great honor to be a member of Christ's church. It is called the family of God, and its members are the children of God. Someone has described the Christian's family tree this way: God is his father; Jesus, his elder brother; the Holy Spirit is the abiding guest within his heart; other Christians are his brothers and sisters; and he is surrounded by that "great cloud of witnesses" (Hebrews 12:1) in Heaven who cheer him on as he runs the race of the Christian life. That is a fine pedigree! One should consider it a blessed privilege to be a part of God's family, the greatest honor that could ever be bestowed upon him.

Church membership is not optional for the Christian. He does not accept Christ, receive His promises, and then decide whether

143

he wants to become a member of His church. No one ever *joins* the church. That idea is unscriptural. Instead, he accepts Christ and automatically becomes a part of it.

The second chapter of Acts gives an example of this. It will be remembered that Peter preached the first gospel sermon there; three thousand persons answered its invitation, and many others later on followed them. It says, "And the Lord added to the church daily such as should be saved" (Acts 2:47). Those who accepted Christ were at the same time added to the church and numbered with the believers. It was God's action, and it was just as certain as the remission of sins and the gift of the Holy Spirit.

The good confession and Christian baptism made the new church member's faith visible. "And all that believed were together . . ." (Acts 2:44). They composed a visible body, an identifiable congregation. It is for this same reason that Paul was later able to write to "the church of God which is at Corinth" (1 Corinthians 1:2), and "the church of the Thessalonians" (1 Thessalonians 1:1), "the church in [Philemon's] house (Philemon 1:2), et. al. They were visible, identifiable bodies of believers.

While one cannot *join* the church, because God adds him to it, he should at the same time see to it that he is identified with a local congregation. This is particularly important for the Christian who moves from one community and relocates in another. He should seek out a Christ-centered, Bible-teaching, undenominational church and become a visible part of it. The opportunity to be identified with such a congregation is usually offered during Sunday and weekday services by most churches. Baptized believers are invited to step forward before the assembled congregation to reaffirm their faith in Christ and become a part of the local congregation. Some churches extend what they call "the right hand of Christian fellowship," which both welcomes the person and identifies him as a member of that body.

However, identification alone is insufficient. In addition to that, the new Christian becomes a working *minister* within the church. *Every* Christian is called to be a minister! This is contrary to the hierarchical clergy concept of ministry within most Protestant and Catholic churches. They separate the clergy from the laity, which makes two classes of Christians: the ordained clergy set apart to do the work of the ministry on the one hand, and the rest of the church members on the other hand. Some refer to them

144

as the *doers* and the *listeners*. The clergy are given lofty titles to designate their supposedly elevated status.

The clergy concept of ministry is unbiblical. Both Barton W. Stone and Alexander Campbell plead for its elimination and the titles that evolved from it, and the "priesthood of all believers" became an integral part of the restoration movement.

Sanctification is another one of those big words in the Bible. But it, like the others, carries a most meaningful truth. It means "to set apart, to consecrate, to ordain." It will be remembered that, when the seven men were chosen to administrate the common fund in Acts 6, the apostles laid their hands on them. It set them apart for that work and sanctified them for that purpose. The Christian may look upon his baptism as the ordination service that sets him apart for the work of ministry because every Christian is, in fact, a minister.

Paul discusses this concept of the ministry of all believers in Ephesians 4. He calls attention to the various offices in which Christians serve in the New Testament church. Two of them, apostles and prophets, were temporary, peculiar to that era. The others, evangelists, pastors, and teachers, remain because they were permanent. He says that these offices are to equip the saints for the work of ministry to build up the body of Christ. Saints are those who have been sanctified, all Christians. The offices mentioned were to equip each church member to enable him to perform his particular ministry.

No discussion of ministry within the New Testament church would be complete without a consideration of what are called the "gifts of the Spirit." Their name comes from the Greek word, *charismata,* which means "gifts of grace." They are discussed in five places: 1 Corinthians 12:4-12; again in that same chapter, verses 27-31; Romans 12:4-8; Ephesians 4:11-16, and 1 Peter 4:10, 11. These gifts were responsibilities (or opportunities) for service given to Christians to be used to build up the church and make it strong. Along with the opportunity came the ability to fulfill it if the recipient would follow the leading of the gift of the Holy Spirit he received when he accepted Christ.

The gifts present an interesting study in diversity. There are over twenty different ones identified in the five Scriptures. However, no one gift appears in all five lists and thirteen appear in only one. A person would also draw the inference that those specified do not compose an exhaustive list. It is almost as if they are only those that came to mind at the moment of the writing and were used illustratively to show how the church is to function like a human body. There may be others given to edify the church that are not mentioned. It should also be pointed out that these gifts were not innate talents received at birth. They were opportunities given to Christians to serve within the church, perhaps music and visitation, for example. God may choose to give a gift to one who has an innate talent to enable him to fulfill his responsibility; however, the gift and the talent should not be confused.

The gifts were always to be used to build up the church. That was their sole purpose. Paul wrote, "Now to each one the manifestation of the Spirit is given for the common good" (1 Corinthians 12:7, NIV). Peter was even more clear on the subject when he said, "Each one should use whatever gift he has received to serve others" (1 Peter 4:10, NIV). The spiritual gifts were not to be used selfishly but were to be used to strengthen other church members, and thus edify the whole church.

It will be helpful to identify the gifts of the Spirit mentioned in Scripture. Notice their diversity, for they vary from the miraculous to the mundane to the prosaic. They are *wisdom, knowledge, faith, healing, miracles, prophecy, discerning of spirits, tongues (languages), interpretation of tongues, apostles, prophets, teachers, helping others, government (administration), exhortation (encouragement), giving, ruling (leadership), mercy, pastors, evangelists, ministry, and to speak*. The gifts vary from miracles to ministry, from prophecy to helping others.

Most discussion of the charismata centers around what are called "the miraculous," or "supernatural gifts"—healing, miracles, tongues and interpretation of tongues. These four create the most interest. It is significant that they are listed only in Corinthians the other Scriptures do not mention them. These supernatural gifts were peculiar to the first-century church and were used to verify the authenticity of the apostolic message. They were appropriate only for that era. Scholars point out that miracles in the Scripture cluster in four groups: (1) Moses, at about the time he received the Law; (2) Elijah and Elisha, as the prophets became prominent; (3) Jesus' ministry; and (4) the beginning of the church. John R. W. Stott observed from this, "And the major purpose of miracles was to authenticate each fresh stage of revelation."[1]

The miraculous gifts served their purpose in the New Testament church, and ceased, even as did the office of apostle. They served somewhat like the scaffolding during the construction of a building. They were needed in the beginning, but scaffolding is removed when the structure is finished. It is no longer needed and would detract from the beauty of the building. Paul explains in 1 Corinthians 13 that when a perfect understanding of the gospel would come, the miraculous elements, the scaffolding, would no longer be necessary. This subject will be discussed at greater length in a subsequent chapter.

However, notice how relevant the other gifts remain for ministry in the church of every age. How could the church become strong without members who teach, lead, encourage, administrate, give, evangelize, shepherd, et. al.? It is certain from the Scripture that the gifts are so widespread and diversified that every Christian has been given one, or perhaps more than one. Paul admonished the Romans to be humble; then he wrote, "I say to every one of you. . . . we have different gifts, according to the grace given to us" (Romans 12:3, 6, NIV). This would seem to imply that *everyone* in the church is given some responsibility by the Spirit. The apostle went on to say to the Ephesians, "But unto every one of us is given grace according to the measure of the gift of Christ" (Ephesians 4:7).

Imagine what a congregation would be like if every member sought his responsibility and fulfilled it to the best of his ability under the leadership of the gift of the Holy Spirit. It would be edified (built up), become strong, and be a blessing to every person who would become a part of it. There would be unity and harmony—a beautiful fellowship!

Paul uses the human body to illustrate how these gifts are to be used. He says that the church is the body of Christ. Jesus is the head that gives directions to it and the Holy Spirit is the life within the church that gives it vitality, or quickens it. Christians are like the various members of a body. Each organ provides a different but vital function on behalf of the others. The apostle says, "For the body is not one member, but many. If the foot shall say, Because I am not the hand, I am not of the body; is it therefore not of the body? And if the ear shall say, Because I am not the eye, I am not of the body; is it therefore not of the body? If the whole body were an eye, where were the hearing? If the whole were hearing, where were the smelling? But now hath God set the members every one of them in the body, as it hath pleased him.

147

And if they were all one member, where were the body? But now are they many members, yet but one body? (1 Corinthians 12:14-20).

Compare the functions of the organs of a human body to those of the members of the church. One Christian may be called of God to preach, for example. This will be his responsibility, and God will give him the ability to perform this ministry. He will work hard to prepare good gospel sermons to build up the other members of the church. Another will be called to teach. This is his ministry, and he will work hard to prepare good Bible lessons. Another may be given the responsibility to shepherd as an elder, or administrate, perhaps as a Sunday-school superintendent. Paul emphasizes that each ministry is essential to the life of the church, and the body is hurt when an organ fails to function. Each depends upon the other for mutual benefit so the whole body may be strong.

One ministry within the church is not to be seen as superior to another. The essentiality of each precludes that. It is significant that each office of the church has a name that denotes service rather than prestige. The word *minister* means "servant" and *deacon* literally means "a waiter at the table." A Greek word for *pastor* is *poimen,* which means "shepherd," and this is more descriptive of ministry than of position. Indeed, Peter admonished elders, who are also overseers, that they should not attempt to be "lords over God's heritage," but examples to the flock (1 Peter 5:3). Jesus himself was a humble servant who came to minister rather than to be ministered unto and even washed the disciples' feet in a lesson of humility.

Peter refers to all Christians as "a royal priesthood" (1 Peter 2:9). There is no such thing as the separation of clergy and laity in the New Testament church. Peter went on to say, "As every man hath received the gift, even so minister the same one to another, as good stewards of the manifold grace of God" (1 Peter 4:10).

This does not preclude one's receiving a livelihood from the Lord's work. To the contrary, this may not only be desirable, but necessary, and the New Testament provides for the necessity. It is true that the apostle Paul conducted a tent ministry in Corinth with Aquilla and Priscilla. He made tents for a living while he preached. But this was a necessity, not a precedent, as he would later plead eloquently on behalf of himself and Barnabas for a living wage. He said to the Corinthian church, "Or I only and

Barnabas, have we not power [or right] to forbear working? Who goeth to warfare any time at his own charges? who planteth a vineyard, and eateth not of the fruit thereof? or who feedeth a flock, and eateth not of the milk of the flock?" Then he proceeds to make a comparison between his work, which was the the work of God, and the aforementioned occupations. He says, "If we have sown unto you spiritual things, is it a great thing if we shall reap your carnal things? ... Even so hath the Lord ordained that they which preach the gospel shall live of the gospel" (1 Corinthians 9:6, 7, 11, 14).

Paul made the same plea for those who labor in word and doctrine. He wrote, "For the Scripture saith, Thou shalt not muzzle the ox that treadeth out the corn. And, the laborer is worthy of his reward" (1 Timothy 5:18).

Some Christians have the privilege of serving Christ vocationally. This opportunity comes from the church itself as the members support them with their tithes and free-will offerings. It does not mean that their work is more important or vital than that performed by the person who must work at another vocation. They both are ministers and servants.

There is another sense in which Christians minister, both to each other and to those who have not yet believed. It is in loving concern for one another. The church, as has been pointed out, is like a family in which the brothers and sisters care about each other. Paul admonished the Galatians, saying, "Bear ye one another's burdens, and so fulfil the law of Christ" (Galatians 6:2). He told the Romans to "Rejoice with them that do rejoice, and weep with them that weep" (Romans 12:15).

The Jerusalem church gives an example of how Christians should minister to one another's needs. Much poverty existed among its members. Many had come to Jerusalem for the feasts of Passover and Pentecost and stayed because they had found Christ. But they had no means of support, and the residents of Jerusalem may have ostracized those who became Christians. The feeling was so strong against them that employers might have fired anyone who walked in the way of the Nazarene. But, for whatever reason, we do know that many Jerusalem church members were destitute, and this evoked some beautiful expressions of loving concern.

The book of Acts says, "And all that believed were together, and had all things common; and sold their possessions and goods, and parted them to all men, as every man had need" (Acts 2:44, 45). "Neither was there any among them that lacked: for as many as were possessors of lands or houses sold them, and brought the prices of the things that were sold, and laid them down at the apostles' feet: and distribution was made unto every man according as he had need" (Acts 4:34, 35). It is a beautiful picture of how they ministered to each other's physical needs.

It would also seem that the gospel demands that the Christian minister to those who do not yet believe. The parable of the good Samaritan teaches this lesson. Also, Jesus told about what will happen when He returns to earth in His glory. He will say to the sheep whom He will set on the right hand, "Come, ye blessed of my Father, inherit the kingdom prepared for you from the foundation of the world: for I was ahungered, and ye gave me meat: I was thirsty, and ye gave me drink: I was a stranger, and ye took me in: naked, and ye clothed me: I was sick, and ye visited me: I was in prison, and ye came unto me." The people will naturally ask, "When did we do these things for you, Jesus?" He will reply, "Inasmuch as ye have done it unto one of the least of these my brethren, ye have done it unto me" (Matthew 25:34-36, 40).

Love always demands service, or ministry, and Jesus calls Christians both to love and serve others. The New Testament church is a wonderful example for ministry. The Lord added to it every person who accepted Christ, and each was given his gift of service. He used it to bless others within the church, to build them up so the whole body would be strong. His function was like that of a member of a human body, coordinated with the ministries of others to carry out the Lord's purposes for His church. When a congregation restores this New Testament concept of ministry, it will have unity and harmony, and will become a strong body of Christ.

NOTES

[1]John R. W. Stott, *The Baptism and Fulness of the Spirit* (Downer's Grove, IL: Inter-Varsity Press, 1964), p. 97.

19

EVANGELISM AND DISCIPLESHIP

"Go and make disciples of all nations"
(Matthew 28:19 NIV)

His acceptance of Christ and becoming a Christian is the most determinative step a person ever takes. He receives three blessings, which determine his eternal destiny: the remission of sins, the gift of the Holy Spirit, and the promise of Heaven. The Lord also adds him to His church, and he becomes a part of the body of Christ on earth, a church member. This blessing gives his life meaning, purpose, and direction.

Jesus said that He would establish His church, "and the gates of hell shall not prevail against it" (Matthew 16:18). He did not mean that it should assume a defensive posture to withstand the onslaught of evil. On the contrary, the church is to be on the offensive, to take the initiative to batter down the citadels of evil in the world. Paul admonished Christians to "put on the whole armor of God," for they "wrestle not against flesh and blood, but against principalities, against powers, against the rulers of the darkness of this world, against spiritual wickedness in high places" (Ephesians 6:11, 12). The church has a divine mission. This is the reason Christians sing with fervor the hymn that says, "Onward Christian soldiers, marching as to war, with the cross of Jesus going on before."

The new Christian is to find his place of service within the mission of the church and fulfill the responsibility given him by the Lord. He is to find his *gift* and become a tool in the providential hand of God. The Scripture compares him to a servant in the household and a laborer in the vineyard of the Lord because every church member is called to serve, or minister.

The New Testament indicates that there are two major areas of Christian service. By both example and command, they stand out above all others. They are *evangelism* and *discipleship*. These are both germane to the mission of the church, and a congregation is not truly one of Christ's churches unless it participates in them. Jesus gave to His followers what is called the Great Commission. He said, "Go ye therefore, and teach all nations, baptizing them in the name of the Father, and of the Son, and of the Holy Ghost: teaching them to observe all things whatsoever I have commanded you: and, lo, I am with you alway, even unto the end of the world" (Matthew 28:19, 20).

The "go," "teach," and "baptize" refer to the *evangelistic* mission of the church. The "teaching them to observe all things" concerns *discipleship.* Consider each of them.

George E. Sweazey, in his book, *Effective Evangelism: the Greatest Work in the World,* defines *evangelism.* He says, "Evangelism is every possible way of reaching outside the church to bring people to faith in Christ and membership into His church."[1] This is a good definition, but perhaps there is a better definition, more germane to the etymology of the word. It would say, "Evangelism is the bringing of people into such a proximity with the gospel of Christ that they can be saved by it."

The word *evangelism* comes from the Greek word *euanggelos,* which means "good news." It carries the same meaning as the word gospel. An evangelist is one who takes the good news or gospel to others. Evangelism, then, is the program, or plan, utilized by the church to disseminate it. This is important because a primary mission of the church is to take the *evangel* to others so they can be saved by it. Paul said, "For I am not ashamed of the gospel of Christ: for it is the power of God unto salvation . . ." (Romans 1:16).

The word *evangelist* is used in two ways in the New Testament. It is, in the first sense, an *office* to which persons are called by God. One will find it listed along with apostles, prophets, pastors, and teachers in Ephesians 4. Paul admonished Timothy, saying, "Do the work of an evangelist, make full proof of thy ministry" (2 Timothy 4:5). There seems to have been those who were set apart to evangelize and were paid so they could spend their full time in that effort.

The New Testament church gives an example of this. It is found in Acts 13. The church at Antioch, in Syria, prospered and became a strong congregation, even the foster brother of Herod the Tetrarch was a member of it. The Holy Spirit instructed it to consecrate Paul and Barnabas to a specific task of evangelism. They were to go with the good news to the Gentiles, which opened up the whole world to the good news of the gospel. The Scripture says, "And when they had fasted and prayed, and laid their hands on them, they sent them away. So they, being sent forth by the Holy Ghost, departed unto Seleucia; and from thence they sailed to Cyprus" (Acts 13:3, 4).

Paul and Barnabas can be called the first *missionaries,* because evangelism is so much of the *mission* of the church. New Testament churches today continue the precedent set by Antioch. They set apart those who feel called to take the gospel to people, both in their own country and also those in foreign lands. Every local preacher, in this sense, is an evangelist because he delivers the good news. Foreign missionaries, likewise, are evangelists because they take the gospel to those in other lands.

Some congregations have missionary societies within them, and they do much good. But it should be understood by all Christians that the church does not *have* missionary societies; it *is* a missionary society. Everyone is not called to take the gospel to others in a full-time, vocational sense. But every Christian is responsible to support those who are so called with his prayers, finances and encouragement. A congregation cannot be a New Testament church unless it is missions-minded and possesses a world-wide vision of evangelism. It must *think* world evangelism.

But there is another sense in which evangelism is incumbent upon each Christian personally. He is to seek the opportunity to present the good news to those with whom he comes into contact daily. Some call this *personal evangelism.* The first method of evangelism calls for the sending of persons to go preach; personal evangelism has them preach as they go. The New Testament church also provides a beautiful illustration of the latter method even as it did the former.

Saul of Tarsus persecuted the church in the early chapters of Acts. He had participated in the martyrdom of Stephen. "He made havoc of the church, entering into every house, and haling men and women committed them to prison" (Acts 8:3). His persecution scattered the church at Jerusalem. But, as is so often the case, God used the devil's work to further His own plan. The Bible says, "Therefore they that were scattered abroad went every where preaching the word (Acts 8:4). It goes on to relate how Philip, a deacon at the time, went up to the neighboring city of Samaria: "But when they believed Philip preaching the things concerning the kingdom of God, and the name of Jesus Christ, they were baptized, both men and women" (Acts 8:12). This deacon preached as he went, and the Lord made him a great personal evangelist.

Every Christian should equip himself to be able to present the gospel and its plan of salvation to his unsaved friends and acquaintances. The apostle Peter told the believer to "be ready always to give an answer to every man that asketh you a reason of the hope that is in you, with meekness and fear . . ." (1 Peter 3:15). Churches should seek to provide instruction to help their members become effective evangelists. A church will grow when its people know how to present the gospel to the unsaved in a winsome way.

The personal evangelist should realize that he never fails. If he feels that he has failed, he possesses an erroneous concept of his mission. Some have been taught that a personal evangelist is like a salesperson who goes with a pitch to make a quick sale. Then, if the person does not buy it, he looks upon himself as a failure. Wrong! This idea of the personal evangelist is not from the New Testament. One who presents the gospel to another in a loving, winsome way can never fail. His witness will always bear fruit because he has done what his Lord has asked him to do. Paul said, "I have planted, Apollos watered; but God gave the increase" (1 Corinthians 3:6), and God promised, "So shall my word be that goeth forth out of my mouth: it shall not return unto me void, but it shall accomplish that which I please, and it shall prosper in the thing whereunto I send it" (Isaiah 55:11).

The Christian should never conceive of himself as a salesperson with a pitch, but rather as a sower who goes forth with the seed of the Word. Jesus told a beautiful parable to illustrate how this works. It is called the parable of the sower, and is found in Matthew 13. He told about a sower, who represents the Christian, who went out to sow his seed, which represents the gospel. Some seed fell on hard ground, which was unreceptive, as the hearts of some people are hard and unreceptive. Other seed fell on shallow soil, which enabled them to germinate, but, because there was no room for roots, the plants quickly died. Are not some people so glib and shallow that they have no room for eternal values? Still others were crowded out by weeds, even as involvement in the world can crowd out faith. However, the parable says that some seed fell on fertile soil "and brought forth fruit, some a hundredfold, some sixtyfold, some thirtyfold" (Matthew 13:8).

154

This is the promise Jesus gives to the personal evangelist who sows the seed of His Word. Some seed will fall upon receptive soil and produce faith in the hearts of people.

A New Testament church must have evangelism, both local and foreign, as a top priority. Jesus said, "Go ye ... ," and that commandment is an imperative. He would later say, "Ye shall be witnesses unto me ... unto the uttermost part of the earth" (Acts 1:8). He used the parable of the wedding feast to emphasize the importance of evangelism. He said in it, "Go out into the highways and hedges, and compel them to come in, that my house may be filled" (Luke 14:23).

But there is another dimension to the mission of the church equal to evangelism. It is *discipleship*. One must be brought into such a proximity with the gospel of Christ that he can be saved by it. That is evangelism. Then he must be enabled to grow in the grace and knowledge of Christ. That is *discipleship*, or *discipling*, or *Christian nurture*, as it is sometimes called.

Evangelism and discipling must never be separated, for the one must flow into the other. Paul and Peter compare the new Christian to a newborn babe in Christ (1 Corinthians 3:1 and 1 Peter 2:2). Jesus said a person must have been "born anew" in order to be in the family of God. The birth, "to walk in newness of life," is the result of evangelism. It could be called spiritual *obstetrics*. However, it is considered not only tragic, but even criminal, to bring a natural child into the world and fail to care for him. Likewise, it may be spiritual infanticide for a church to bring babes into its fellowship and fail to nurture them. As evangelism is spiritual obstetrics, discipling may be considered spiritual *pediatrics*.

The Christian should become acquainted with the word *edification*. It means "building up, making strong." A New Testament church must work hard to provide the care and nourishment that will enable a new member to grow strong in the Lord. Paul spoke of spiritual gifts and said, "Let all things be done unto edifying" (1 Corinthians 14:26). And again, "Wherefore comfort yourselves together, and edify one another, even as also ye do" (1 Thessalonians 5:11). Edification is the means by which individual Christians are made spiritually strong to build up the entire body.

The goal of edification is *perfection*. Impossible? Yes. But the same spiritual perfection found in Christ remains the goal of the Christian's life. Paul discusses this in Ephesians 4 as he identifies several offices in the church—apostles, prophets, evangelists, pastors, teachers—and defines their purpose: "for the *perfecting* of the saints, for the work of the ministry, for the edifying of the body of Christ: till we all come in the unity of the faith, and of the knowledge of the Son of God, unto a *perfect* man, unto the measure of the stature of the fullness of Christ: that we henceforth be no more children, tossed to and fro, and carried about with every wind of doctrine . . ." (Ephesians 4:11-14).

Some contemporary translations use the word, *mature* or *complete* instead of *perfect,* which may be an improvement. However, if one were completely mature in Christ, he would be perfect. The goal of the Christian is to grow in His grace and knowledge until he becomes spiritually mature, whole, complete—perfect. God has provided the means whereby he can grow. Consider four of them.

THE WORD. There is no substitute for a Christian's learning the Scripture. It must be ranked at the top of the list among means for edification. The Word represents itself as "meat, bread, and milk" to nourish the soul, and "the water of life" to slake spiritual thirst. The Corinthians were weak, carnal Christians for the most part. Paul wrote them and said, "And I, brethren, could not speak unto you as unto spiritual, but as unto carnal, even as unto babes in Christ. I have fed you with milk, and not with meat: for hitherto ye were not able to bear it, neither yet now are ye able" (1 Corinthians 3:1, 2). The apostles' doctrine was like both "milk," to nourish the immature Christians and as "meat" for the more mature ones who could receive it.

The writer of Hebrews uses the same metaphor in the fifth chapter of his epistle (Hebrews 5:12-14). And Peter wrote, "As newborn babes, desire the sincere milk of the word, that ye may grow thereby" (1 Peter 2:2).

The Christian should make every effort to learn God's Word. This is a reason for him to seek membership with a Bible-believing church, where the Word is both taught and preached. His spiritual life will become weak and emaciated without a steady diet of this "milk", "meat", and "bread." This is the great tragedy of many liberal churches. People find there no food to sustain them and often become both discouraged and carnal.

The Christian must also seek a time for personal study of God's Word. Much should be committed to memory. Many find that early morning is the best time for them. He will also need some aids, such as a reputable commentary and concordance. A contemporary language translation of the Bible, such as the *New International Version,* can be of great help, and he should become a part of a Bible study group, such as a Sunday-school class, where he can discuss God's Word with his peers.

Edification, to a large extent, depends upon a knowledge of the Scripture. Paul admonished all Christians when he wrote to Timothy and said, "All Scripture is given by inspiration of God, and is profitable for doctrine, for reproof, for correction, for instruction in righteousness: that the man of God may be perfect, thoroughly furnished unto all good works" (2 Timothy 3:16, 17), and Luke commended the Bereans because they "searched the Scriptures daily" (Acts 17:11).

PRAYER. Jesus told the parable of the widow and the judge to teach that "men ought always to pray, and not to faint," or give up (Luke 18:1). The Scripture is God's Word to man, while prayer could be called man's word in return to Him. Edification is impossible without this two-way conversation with God.

The twelve apostles made a significant request of Jesus in Luke 11. He had been praying, as He so often did, when one of the disciples came up to Him. He did not ask that Jesus teach His followers to preach, or teach, or evangelize. But, after living with Christ and noting the power in His life, the request was, "Lord, teach us to pray" (Luke 11:1).

There can be no doubt but what there is power in prayer. Jesus said, "Ask, and it shall be given you . . ." (Matthew 7:7). James wrote, "The effectual fervent prayer of a righteous man availeth much" (James 5:16). If a Christian feels that something he desires is in God's will, within His providential plan, he is told to pray with *importunity,* which means that he is to keep on praying and praying for it.

The Christian must seek a quiet time for prayer in order to grow strong in the Lord. Some prefer morning, others evening; perhaps it should be in conjunction with his Bible study. Prayer remains essential for edification whenever and under whatever circumstances it occurs.

FELLOWSHIP. Christians need Christians. They must come together and minister to each other. That is the purpose of spiritual gifts; to edify the body (Ephesians 4:12). The tenth chapter of Hebrews explains the necessity of fellowship when it says, "And let us consider how we may spur one another on toward love and

157

good deeds. Let us not give up meeting together, as some are in the habit of doing, but let us encourage one another—and all the more as you see the Day approaching" (Hebrews 10:24, 25, NIV). What was to be the purpose of believers' coming together? To "spur one another on" and to encourage each other in Christ.

A live coal burns brightly in the fireplace while it is with the others. But if it is removed, and laid on the hearth alone, it quickly dies. There is a great lesson to be learned by the Christian from the coal. If he moves into another community, he should immediately seek fellowship with a New Testament church there, lest he be left alone and his faith grow cold and die.

Christians need to come together, to encourage each other, to bear one another's burdens, to weep with them that weep, and rejoice with them that rejoice, as Paul says. Fellowship can help make one strong in Christ. That is the reason the early Christians met daily. It says, "And all that believed were together, and had all things common.... And they, continuing daily with one accord in the temple, and breaking bread from house to house, did eat their meat with gladness and singleness of heart, praising God, and having favor with all the people" (Acts 2:44-47).

EXERCISE. Every growing body must exercise, even as it must have nourishment. The Christian cannot grow spiritually strong unless he actively participates in the mission and ministry of the church. This is the reason it is important for him to find his gift, equip himself to fulfill its responsibility, and work at it. Someone has said, "Impression, without expression, leads to depression." True. The Christian must translate, or express, his faith into ministry, or it becomes dull and dies. James knew this when he said, "Be ye doers of the word, and not hearers only" (James 1:22). He uses Abraham as an example of how fulfilling one's ministry makes a person spiritually strong. He said, "You see that his faith and his actions were working together, and his faith was made complete by what he did" (James 2:22, NIV).

We used the example of the coal to illustrate how the Christian must have fellowship with other Christians to grow strong in Christ. Perhaps we can use the human arm to show how exercise of one's faith is essential. If a person straps his arm tightly to his body so that he cannot move it and leaves it in that condition for a long time, what will happen to the arm? It will atrophy, grow weak, and become useless, will it not? Likewise, faith, unless it is put to work and used, dies.

158

The mission of the New Testament church can be expressed to a great extent by two words: *evangelism* and *discipleship.* People must be brought into proximity with the gospel of Christ so that they can be saved by it and enabled to grow up toward spiritual maturity in Him.

NOTES

[1]George E. Sweazey, *Effective Evangelism: The Greatest Work in the World* (New York: Harper & Row, 1953), p. 19.

20

CHRISTIAN WORSHIP

An ice storm spread across a Midwestern city. It broke down the electric lines, curtailing the energy. A notice was put on a church bulletin board which read, "Because of the lack of power, there will be no worship service tonight." Without electric power, the building could not be lighted or heated, and the worship had to be cancelled. The sign might be turned around for many congregations. It would read, "Because of the lack of worship, there will be no power in the church."

Dr. Frank Albert, a beloved professor at the Butler School of Religion, would say, "Persons who worship well, live well." His students would question him as to cause and effect. They felt Christian living would result in rich worship. But the professor insisted that the opposite is also true, and his pupils would come to agree as they developed maturity. A Christian who worships well in the way God has prescribed cannot help but live a life of fruitful service. It furnishes him with the spiritual power to enable him to be a victorious Christian.

One cannot even be religious unless he worships. The word is a combination of two Anglo-Saxon terms: *worth,* and *ship.* It means to extend to one expressions of his worth or worthiness. One who worships God ascribes to Him holiness, majesty, and sovereignty. The word appears in its various forms 197 times in the Bible—117 times in the Old Testament and 80 times in the New Testament. The Greek word most often used for it in the New Testament is *proskuneo.* It means to do reverence or homage to a superior, usually with the picture of bowing down or prostrating oneself before him. Jesus said, "The true worshippers *(proskunetai)* shall worship *(proskunesousin)* the Father in spirit and in truth: for the Father seeketh such to worship *(prokunountas)* him" (John 4:23). This teaches that one who worships God in the

161

name of Christ pays reverence and homage to Him, spiritually prostrating himself before Him.

The worship experience may be too personal to define, although many have tried. Perhaps the most satisfying definition comes from James S. Dobbins in his book, *A Ministering Church.* He quotes a thoughtful student:

> Worship is an individual or corporate awareness of God, involving a direct relationship with him as he is revealed to us in and through the person of Jesus Christ. It is a recognition of God's worth, involving direct inner contact, a mutual intercourse, a conversation—which should result in action in accordance with his will.[1]

This definition indicates that corporate Christian worship occurs when God's people, the church, gather to extend to Him their homage, love and devotion in Christ's name, which results in a closer walk with Him in life.

Those who would restore the New Testament church must restore New Testament worship because the New Testament church was a worshiping church. As soon as people accepted Christ and became Christians, they began to assemble with the other believers to express the high esteem (worth) in which they held their God. You will find that in each of the early chapters of Acts they worshiped. The second chapter says, "And they [the new Christians], continuing daily with one accord in the temple, and breaking bread from house to house, did eat their meat with gladness and singleness of heart, praising God, and having favor with all the people" (Acts 2:46, 47). The next chapter tells about Peter and John going to the temple at the hour of prayer—which one would have to infer was for the purpose of worship. These same two apostles were imprisoned in the fourth chapter, but, on being released, they returned to the assembled church and found it in a prayer meeting as it prayed for their safety. The fifth chapter may even imply that the early disciples worshiped every day, as it says, "And daily in the temple, and in every house, they ceased not to teach and preach Jesus Christ" (Acts 5:42). No doubt about it: the New Testament church was a worshiping church.

Acts 2:42 may best describe New Testament worship. It says, "And they continued steadfastly in the apostles' doctrine and fellowship, and in breaking of bread, and in prayers." This description contains four elements that should be in the worship of those who want to worship Biblically.

162

First, "they continued steadfastly in the *apostles' doctrine*," which means teaching. This precedent reveals that when the believers gathered for worship, the inspired apostles spoke to them God's Word. They were divinely appointed to deliver it, and the opportunity to do so presented itself when the Christians assembled to praise God. Churches that seek to follow after the New Testament order include the apostles' doctrine in their worship. The apostles themselves have long departed, but they left their doctrine in the New Testament, which remains their authoritative word. Therefore, when it is read, taught, and preached, it is almost as if the apostles were present. Churches that seek to do Bible things in Bible ways will have a message from God's Word in their worship.

Then it says that "they continued stedfastly in . . . *fellowship*." The Greek word used is *koinonia,* which describes the very nature of the church. It means a "fellowship of sharing." New Testament Christians would gather together and share in the things of Christ. The writer of Hebrews encouraged the believers to be faithful in worship when he said, "Let us hold fast the profession of our faith without wavering; for he is faithful that promised; and let us consider one another to provoke unto love and to good works: not forsaking the assembling of ourselves together, as the manner of some is; but exhorting one another: and so much the more, as ye see the day approaching" (Hebrews 10:23-25). The word translated "exhorting" means encouraging. A purpose in the fellowship's coming together for worship was for the members to encourage each other to love and good works.

God never intended for the Christian to live in isolation. This is a reason He created the church. The book of Acts says, "And the Lord added to the church daily such as should be saved" (Acts 2:47). God knew that the believers would need the support of other believers to stay spiritually alive. They would be like a branch torn from the vine; unattached, it quickly dies because it has nothing for nourishment and support. So does the Christian wither without nurture and support from other Christians.

God created fellowship for His chosen people in the church. They gather often in order to encourage each other and to grow in Christ as they feast upon the apostles' doctrine. Worship, the gathering of Christians to praise God, is an integral part of that fellowship that will make one spiritually strong.

Many believe the central element in New Testament worship is the Lord's Supper, or, as Acts 2:42 refers to it, the *breaking of bread*. It is also sometimes called "Communion" (1 Corinthians 10:16), or "the Lord's table" (1 Corinthians 10:21). It involves the congregation's partaking of unleavened bread to remind them of Christ's body and fruit of the vine as a reminder of His blood. Thomas Campbell believed in this act of worship so deeply that he would say, "New Testament worship ceases" when the Lord's Supper is not observed every Lord's day.[2]

Indeed, Jesus did command His disciples to participate in this Communion. He instituted the Lord's Supper in the upper room at the Passover Feast, which He ate with the apostles just before His crucifixion. Luke describes the occasion: "And he took bread, and gave thanks, and brake it, and gave unto them, saying, This is my body which is given for you: this do in remembrance of me. Likewise also the cup after supper, saying, This cup is the new testament in my blood, which is shed for you" (Luke 22:19, 20). Notice the imperative: "This do in remembrance of me."

We know the early church kept that command. Evidence of this is found when Paul rebuked the Corinthians for their irreverence at the Lord's table. He said they were weak because they did not participate in it reverently and thoughtfully. He introduced the rebuke by repeating Jesus' command. He said, "For I have received of the Lord that which also I delivered unto you, That the Lord Jesus, the same night in which he was betrayed, took bread: and when he had given thanks, he brake it, and said, Take, eat; this is my body, which is broken for you: this do in remembrance of me. After the same manner also he took the cup, when he had supped, saying, This cup is the new testament in my blood: this do ye, as oft as ye drink it, in remembrance of me. For as often as ye eat this bread, and drink this cup, ye do show the Lord's death until he comes" (1 Corinthians 11:23-26).

There can be no doubt but what Christ expects Christians to commune about the elements of the Lord's Supper. The early leaders of the restoration movement believed it was central in the Lord's day worship. Alexander Campbell wrote, "The commemoration of the Lord's death must . . . be a weekly institution."[3] He went on to quote John Calvin, a sixteenth-century reformer to whom the Reformed churches of today trace their origin. Calvin said, "Every week, at least, the table of the Lord should have been spread for Christian assemblies, and the promises declared, by which, partaking of it, we might be spiritually fed."[4]

The early leaders of the movement found Scriptural precedent for the weekly partaking of the Lord's Supper. Acts 20 tells of Paul's visit to Troas. "And upon the first day of the week, when the disciples came together to break bread, Paul preached unto them, ready to depart on the morrow; and continued his speech until midnight" (Acts 20:7). The reader will note that the congregation did not gather for the purpose of Paul's preaching. It does not say that the inspired apostle came and so the church assembled in order to hear him. No! Instead, they gathered, as was their custom, on the first day of the week (Sunday) to partake of the Lord's Supper. Communion was what brought them together, and that presented the opportune time for Paul to preach.

The New Testament church grew much more rapidly than it could provide preachers for itself. The apostles themselves could not be everywhere. So the early Christians would meet on Sunday, oftentimes in homes, and commune together in the Lord's Supper. It reminded them of the central fact of the gospel message, "Christ died for our sins." The Lord's Supper in the worship service today still centralizes that truth. The preacher and the choir may miss the mark; no gospel content may be in their messages. But the Lord's Supper will always bring to remembrance the love of Christ in the cross for the sincere worshiper.

One's attitude must be right when he communes. Paul warned that those who partake in an unworthy manner, that is, irreverently, drink damnation to their souls (1 Corinthians 11:29). He tells us that the Lord's Supper should take one's thoughts in three directions: 1) *backward,* "This do in remembrance of me," Jesus said; 2) *inward,* "But let a man examine himself, and so let him eat of that bread, and drink of that cup" (1 Corinthians 11:28); 3) *forward,* "Ye do show the Lord's death till he come" (1 Corinthians 11:26).

Finally, Acts 2:42 says the early Christians continued steadfastly in *prayer*. This refers to corporate prayer, the assembly praying together, without which no worship could be complete. As the Scripture reading is God's speaking to the worshiper, prayer is the worshiper's speaking to Him. Prayers can be divided into several kinds: forgiveness, praise and adoration, intercession for others, and petition. The Bible makes it clear that God wants the prayers of His people. He also promises that "the effectual fervent prayer of a righteous man availeth much" (James 5:16).

The congregations that try to do Bible things in Bible ways

PRAYER

usually include two other elements in the Lord's-day worship, which they believe to be scriptural. One is the *offering*. Paul told the Corinthians, "Upon the first day of the week let every one of you lay by him in store, as God hath prospered him, that there be no gatherings when I come" (1 Corinthians 16:2). Communion reminds the Christian of how much God has given; the offering provides him an opportunity to give a small portion of his blessing back to God. The Christian brings his offering on the Lord's day, not to enable the church to pay its bills or meet the budget, or as dues: instead, he brings it as an act of oblation.

Most churches of the restoration movement include *singing* in the Lord's day worship. It expresses praise to God, and edifies the saints. Paul said, "Let the word of Christ dwell in you richly in all wisdom; teaching and admonishing one another in psalms and hymns and spiritual songs, singing with grace in your hearts to the Lord" (Colossians 3:16). Congregational singing is one act that the church members do as one body, together.

One can conclude from Scripture that the Lord's day worship should include these elements: 1) *apostles' doctrine*—reading, preaching, teaching; 2) *fellowship*—encouraging one another to love and good works; 3) *the Lord's Supper;* 4) *prayer;* 5) *offering;* and 6) *singing*. Christians who worship with these ingredients will receive the spiritual power to make the church strong.

God specified the first day of the week, Sunday, to be the Christians' day of worship. This should not be confused with the Old Testament Sabbath, which was the seventh day and was filled with legalistic prohibitions. The law of Moses established it, but Paul tells us that Christ nailed this law to the cross and replaced it with grace. The Sabbath was part of that law which passed away. On the Lord's day, Sunday, the believers met in New Testament times to celebrate all that God had done for them. They came together on the first day of the week for that purpose in Troas in Acts 20; Paul told the Corinthians to bring their offerings on the first day of the week (1 Corinthians 16:2), and John said he was in the Spirit on the Lord's day (Revelation 1:10).

Alexander Campbell testified as to how the Brush Run Church, of which he was a member, observed the Lord's Day. He wrote:

The morning of the day we freely consecrate to the Lord in reading, meditation, prayer, with other necessary duties. During the day we assemble to commemorate the death, resurrection, and works of

Christ—to pray, to praise, to comfort and edify one another. . . . In the evening of the day we conclude as we began. So that there are no professing Christians of any denomination, even those who call the Lord's day a Sabbath, who pay a more rational, scriptural and sacred regard to the Lord's day than *we*. [5]

God seems to have singled out Sunday and made it special for Christians. The great events of the Christian faith occurred on that day: Jesus arose from the dead on the first day of the week, and Christian worship is a celebration of that victory. The church was established, the Holy Spirit came in power, the gospel was first preached, and the plan of salvation defined—all on the first day.

The assembling of the church on the first day of the week around the Lord's table should be looked forward to with keen anticipation by every Christian. It is not merely a duty, but an opportunity without which he will grow weak. Alexander Campbell expressed the joy he experienced in worship. He wrote:

Next to the beautific vision of God in his own glorious heaven, there is nothing on earth to compare with the pleasures of—prayer with God; or in the celebration of the Lord's supper in the solemn assembly of a sincerely pious and well-informed Christian community, while . . . in . . . devotion all unite, each in his own bosom, in adoring him who so loved us, "dead in trespasses and sins," as to send his Son . . . to redeem us to himself by the sacrifice of himself, symbolized and set forth in this hallowed institution.[6]

NOTES

[1]James S. Dobbins, *A Ministering Church* (Nashville: Broadman Press, 1960), p. 114.

[2]W. E. Garrison and A. T. DeGroot, *The Disciples of Christ: A History* (St. Louis: Christian Board of Publication, 1948), p. 163.

[3]Alexander Campbell, *The Christian System* (Cincinnati: H. S. Bosworth, 1866), p. 338.

[4]Alexander Campbell, *The Christian Baptist,* 1825, p. 195.

[5]Robert Richardson, *Memoirs of Alexander Campbell* (Cincinnati: Standard Publishing Co., 1868), Vol. 1, p. 435.

[6]Alexander Campbell, *The Millenial Harbinger,* 1849, pp. 9, 10.

21

CHURCH GOVERNMENT

The smartest man in the restoration movement should sharpen his pencil and write in the area of church government, sometimes called "church polity." This deals with who leads the congregation, and by whom and how decisions are made for it. Many believe answers must be found in this area to enable the churches of the movement to grow as they must. However, its early leaders made some decisions upon which a consensus still remains.

The early leaders of the restoration movement rejected all hierarchical and episcopal systems of church government. The Roman Catholic Church has most elaborately developed the hierarchical system. It is a pyramidal organization, at the top of which presides the pope, who is described as the vicar of Christ on earth, standing in His place. The Curia, which is an ecclesiastical cabinet, surrounds the pope. The pyramid then descends in order with cardinals, archbishops, bishops, priests, and laity. Some believe this system parallels the monarchy of ancient Rome, where decisions came from the top, the pope being like Caesar. Roman Catholic doctrine states that "when the Pope speaks in the capacity of his office *(ex cathedra),* he speaks without error in matters of faith and morals." The faithful within the Roman church are to be obedient to these dictums; however, evidence does exist of erosion of papal authority in modern times since Vatican Council II in 1962. However, the hierarchical system remains the governmental philosophy of the Roman Catholic Church.

The Eastern Orthodox churches use an oligarchical system of government in contrast to the monarchial system. It differs in that the seat of authority within the denomination centers in several men in different geographical areas who are called patriarchs. They govern and speak authoritatively from several sees: Constantinople, Alexandria, Antioch, and Jerusalem. Some national churches have their own patriarchs, such as the Russian Orthodox Church, Greek Orthodox Church, and Syrian Orthodox Church. Both the Roman Catholic and Eastern Orthodox Churches lay heavy emphasis upon "apostolic succession." This doctrine means that they believe their priests have been ordained by the laying on of hands in succeeding generations back to the apostles.

The Episcopal Church has the same emphasis upon "apostolic succession." It traces its history back to the Church of England, which separated from the Roman Church under the leadership of Henry VIII in 1534. Archbishops and bishops administer over areas of churches. Other Protestants have church governments that allow decisions to be made at the top by those who speak for the whole denomination to a lesser degree. The Methodists have bishoprics and districts; Presbyterians have synods and presbyteries.

The early leaders of the restoration movement rejected all forms of episcopal government. They found no Scriptural precedent for them and looked upon them as counterproductive. Barton Warren Stone said in *The Last Will and Testament of the Springfield Presbytery:* "We will that each particular church, as a body, actuated by the same spirit, choose her own preacher, and support him by a free-will offering, without a written call or subscription—admit members, remove offenses; and never herewith delegate her right of government to any man or set of men whatever." Alexander Campbell agreed. He expressed the principle of interdependency in a speech in defense of his father's *Declaration and Address*. He said, "Each congregation should have its own internal government by elders and deacons, and while regarded as an independent body, should have fellowship with other churches of like faith."

These men saw the New Testament church as composed of autonomous, interdependent congregations. By autonomous they meant that each congregation was to conduct its own affairs under the leadership of elders with the help of deacons as guided by Scripture. There was to be no higher human authority. However, they did find precedent for the congregations being interdependent. Interdependency meant they were to cooperate with each other to forward the cause of Christ, even as the churches in Asia Minor received an offering for the church in Jerusalem (1 Corinthians 16). Practical expressions of the principle of interdependency can be seen within the restoration movement today.

Autonomous congregations willingly come together to support Christian service camps, evangelistic fellowships, colleges, and other ministries.

The churches of the restoration movement universally accept local autonomy; few would want to see it lost. The vast majority still look upon any episcopal form of church government as unscriptural and counterproductive.

It is about the organization of the local congregation that the "smartest man" in the movement needs to write. What relationship does the minister have to the elders, the elders to the deacons, the deacons to the congregation? Who has purview of what areas of church life? How shall the fellowship structure itself to most fruitfully serve Christ? These questions need thoughtful consideration and expression from the "smartest man" in the movement.

Some of the ambiguity comes because the New Testament gives no set pattern for congregational life. Some of it seems to have evolved as need came. In the early days of the church, temporary offices led; notable among them were the apostles. The Jerusalem church in Acts centered around these men. There were twelve after Matthias joined them, and later Paul increased their number. The New Testament calls others apostles in the sense that they were messengers, such as Barnabas, Andronicus, Junius, and James, the Lord's brother. But God chose the Twelve and Paul to be the leaders of the church in its infancy, and the Holy Spirit gave them personal inspiration so that they spoke God's will without error. They could perform miracles and pass on the power to perform miracles. It also seems that they had to be directly called by God, and Acts 1:21-23 implies that they had to witness the resurrected Christ. The last apostle alive, John, died at about the turn of the first century, and the office ceased.

There were prophets in the early church. That office, too, had a dual meaning in that it, too, could refer to any spokesman for God in its broadest sense. But some prophets in the New Testament church had special powers as the Holy Spirit personally inspired them to reveal God's will inerrantly. They rendered an indispensable service to the early church, but when the New Testament became complete, the church no longer needed their ministry.

However, Ephesians 4, Titus 1, and 1 Timothy 3 identify three permanent, divinely appointed places of service in the church: evangelists, elders, and deacons. An evangelist is anyone who carries the good news, but the New Testament church set apart some men specifically for this ministry. They called Philip "the evangelist" (Acts 21:8), and Paul told Timothy "to do the work of an evangelist" (2 Timothy 4:5). One would infer from the letter which bears his name that Titus also fit into this category. The evangelist seems to have been a preacher who would come into the church from outside the community to shape it up. Paul told Titus to do exactly that (Titus 1:5) when he left him in Crete to "set in order the things that are wanting, and ordain elders in every city." It would also appear that their service with any one congregation was rather short in duration.

Elders would become the long-term leaders in most New Testament churches. The apostles could not be everywhere and not enough evangelists existed to go around. So congregations chose spiritual men within the fellowship to care for them. The New Testament uses three Greek words to denote the office, and they describe its ministry. The first is *presbuteroi,* which literally meant in its origin "old men," then came to represent those with maturity of spiritual experience. The Jews used it to represent the elders in their synagogue long before Christ came. In the New Testament church, they were spiritually mature men, able to lead the people of God in His truth. They were also called the *episcopoi,* which is translated bishops, or overseers. It describes their responsibility as they superintended the work or ministry of the church. The third term is *poimen,* which means pastor in the New Testament and says something about the elder's heart. It refers to a shepherd, one who loves and cares for the sheep in God's flock.

No one could doubt that the eldership remains a high office within the church and carries great responsibility. The writer of Hebrews referred to it when he said to the church, "Obey them that have rule over you, and submit yourselves: for they watch for your souls, as they that must give account, that they may do it with joy, and not with grief: for that is unprofitable for you" (Hebrews 13:17). Paul met with the elders from Ephesus in an emotional farewell at Miletus in Acts 20, and impressed them with their responsibility. He charged them saying, "Take heed therefore unto yourselves, and to all the flock, over the which the Holy Ghost hath made you overseers, to feed the church of God, which he hath purchased with his own blood (Acts 20:28). Peter added his emphasis in regard to the responsibilities of elders. He said, "The elders which are among you I exhort, who am also an elder:

... Feed the flock of God which is among you, taking the oversight thereof, not by constraint, but willingly; not for filthy lucre, but of a ready mind; neither as being lords over God's heritage, but being ensamples to the flock" (1 Peter 5:1-3).

Titus 1:5-9 and 1 Timothy 3:1-7 describe the kind of men who should serve as elders. They make it obvious that they should be deeply dedicated, with great character and reputation, who are willing to serve. One would infer from Acts 14:23 and Titus 1:5 that, as a rule, a plurality of elders served within the local church. The method by which they were chosen is somewhat vague, but the evidence indicates that they elected them by the stretching forth of hands (Acts 14:23).

The word deacon is a transliteration of the Greek word *diakonos,* which means "servant." Many believe the first deacons were the seven chosen by the Jerusalem church in Acts 6 to disseminate the common fund to the poor. Deacons worked under the purview of elders, but this does not mean that they do not serve in a most responsible way. The Scripture says, "For they that have used the office of deacon well purchase to themselves a good degree, and great boldness in the faith which is in Christ Jesus" (1 Timothy 3:13). The qualities of the men that fill this office appear very similar to those of the elders (see 1 Timothy 3:8-12).

Our "smartest man" would render the movement great service if he would write about the interrelationship of these offices. Probably, flexibility should be the policy since no prescribed pattern exists. Most of the older congregations in the restoration movement have three separate entities in church government. They have a minister or ministers, a term probably derived from Peter's statement in Acts 6:4 that the apostles would give themselves to the "ministry of the word." The church calls them from the outside and expects them to serve under the authority of the elders. They pay them so they do not have to do work in other employment, and the vast majority have received college-level training to prepare them for church vocation. These churches will also have elders and deacons, whom they elect from within the congregation, who are not paid. The congregation usually conducts its business when the three groups come together in what they call the board meeting. The paid ministers attend but most of the time do not vote.

Some congregations, particularly newer ones, have come to

question the effectiveness of this church polity and look for variables within the Scriptural context. Some, for example, say the preaching minister, and perhaps other paid ministers, serve as *de facto* pastors-teachers and should be considered as such. They feed, shepherd, and oversee the flock of God, which is the ministry of the elders (pastors). They would not want them to be *the* pastor in a ruling sense, but an elder among other elders within the church. Some feel that a period of time should elapse before a man called into the congregation from the outside should be considered an elder. It would be a time of testing, but, if he proved himself worthy, he would become one and be equal with them. They believe this would minimize the adversarial relationship that sometimes develops between preachers and elders. It would enhance collegiality.

Another concept emerging is called elder administration or elder rule (Hebrews 13:17). Those coming to this concept believe an inequity exists when a congregation uses an official board composed of both elders and deacons in joint session. This group becomes the decision-making body of the church. In most cases, the deacons outnumber the elders considerably and, therefore, control the vote. Some believe this to be unscriptural because they have concluded that the New Testament gives oversight of the church to the elders (Acts 20:28 and 1 Peter 5:1-3). Also, they consider deacons to be usually less spiritually mature.

Elder rule means that the elders become the decision-making group and assume responsibility for the church. Then the elders appoint persons to serve as deacons. The deacon assumes specific, prescribed responsibilities within the whole. It may be in property maintenance, finance, or in benevolence, *et cetera*. The elders seek men gifted in the areas in which they serve and appoint them for a tenure or until they finish their prescribed task.

The Mason Church of Christ, near Cincinnati, Ohio, recently took a new look at its old church polity with an official board and reorganized its structure. Thomas D. Thurman, then minister of the congregation, wrote (in *Recovery,* Grayson H. Ensign, editor [Cincinnati: Recovery Publications, March 1985]):

> Some time ago at Mason Church of Christ we determined to try to structure the church after the pattern which we believe is in the New Testament. In the process of doing this, we devised the following chart:

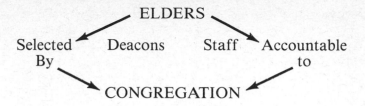

There are several things we observe about the chart. One: the preacher and other staff members and the deacons, as well as all other members, function under the elders who, of course, function under Christ. Deacons are "special servants." Preachers are too. Two: although the elders have authority over the congregation, they are selected by it and are accountable to it. They are not overlords, but overseers.

Thurman goes on to say: "The plan has been in operation several years and is improving with age. We believe the reason for its success is that it is God's plan for operating His church."

The New Testament allows a great amount of flexibility within the framework of local autonomy and interdependence. This allows the church to adjust to particular needs and circumstances. However, some spiritual principles of leadership need to be effected in order for the church to receive God's blessing.

1. Every church leader must realize that God calls him to sacred service. The church remains the only eternal institution and the holiest. God purchased it with His own blood, and the New Testament refers to it as the body of Christ on earth. Therefore, it honors one to serve in it, but with the honor comes responsibility. Self-interest must be laid aside as the leader always bases his decisions on what is best for the Lord's church.

2. Every church leader must look upon himself as a humble servant, or minister. How important this is! Even Jesus said He came to minister and not to be ministered unto, and they called Him the "Suffering *Servant*." Most of the titles for church offices in the New Testament carry humble connotations as was mentioned in the chapter on "Membership and Ministry." *Deacon* means "household servant," or "a waiter upon the tables"; *minister* means "servant"; and *pastor* means "shepherd," one of the humblest servants in the Near East. Peter warned elders about arrogance when he wrote, "Neither as being lords over God's heritage, but being ensamples to the flock. . . . Yea, all of you be subject one to another, and be clothed with humility: for God

resisteth the proud, and giveth grace to the humble. Humble yourselves therefore under the mighty hand of God, that he may exalt you in due time" (1 Peter 5:3, 5, 6). When Christians begin to serve each other in a church, it will create a happy fellowship that will make people want to become a part of it.

3. Love must abound within the hearts of church leaders—love of God, Christ, the church, and the persons who comprise the church. Paul said, "Let love be without dissimulation" (Romans 12:9). John wrote, "If God so loved us, we ought also to love one another" (1 John 4:11). Jesus tells us how important love is within the fellowship, "By this shall all men know that ye are my disciples, if ye have love one to another" (John 13:35). Church leaders must be examples of Christian love that the church might be a fellowship of love.

4. Church leaders must work hard to keep avenues of communication open. It is the vehicle that carries one's thoughts and feelings to others. It enhances understanding, which makes unity possible. Some elders and ministers meet weekly for prayer and deliberations, oftentimes with no planned agenda. They simply gather to seek the Lord's guidance and to be sure that there is understanding among themselves. Good leaders will also strive to communicate well with the congregation they lead.

A legend out of antiquity illustrates the necessity of good leadership within the church. It tells about Jesus' ascension back to Heaven after the resurrection. The archangel Michael approached him and said, "Jesus, you went down to earth to accomplish the redemption of mankind. There people despitefully used you; some cursed you, others blasphemed you; still others spat upon you, stoned you, and at last they crucified you. Now you have come back to Heaven and have left the task of redeeming man in the hands of eleven disciples—disciples who have not always proved faithful; one denied you, another doubted you, and a third of like kind betrayed you. Now, Jesus, what other plan do you have to redeem mankind if these eleven men fail you?" Jesus is supposed to have replied, "If those eleven men fail me, I have no other plan."

So God's Word teaches concerning the church of this age. Jesus depends upon it for the redemption of mankind; it is to be His agency of salvation. If church leaders of today fail Him, He has no other plan to redeem man. A congregation can rise only as high as its leadership's vision.

22

CHRISTIAN STEWARDSHIP

Christians within the restoration movement need to do more to restore the New Testament concept of stewardship. The subject remains most important. The Gospels record thirty-eight of Jesus' parables, of which sixteen deal with man's responsibility as a steward. One of every six verses in the synoptic Gospels (Matthew, Mark, and Luke) concerns the stewardship of possessions.

A group of Protestant church leaders met and formed a classical definition of stewardship. Its says, "Christian stewardship is the practice of systematic and proportionate giving of time, abilities, and material possessions based on the conviction that these are a trust from God to be used in His service for the benefit of all mankind, in grateful acknowledgment of Christ's redeeming love."[1] Restoration movement Christians must seek to embody this definition. Fulfillment of the church's mission depends on it.

Jesus told a story that explains what He would have His people understand about stewardship. It has been popularly known as the parable of the talents, found in Matthew 25. He said a certain rich man, who represents Jesus himself in the story, prepared to take a long journey, which represents His ascension back into Heaven. Before leaving, he called in his servants, who represent Jesus' disciples, and divided among them his living. He gave to the first servant five talents. A talent in Jesus' day was a weight of money worth about a thousand dollars. The second servant received two talents and the third, one.

It should be understood at the very outset of Jesus' story that the rich man parcelled out to the servants that which still belonged to him. He gave it to them not to own, nor could they use it as they desired, nor did they have the right to pass it on to their posterity. He merely loaned the money to them for a short time.

They were to manage it for him during that time in such a way that it would bring a profit to his household.

This illustrates the Biblical word *oikonomos,* which we translate "steward." It represents one who manages that which belongs to another. In New Testament times, it was usually a farm, household, or an estate; but the steward owned nothing. Instead, he just managed it for its owner.

The basis for Christian stewardship goes back to Psalm 24:1, which says, "The earth is the Lord's and the fulness thereof; the world, and they that dwell therein." This means that all the Christian is and all he has belongs to God by right of creation.

An old story tells about the preacher who went home with the rich farmer for Sunday dinner. It illustrates how all one has belongs to God. The farmer had acquired many possessions because he had worked hard, lived frugally, and invested well. This enabled him to build large barns, acquire fields of grain, and a fine herd of registered cattle. After dinner, the farmer took the preacher out to show him the farm. But everywhere they went the minister would say, "My but the *Lord* has a fine barn over there," and, "The *Lord* has a fine stand of wheat in that field," and, "The *Lord* has a fine herd of cattle on the other side of the fence."

This hurt the farmer; he took great pride in his possessions. When he could stand it no longer, he exclaimed, "Do you mean to say these barns are not mine, and the fields and the cattle do not belong to me?" To which the preacher replied, "Ask me that question a hundred years from now."

Do you see the point? Nothing the Christian possesses will belong to him a hundred years from now. A rather vulgar truism says, "You can't take it with you." Vulgar? Perhaps. But true. A Spanish proverb observes, "They don't put pockets into funeral shrouds." I used this at a church service in Plainfield, Indiana. Afterwards, an old elder emeritus of the congregation passed by me as he left, dressed in an old tattered overcoat and leaning on his cane. He said, "Preacher, you talk about no pockets in funeral shrouds. I've got one for you better than that." He said, "I never seen a Brink's truck in a funeral procession, and I never seen a hearse pulling a U-Haul-It trailer." He cackled and went on out the door. But he had made a good point. Job said, "Naked came I out of my mother's womb, and naked shall I return thither" (Job 1:21). Many people live comfortably in this world. They have large homes, take long vacations, have country club memberships, but at some point they will leave all of it behind and will have no treasure laid up for themselves in Heaven for eternity. And Jesus asked, "For what is a man profited, if he shall gain the whole world, and lose his own soul? or what shall a man give in exchange for his soul?" (Matthew 16:26).

God makes every Christian a steward of His creation. He gives him time, abilities and possessions, and He expects him to use them to bring a profit to His household. The Christian may be a good steward, or a poor steward; a faithful one or an unfaithful one; fruitful or unfruitful. But he nevertheless remains a steward of what the Lord has invested in him.

The good steward recognizes that life itself is the gift of God—that his time belongs to Him. Someone said, "Life is God's gift to us; but what we do with it is our gift back to Him." Benjamin Franklin saw the importance of this gift. He said, "Time is important; it is the stuff life is made of." And the apostle Paul possessed an acute sense of the value of days and hours. He admonished the Colossians saying, "Walk in wisdom ... redeeming the time" (Colossians 4:5), which means, seize your opportunities, you only pass this way once.

The apostle went on to drive home the essentiality of the stewardship of life. He wrote to the Corinthian Christians and said, "What? know ye not that your body is the temple of the Holy Ghost which is in you, which ye have of God, and ye are not your own? For ye are bought with a price: therefore glorify God in your body, and in your spirit, which are God's" (1 Corinthians 6:19, 20). He reiterated the same sentiment when he admonished the Romans saying, "I beseech ye therefore, brethren, by the mercies of God, that ye present your bodies a living sacrifice, holy, acceptable unto God, which is your reasonable service" (Romans 12:1). These Scriptures teach that the very hours of a steward's life belong to Him who created it.

God has a plan He wants to effect to evangelize the world, and, He gives the Christian opportunities to be used in this plan. The Christian must, as a good steward, find his place of service in that plan and invest his life in it. His hours and his days belong to God.

The good steward will also use his abilities in God's plan because they belong to Him, too. Some of these abilities may be innate, others acquired. He might have been born with the talent to sing; or he might have gone to school and developed business acumen, both of which can be used in the Lord's work. It should be noted that these abilities, or talents, differ from the gifts of the Holy Spirit. The gifts are given only to Christians to be used to bless the lives of others in the church. Talents are given to, and other abilities are developed by, unbelievers as well as believers. However, the Christian takes his abilities and uses them as a faithful steward. Sometimes the Holy Spirit will give him a gift to be used in the church for which his talents are most suited. His gift may be to sing, or preach, or oversee finances, for which he has innate ability.

Jesus' parable reminds us that some people have more ability than others; one servant received five talents, the second two, and the third but one. This accurately describes life, does it not? All men are created equal as far as their *rights* are concerned; but not all men are created equal as far as their *abilities* are concerned. Some are much more superbly endowed with talent than others. However, God does not hold the steward responsible for an ability He does not invest in him. He does not expect every Christian to be multi-talented, brilliant, or clever. All he has to be is committed and available. The Scripture says, "Moreover it is required in stewards, that a man be found faithful" (1 Corinthians 4:2).

Sometimes it seems that God chooses those with little ability, even the handicapped, to accomplish His purposes so that He can receive the glory. We know He did this in the case of Gideon's army. He reduced it to three hundred so that the people would depend on Him and give Him credit for the victory. Consider other crooked sticks God has used to work out His plans. Moses could not speak well, but God used him to be His spokesman before Pharoah, the most powerful man on earth at that time. There is much evidence that Jeremiah was a timid soul who did not like to appear before people in public. But God took him and made him one of His most beloved prophets. The greatest preacher who ever lived may have been a crooked stick. Tradition calls Paul "the ugly, little Jew." Herbert Lockyear in his book, *All the Apostles of the Bible,* says that he probably was a little dwarf who did not stand five feet in height. He was neither pleasant to look upon nor to listen to, but God empowered him to become His greatest preacher. Others of more recent vintage suffered impediments but rendered magnificent service. John Wesley contended with poor health all his life and his marriage was less than ideal, but God used him to revive England. Dwight L. Moody had a limited education; he pronounced Gideon as Gidjun. One evening a woman said to him, "Mr. Moody, you made seventeen grammatical errors tonight." "Well," he replied, "that's all the Lord gave me. If He had given me any others, I would have delivered them, too." With little formal education, he became the most renowned evangelist of his era.

The steward will not be judged by the amount of talent he possesses. However, he will be held responsible for how faithfully he uses that which has been invested in him.

Jesus talked much about the stewardship of possessions. Only upon one occasion did He call a person a fool, and it concerned this subject. It was prompted by a farmer's misuse of his possessions in a story found in Luke 12. The farmer, it says, had been successful because the Lord had blessed him with many possessions. He resolved to build larger barns in which to bestow his goods, then he would eat, drink, and be merry. He thought he had it made. "But God said to him, Thou fool, this night thy soul shall be required of thee: then whose shall those things be, which thou hast provided?" (Luke 12:20).

That question speaks to the heart of Christian stewardship—"then whose shall these things be?" One's possessions must be looked upon as an opportunity to serve God, to forward His plans.

Stewardship of possessions necessitates consideration of the tithe. Tithing means to give a tenth of one's income to the Lord's work and is a practice that goes back deep into Hebrew history. It begins in Genesis. Abram defeated the kings who had sacked Sodom and Gomorrah and taken his nephew, Lot, prisoner in Genesis 14. Later in the same chapter it says he met Melchizedek, who was both a king and a priest, and presented him with a tithe of his spoils. Later on in Genesis 28, Jacob pledged a tenth of all his blessings to God from whom they had come.

The Law of Moses made tithing a necessity for the Hebrews. Leviticus 27:30-32 says, "And all the tithe of the land, whether of the seed of the land, or of the fruit of the tree, is the Lord's: it is holy unto the Lord. And if a man will at all redeem aught of his tithes, he shall add thereto the fifth part thereof. And concerning the tithe of the herd, or of the flock, even of whatsoever passeth under the rod, the tenth shall be holy unto the Lord." The Hebrews used the tithe to support the work of the priests and the Levites.

God not only expected His people to tithe, but He also promised to bless those who did. He gave this promise in Malachi 3:10. He said, "Bring ye all the tithes into the storehouse, that there may be meat in mine house, and prove me now herewith, saith the Lord of hosts, if I will not open you the windows of heaven, and pour you out a blessing, that there shall not be room enough to receive it."

Many Christians who tithe testify to its blessing because they believe God still honors this promise. They testify that one who enters into a tithe covenant with God receives a special blessing from Him. These Christians say that if the Hebrews were required to tithe, how can Christians who know the love of God in Christ want to do less?

However, others point out that the New Testament never specifically commands the Christian to tithe. Jesus did commend the practice in a backhanded way when He condemned the Pharisees for their lack of compassion. He said that they passed over the judgment and love of God as they tithed their "mint and rue and all manner of herbs." Then he added, "These ought ye to have done, and not to leave the other undone" (Luke 11:42). But Jesus, in this Scripture, spoke to people who still lived under the law of Moses. Neither He nor the apostles specifically commanded it for those who live in the age of grace.

The New Testament does teach that the Christian should give proportionately. Paul said, "Upon the first day of the week let every one of you lay by him in store, as God hath prospered him, that there be no gatherings when I come" (1 Corinthians 16:2). The key phrase there is "as God hath prospered him." Those who tithe believe that the practice helps them give proportionately. If they make more, they give more, and when less comes, they are expected to give less. It may not be quite that simple because of the complexity of modern-day economics where taxes enter into the picture. But many still insist that the tithe is the place for the Christian to begin his stewardship responsibilities.

Whether the Christian decides to tithe or not, there are some rules that will help him be a good steward of his possessions:

1) First, he must recognize that his possessions, as well as his time and abilities, belong to God. He merely manages them for Him for a little while.

2) He must give as unto the Lord. He should not look upon his contribution as a tax or assessment. It is to be presented as an act

of worship. Many Christians divide their income into fifty-two equal parts so they can bring it with them each week to the Lord's day worship. Remember Paul said, "Upon the first day of the week let every one of you lay by him in store...."

3) The steward must give with the right attitude. The Scripture says, "Every man according as he purposeth in his heart, so let him give; not grudgingly, or of necessity: for God loveth a cheerful giver" (2 Corinthians 9:7). The good steward gives from a grateful heart in recognition that God's grace can never be repaid.

4) He should also remember that he cannot outgive God. Jesus said, "Give, and it shall be given unto you; good measure, pressed down, and shaken together, and running over, shall men give into your bosom. For with the same measure that ye mete withal it shall be measured to you again" (Luke 6:38). It appears that God is generous toward the generous and will not let anyone give Him more than He returns. The apostle Paul seems to have learned this lesson. He wrote, "He which soweth sparingly shall reap also sparingly; and he which soweth bountifully shall reap also bountifully" (2 Corinthians 9:6).

Jesus' parable of the talents concludes with a promise and a sober warning. The rich man in the story returns and calls in the servants. The one given five talents brings in ten, for he had used them well and made a profit. His lord commended him and said, "Well done," and bade him enter into his own joy. Likewise, the second servant, who had been given two talents, had used them to make an additional two. He, also, received a commendation because he had been a "good and faithful servant."

Later, the one who had received the one talent came. He had buried it and failed to use it profitably. His lord called him "a wicked and slothful servant" and condemned him to outer darkness. One can trace an element of surprise in this condemnation. The man had neither murdered nor robbed anyone, nor can we infer from the story that he had even cheated a neighbor. He may have been a morally upright citizen, but he was condemned because he failed to be a good steward of that which the lord had invested in his life.

Jesus' story illustrates the New Testament concept of stewardship. It teaches that God has invested time, abilities, and possessions in the Christian's life, and he is to manage them as a good steward in such a way that they will bring a profit to God's household. Some day, every Christian will stand before God on the occasion of judgment and give an account of his stewardship. The goal of the good steward is to hear, "Well done," from his Lord on this occasion (Matthew 25:23).

NOTES

[1]Julian Stuart, *Christian Stewardship* (Indianapolis: National Church Coordinating Council, no date), p. 23.

23

THE A CAPPELLA CHURCHES OF CHRIST

Coming from within the restoration movement is a large group who call themselves only by the name Churches of Christ. Within their congregations are some of the most dedicated Christians, who are deeply committed to Christ, His Word, and the ideal to restore His church to its pristine state. Some of their churches are quite large, vibrant, and alive. The most obvious distinction between them and others in the movement is their choice not to use a musical instrument in their worship services. For most of them, also, its use constitutes a test of fellowship: i.e., they do not consider those who have the piano or organ in their worship to be full brothers and sisters in Christ.

The separation has come primarily from a different understanding of a verse of Scripture and two restoration movement mottoes. The Scripture is Ephesians 5:19; and the two mottoes are: "Where the Scriptures are silent, we will be silent," and "We are Christians only."

But before we consider these differences, let us learn something about who these dedicated people are.

The Churches of Christ number over one million members with the greatest concentration in Tennessee and the Southwest. Leroy Garrett, in his book, *The Stone-Campbell Movement,* says that the Churches of Christ are themselves divided into six major segments. The largest he calls the "Mainline Group." They number 935,439 members in 10,165 congregations. They wear the name Church of Christ and no other, they neither sing with the accompaniment of a musical instrument nor have instruments in their church buildings, and generally do not fellowship with those who do. Affiliated with them are some fine educational institutions such as Abilene Christian College, Pepperdine University, and David Lipscomb College. *The Gospel Advocate* is an influential journal that circulates among them, and they sponsor a radio-television ministry called "The Herald of Truth."

Separating themselves from the "Mainline Group" are about 100,000 members in 2,800 congregations primarily located in the deep South who call themselves the "Non-Cooperatives." They pulled apart over the issue of the cooperative effort among the churches to have "The Herald of Truth." These dissenters say there is no more Scripture for this kind of effort than there is for cooperating in a missionary society. Another separatist group is called the "Non-Sunday School Churches of Christ," who can be found in about 600 congregations. They say they do not have Sunday-schools for the same reason they don't use musical instruments—the New Testament is silent on the subject. Some of their congregations have large commodious buildings, but no Sunday-school rooms. One of their leaders says, referring to the New Testament and post-Biblical writings, "So far as we can tell from these accounts, when the congregation met for teaching and worship, the saints always came *together*." They did not separate into classes, which the non-Sunday-school people believe should constitute a precedent. Neither do they fellowship with those who have a graded Sunday-school.

Garrett identifies three other groups within the Churches of Christ. The first of these is called the "One Cuppers." They withdrew fellowship over the use of multiple cups in which to serve the Lord's Supper. They feel when the Scripture says "the cup," it sets a precedent for using just one cup, and it is passed to all who are present. Their congregations number 400 with 15,000 members. There are also the "Pre-millenial Churches of Christ." They feel that they did not leave the "Mainline Group" but were disfellowshipped by it. They believe Jesus will set up His kingdom on earth and rule one thousand years following the removal rapture of Christians from it and subsequent punishment of those left, called "the tribulation." This theory was espoused by John Nelson Darby (1800-1882), a Plymouth Brethren preacher in England. It is popularized in America by such as Hal Lindsey and the Scofield Reference Bible. Most early leaders of the restoration movement believed the church would win the world to Christ before He returned. This was called "post-millenialism," as opposed to "pre-millenialism." Finally, there are the black Churches of Christ. They have no doctrinal differences with the "Mainline Group," but there exists *de facto* separation. One of the black leaders is quoted as saying, "The cold truth is that black and white Churches of Christ represent two distinct fellowships."

These are the "Churches of Christ"—over a million members in at least six distinct groups.

The official beginning of the a cappella Churches of Christ came in 1906. The United States Census Bureau wrote two leaders in the non-instrument group, David Lipscomb and J. W. Shepherd, and asked if they wanted those churches not using the musical instrument listed separately from the other Christian Churches/Churches of Christ. They did, and for the first time those who held the use of a musical instrument as a "test of fellowship" were listed separately.

If the *official* beginning of this group is 1906, the *historical* beginning must go back to August 18, 1889. A document was read on this occasion at Sand Creek, Illinois, to about 6,000 persons who had gathered for the annual meeting of the brethren of that area. It was written by an elder named Peter Warren at the urging of one Daniel Sommer, editor of *The American Christian Review.* It was entitled *The Address and Declaration,* a play on words which, of course, alluded to Thomas Campbell's *Declaration and Address.* The document protested the use of what its author considered unscriptural innovations. They included use of instrumental music in worship, the located minister who might be brought into the local congregation from outside, choirs, and missionary societies. It concluded by saying that those who use such innovations should not be considered as "brethren." The document became known as *The Sand Creek Declaration,* and separated the a cappella churches from the others in that part of the country.

However, the instrument controversy goes back further than Sand Creek. It smoldered for many years beneath the surface. Some historians believe that several factors led to the open rupture of fellowship over this issue, including the Civil War. Although Sand Creek was located in the North, the a cappella Churches of Christ gained most of their strength in the South. The American Christian Missionary Society, which was mostly led by Northerners, had denounced both slavery and pro-slavery states. David Lipscomb of Tennessee would later revive the journal he called *The Gospel Advocate* so, as he said, Southerners could read something without hurting their feelings. The journal, published in Nashville, has served the Churches of Christ ever since.

Also, sociological factors put the musical instrument under suspicion. The restoration movement moved west with the pioneers. Cultural advantages were few on the frontier and settlers could not afford pianos and organs. Saloons were the first to import them because they helped make business profitable. The instruments, as a consequence, became tainted in people's minds. Their association with the saloon crowd seemed to make them inappropriate items for worship.

Historical and sociological factors played a part in the division over the use of musical instruments. However, many believe the crux of the issue lies in different interpretations of the verse in Ephesians 5 and the two mottoes mentioned earlier.

Ephesians 5:19 says, "Speaking to yourselves in psalms and hymns and spiritual songs, singing and making melody in your heart to the Lord." The a cappella brethren say the verse contains "singing," but does not say "to the accompaniment of a musical instrument." Therefore, they reason, the absence of a specific mention of the instrument prohibits its use in worship. It is an argument from silence.

However, those who disagree with this interpretation point to the context of the verse. A study of it shows that the verse does not speak specifically to a Lord's day worship service. Verse 18, 20, and 21 are in the same sentence with verse 19. They contain such admonitions as: "Be not drunk with wine . . . be filled with the Spirit . . . giving thanks always . . . submitting yourselves to one another in the glory of God." Those who believe the musical instrument to be permissible point out that none of these pertain to the assembled gathering of the church on the Lord's day. They refer to a Christian's attitude and life-style every day. For example, one is not to be "filled with the Spirit" just on Sunday at worship. It is to be his life-style. Also, one is to "give thanks *always.*" The context would demand that people refrain from gathering around the piano in their homes to sing praises, if they infer from it the prohibition of singing with it in church. Few Church of Christ members apply the verse to the use of musical instruments in their homes.

The argument for the prohibition of the use of musical instruments in worship is one that comes from silence. It reasons this way: no mention of the musical instrument's use in the New Testament eliminates its use in contemporary Christian worship. However, many believe this argument would eliminate other accepted practices if followed to its logical conclusion. It led to the divisions of the "one cuppers" and the "anti-Sunday schoolers." It would also preclude such items as church buildings. Acts 2:46 says that the early Christians met in the temple and from house to house. Later, Paul would speak of the church meeting in the homes of Aquilla and of Nymphas (Romans 16:5 and Colossians 4:15). The approved precedent is for the churches to meet in the homes of members or in the temple that no longer exists. No building as a place of worship in the name of Christ is mentioned until at least the second century. Paul said, "Preach the word" (2 Timothy 4:2). Does this mean a minister cannot use a pulpit because it is not specifically mentioned?

Some of the a cappella churches use what they call "the law of exclusion." It says, "The expression of one thing is the exclusion of another." They reason that there are only two kinds of music, vocal and instrumental. Since the Scripture says "singing," it excludes instrumental music. That is a dangerous conclusion. Consider James 5:14. It says, "Is any sick among you? let him call for the elders of the church; and let them pray over him, anointing him with oil in the name of the Lord." The "law of exclusion" would prohibit Christians from summoning a medical doctor. "Call the elders" is the *expression of one thing* which would exclude another, the summoning of a medical doctor for the sick. No Christian would want to push "the law of exclusion" that far. Other Scripture corroborates the danger of legalistically pressing this law. Paul told Timothy to "use a little wine for thy stomach's sake" (1 Timothy 5:23). Does this preclude all other medicine for digestive ailments? It says, "Greet all the brethren with a holy kiss" (1 Thessalonians 5:26). Does that eliminiate the possibility of a handshake between brethren?

Some believe that when Paul put the "singing of psalms" in Ephesians 5:19, he made provision for the use of musical instruments in worship. R. M. Bell, for many years the respected president of Johnson Bible College, notes the possibility in a tract entitled, *Concerning Instrumental Music in Worship.* He points out that Psalm 33:1-4, (ASV) says, "Rejoice in Jehovah, O ye righteous: Praise is comely for the upright. Give thanks unto Jehovah *with the harp:* Sing praises unto him with the *psaltery* of ten strings. Sing unto him a new song; play skillfully with a loud noise. For the word of Jehovah is right: And all his work is done in faithfulness." Psalm 92 commends the use of the musical instrument in worship. "It is a good thing to give thanks unto Jehovah, and to sing praises unto thy name, O Most High: to show forth thy lovingkindness in the morning, and thy faithfulness every night, with an *instrument of ten strings,* and with the *psaltery;* with a solemn sound upon the *harp*" (Psalm 92:1-3, ASV). The Psalms are saturated with admonitions to praise God with musical instruments.

The apostle Paul had been reared to become a strict Pharisee. He had sat at the feet of the noted rabbi, Gamaliel, and he knew the Old Testament Scripture well. No doubt, some in the Ephesian church had Hebrew backgrounds and knew what the Psalms said. President Bell reasoned that surely, if Paul had felt the use of musical instruments in the worship of God was wrong, he would have said, "Speaking to yourselves in psalms (but don't *use musical instruments as the book of Psalms instructs you to. This is now outlawed in the new covenant)* and hymns and spiritual songs, singing and making melody in your heart to the Lord" (Ephesians 5:19). But, of course, the apostle makes no such prohibition.

Thomas Campbell spoke one of the great principles of the restoration movement at that epic meeting in the home of Abraham Altars in 1809. He arose and said, "Where the Scriptures speak, we speak; and where the Scriptures are silent, we are silent." No motto has had greater influence on the movement than that one. But what does "silence" allow, and what does it deny? Many believe that when the Scripture is silent, it permits, when expedient, that which is not specifically denied. This, in their thinking, would include church buildings, song books, pews, and cooperative efforts such as missionary endeavors and radio/television ministries—as well as the musical instrument in worship. They say we cannot know whether someone at a first-century church in Corinth, or Ephesus, or wherever, took out his fife or harp at a Lord's day service and said, "Let me teach you this spiritual song." We just do not know; the Scripture is silent.

Those who worship with the musical instrument in no way want to deny anyone, or even criticize him, for singing a cappella in his services. Some of the most beautiful praise to God can be rendered that way. A negative attitude toward it would itself constitute a violation of being silent where the Scriptures are silent. They do earnestly seek fellowship with their a cappella brethren with whom they have kinship within the movement.

The difference in understanding of the other restoration motto is more subtle. Most people express it this way: "We are not the only Christians, but we seek to be Christians only." This is a most noble attempt. One will remember Barton W. Stone's emphasis upon the name Christian. He believed God had ordained it as the divinely given name for the followers of Jesus and plead for all others to be discarded and forgotten. He was also convinced that it was the one name around which all believers could unite because anyone who loves Jesus is proud to wear the name Christian. Therefore, he earnestly besought all to be Christians—and Christians only.

However, Stone did not conceive the restoration movement to be the only church and its constituency the only Christians. Indeed, he and the other early leaders of the movement did not look upon it as a church at all. It was rather a movement within the church calling all believers to unite on the basis of the Bible. These men believed that this unity could never be realized and the world subsequently won to Christ until the church returned to the New Testament order and was composed of Christians only.

Later on, some who followed in their train, perhaps unconsciously, rearranged the words in the motto from "Christians only" to "the only Christians." They have assumed an exclusivist posture in relation to other believers. George Bernard Shaw said, "You can tell what a man believes, not by his creed, but by the assumptions upon which he habitually acts." Many within the movement have so isolated themselves that it appears that they assume they are the only children God has. This is counter-productive. Few in this age will pay much attention to a group that sits back and says, "We are the only Christians."

Congregations of the movement and the members of them, whether a cappella or otherwise, should continue to look upon themselves as a movement. It will allow them to respect the integrity of others and rejoice in their good works, while at the same time calling them back to the church as it was given. The ideal to restore the essential marks of the New Testament church will be much more respectfully heard from that posture.

Another motto that has not been mentioned in this chapter becomes relevant at this point. It says, "In essentials, unity; in non-essentials, liberty; and, in all things, love." It is important for the movement that it seeks to speak the truth in love. Too often a mean spirit divides brethren. P. H. Welshimer used to say, "We can disagree without being disagreeable." Those in the restoration movement must allow love to guide their attitudes toward others—even toward others with whom they disagree.

The tragedy of the unfortunate division between the a cappella Churches of Christ and the others lies in what the restoration movement might have become if it had not occurred. The poet wrote:

> "Of all sad words of tongue or pen,
> The saddest are these: 'It might have been.'"

What would have happened if those who believed in the restoration ideal had moved forward with a united front? Even in their divided state, the combined groups who have come out of the restoration movement rank as the third largest non-Catholic group in the United States. But that is nothing compared to what the movement might have become. It represents just the tip of the iceberg. There is little doubt but what the momentum gained in the nineteenth century would have spilled over into the twentieth and increased. No one could possibly guess the propensity of its strength. It is incumbent upon those who believe in the restoration ideal to seek reconciliation. They must become "one" before they can lead all believers to unity that the world might be "won" in answer to Jesus' prayer (John 17:20, 21). Twentieth-century followers of that ideal must always keep in mind that its ultimate purpose is to bring all God's people together so that the world might be evangelized. It must always keep in sight the goal of Christian unity and world evangelization.

James DeForest Murch, in his book *Christians Only,* quotes a minister for the a cappella churches who saw the harm done from the failure to do all things in love.

> If the church of the first century had been ruled by men of the type of certain preachers and elders in the conservative churches of today, or of the type of certain leaders and preachers in the liberal churches of this age, Christianity would have perished before the end of the century in which it was born. But it was not, and the great majority of the churches today are free from these excesses. I verily believe that there are tens of thousands of good people in both the Christian Church and the Church of Christ who are heartbroken because of the excesses to which some preachers and churches have gone in both directions.

But then he adds sadly:

> I do not expect, however, to see fellowship restored in these churches in a day. Fellowship was not broken in a day, nor will it be restored in a day. But it was broken; and in the providence of God I believe it will be restored.

David H. Bobo, a veteran Church of Christ minister, calls for his brethren to reach out in love toward others, and to move away from an isolationist, exclusivist position. He wrote an article entitled, "The Church of Christ—Where from Here." In it he says, "I think the time may well come when the whole Church of Christ tradition may grow out of its *sect* mentality and come to perceive itself not as God's *only* children, but a group of God's *true* children in the midst of all his other children."

It may well be that the "time" of which Bobo speaks has begun. There seems to be a reaching out on the part of some within the a cappella churches. Indeed, there may have been a first step taken toward rapprochment between the Churches of Christ (a cappella) and the so-called independent Christian Churches/churches of Christ. Fifty ministers from each fellowship met on the campus of Ozark Bible College (now Ozark Christian College), August 7, 8, and 9, 1984. E. Richard Crabtree, former minister of the historic First Christian Church, Canton, Ohio, said of the gathering, "This is the most significant meeting I have attended in my thirty-five-year ministry." The two groups were called together by the urging of Don Dewelt, of College Press, Joplin, Missouri, and Alan T. Cloyd, evangelist for the Vultee Church of Christ, Nashville, Tennessee.

The meeting was not an attempt to produce any document that would pronounce a reunion of the two groups. Nothing that ambitious was expected. It was merely an attempt to come together to get to know each other better. That goal was accomplished along with several other tangible manifestations of success such as the following:

1. Each group learned some of its ignorance of the other. For many, the other fellowship was almost a non-entity. One of the a cappella ministers said, "I feel that I have found a million brothers and sisters in Christ I didn't know I had."

2. It fostered personal friendships that could grow into larger expressions of brotherhood. Some found that what they shared in

common produced a kind of friendship in Christ that they could carry home and continue to share. Several congregations planned joint services where both sides could come together to praise God.

3. It was decided that subsequent meetings should be planned. This is significant because it demonstrates that the kinship found in this first meeting merited more exploration.

4. Perhaps the most tangible evidence of progress that came from the meeting was the seemingly natural desire to call each other brethren. A kinship, overriding all differences, bound the groups together.

No one knows what will come of these efforts toward rapprochment. Some within the a cappella churches reacted negatively to the Joplin meeting. *The Gospel Advocate* editorially denounced it. But who knows? Perhaps the time Bobo mentioned has arrived for men of goodwill with irenic spirits, who want to do "all things in love," to reach out to each other. Where there is kinship, there ought to be fellowship.

Would it not be a momentous victory for Christ if in the year 2006, a hundred years after the census first listed separate groups, it could reflect one movement united, calling all believers to unity on the basis of the Bible? Brothers and sisters who want to do "all things in love" will seek that end.

24

THE DISCIPLES OF CHRIST

Another disappointment came to the restoration movement a few years after the instrumental music issue precipitated the separation of the a cappella Churches of Christ. It was struck a blow by theological liberalism, which almost proved fatal. Norman A. Furniss, a church historian, said liberalism was to be more devastating upon the Christian churches than any other communion, with the possible exception of the Presbyterians.[1]

Liberalism, like the use of the instrument in worship, would separate brethren into two groups: The Christian Church (Disciples of Christ) and the fellowship known as Christian churches and churches of Christ. The separation would cause much deep personal hurt. This author's home church divided over issues emanating from liberalism when he was just a child, but the memory of the heartache lingers vividly. His father felt compelled, because of his convictions, to leave the Disciples Church, in which he had been an elder, and become a leader within the Christian churches/churches of Christ in eastern North Carolina. But the hurt of that separation remained to his death.

It is difficult to identify the historical origin of theological liberalism because it resulted from several sources. Many students of the subject believe it had its roots in the same scientific methodology that gave birth to evolution.

The biological evolutionist thought he could see the evolving of man from the lower species to the higher species, then to the highest species, *homo sapiens*. The sociological liberal concluded that he could trace the evolution of man's morals and manners in the pages of history: from primitive man, to medieval man, to modern man, whom he conceived as having evolved to the place that he had become "God." He believed man had progressed to where he himself could build the kingdom of Heaven on earth. He would accomplish the task with three tools: science, education, and democracy. The sociological liberals used such optimistic mottoes as "Mankind, ever onward and upward," and sang hymns that said, "Glory to man in the highest; God is no longer necessary." They had an ebullient view of man's inevitable upward moral evolution.

Then came World War I with its mustard gas that would sear and destroy one's lungs. Optimism about man's moral progress began to wane when such philosophers as Karl Barth became doubters. World War II completely obliterated this optimism. It produced Dachau, Buchenwald, Auschwitz, Belden—German concentration camps in central Europe. They found lamp shades there in the warden's quarters made of human skin. The tattoo on the skin served as the decoration of the shade. For several months during the middle of World War II, one could buy soap on the open market in Central Europe with a label that said, "This soap is made of genuine Jewish fat"—human flesh boiled, processed, packaged, and sold on the open market. The middle of the twentieth century also produced the worst genocide in history when six million Jews were systematically eliminated by the Nazis. This presented the sociological liberal with an ironic dilemma. For T. L. Jarman noted, "In 1939 Germany had the most efficient educational system in the world."[2]

Few now cleave to the notion that mankind progresses inevitably toward moral perfection. Will Durant, the famous historian, says, "In the last twenty-five years, the world has advanced in science, knowledge, and industry, but has retrogressed in morals, art, and manners."[3]

The theological liberal used the same approach as did his biological and sociological counterparts. He taught that the Bible recorded the evolution of man's thinking about God down through the centuries, primarily through the Hebrews, from the primitive Hebrew to the prophets, to Jesus of Nazareth. They considered Him to be the best of human nature and the greatest teacher of ethics in history. One can see what this theory did to the Bible. It made it *man's* book, *his* thinking about God. The traditional view looked upon it as *God's* book; His inspired revelation of himself, His will, and His love for man, and considered it the only authoritative word man had from Him.

Theological liberalism also found philosophical rootage in what is called "German rationalism." This school of thought gained prominence in the nineteenth century. It put man at the center of the universe and his mind above everything. It sought to eliminate the supernatural altogether. Only that which could be understood by the rational processes of human thinking would be accepted. Therefore, it concluded that miracles in the Bible could not have happened; they were misunderstandings or superstitions on the part of ancient people.

Two major schools of thought concerning God came from liberalism. Humanism is one. It accepts a purely naturalistic concept of the universe, and because of this, does not accommodate any concept of "God." The humanists consider such a concept unwarranted because it does not fit into a scientific understanding of reality. Man, according to them, must solve his own problems with no divine help.

Another school of thought which came out of liberalism is Modernism. It accepted the presuppositions of liberalism, but sought to redefine God so that He would fit into them. The modernists gave up miracles, prophecy, and the fundamental doctrines of traditional faith, such as substitutionary atonement, redemption through the blood of Christ, the Bible as the infallible rule of faith and practice, and others. This caused a wide cleavage between those who held to the traditional doctrines (sometimes called "conservatives," sometimes "fundamentalists"[4]) and the modernists. An editor wrote in 1924, "There is a clash here as grim as between Christianity and Confucianism—the God of the fundamentalist is one God; the God of the modernist is another. The Christ of the fundamentalist is one Christ; the Christ of the modernist is another. The Bible of the fundamentalist is one Bible; the Bible of the modernist is another. The church, the kingdom, salvation, the consummation of all things—they are one thing to the fundamentalist and another to the modernist— what is the true religion? The future will tell."[5]

Modernism took a devastating toll on "the faith . . . once delivered to the saints." Harry Emerson Fosdick became the most renowned modernist preacher. James DeForest Murch quotes him in response to a letter he had received. Fosdick said: "Of course, I do not believe in the Virgin Birth or in that old-fashioned substitutionary doctrine of atonement, and do not know of an intelligent minister who does."[6]

Francis J. McConnell, former president of the liberal Federal Council of Churches, wrote:

Critics point out to us that in the early days of the church it was quite common even for popular thought to deify a man—is not this tendency to deify Jesus more heathen than Christian? Are we not most truly Christian when we cut loose from a heathen propensity and take Jesus simply for the character he was and for the ideal he is?[7]

Perhaps a comparison of the modernists' faith with the traditional or conservative will be helpful:

TRADITIONAL
Jesus is *fully God.* "In him is the fullness of deity in the flesh." He is the express image of God. Jesus is also the *Savior:* "There is no other name under heaven given among men whereby we must be saved." Christ died for our sins.

The Bible: The only inspired, authoritative written Word of God; His revelation of himself, His will, and His love for man. The record of God's action to redeem man.

Miracles: Historical events that attest to God's action within the human realm. Jesus' virgin birth, ministry of miracles, and resurrection substantiate His claim to be God.

The Cross: Christ, who was the Lamb of God prepared from the foundation of the world, went to the cross and paid the penalty for man's sins so that we can be justified before God.

The Gospel: "Christ died for our sins." Those who accept the grace He provided on the cross will be saved from the eternal consequences of their sins.

The Church: The fellowship of the redeemed, the called-out by God, His agency to go into all the world to tell this good news of salvation to be found in Christ.

MODERNISTIC
Jesus: Exemplary man, great man, teacher, and philosopher, but in no way is He to be looked upon as the fullness of God or one to be worshiped.

The Bible: "The Bible (is) viewed as a product of natural evolution—a collection of books displaying man's progressive understanding of God as he grows in moral an religious insight, rather than a supernatural disclosure of absolute truth."[8]

198

Miracles: Legendary explanations of epic events ancient people could not understand. They did not historically occur and prove nothing about the supernatural.

The Cross: An inconsequential irrelevancy. The disciples used it to express the love of God. Its meaning will change from generation to generation. It has nothing to do with forgiveness of sins.

The Gospel: It is the "good news" that God loved people of all religions and they shall be called together into the family of man.

The Church: Organization to be used for human betterment. It is to be a social action task force.

Modernism began to make inroads into the Christian churches and Churches of Christ at the beginning of the twentieth century. Some of their ministers had gone to Eastern seminaries that had imported liberalism from Europe. They absorbed it. A few of them organized what they would call the Campbell Institute, which became a cutting edge for the invasion of liberalism within the movement. Its members committed themselves to make modernism the accepted theology of the churches. The liberals used two other organs effectively in their attempt to gain control: the Disciples Divinity House, which was affiliated with the University of Chicago, and a journal they called *The Christian Century.*

Several leaders within the movement began to look with alarm at the inroads liberalism made. Notable among them was John W. McGarvey, president of the College of the Bible, Lexington, Kentucky. He called modernism "the new infidelity," and he began a column in *The Christian Standard* entitled "Biblical Criticism" to combat it.

McGarvey died in 1911. This set the stage for confrontation on the campus of the College of the Bible between traditional conservative faith and modernism. R. H. Crossfield, a liberal, succeeded McGarvey as its president. He began to hire professors of his own ilk, and students began to report strange doctrines being taught in class. Some of these were 1) immersion as Biblical baptism would have to be abandoned for the sake of union; 2) the apostles wrote out of great lives rather than under the infallible direction of the Holy Spirit; 3) nowhere in the New Testament can we pause and say, "Here is finality in matters of faith and doctrine"; 4) the Biblical version of angels and demons is not true, neither are we to believe the miracles of the Old Testament.

These reports led to a heresy trial presided over by Mark Collis, beloved minister of Broadway Christian Church in Lexington. The liberals won. It was a landmark decision. Stephen J. Corey in his book, *Fifty Years of Attack and Controversy,* wrote, "The outcome really turned the tide in our brotherhood for educational institutions."[9] He would go on to report that liberalism would become the "working principle of the faculties in all our schools holding membership in the Board of Higher Education of the Disciples of Christ."[10]

This proved an accurate observation. Modernism inundated Christian church colleges and many of them were swept away in its tide. Some became quickly secularized, such as Texas Christian, Drake, and Butler University. This author remembers hearing W. R. Walker speak at the funeral of P. H. Welshimer in Canton, Ohio. He said, "We stood back-to-back in the conventions trying to stem the mounting tide of modernism." But the mounting tide of modernism could not be stemmed.

It seemed to many that its wake left only a small minority in the movement that still believed in the restoration ideal. Its impact was devastating. The minority could salvage only two colleges in existence when McGarvey died—Johnson Bible College and Milligan, a liberal arts college. Many large congregations were swept away in its tide, although most rank and file members did not know the implications of modernism. They continued personally in the traditional faith, and this caused some congregations to be internally divided over the issues. Missionaries were affected. A number of brave overseas missionaries saw where modernism would lead and raised their voices in protest. They withdrew from their sponsoring society because they believed it had abandoned the restoration ideal. They gave up much security when they took that step.

Many within both the liberal and conservative camps sought to work with each other in spite of differences. But it became increasingly difficult. More reports kept coming from the mission field of widespread "open membership," which was the admission of the unimmersed into the fellowship of the churches of the world. The liberals, who no longer believed in the restoration ideal, applauded the practice. Scriptural baptism meant little to them because they no longer sought to do Bible things in Bible ways. The International Convention, a gathering of the movement's constituency, passed a resolution to curtail open membership on foreign fields. But the United Christian Missionary Society, which was in the tight control of liberals, frustrated this effort.

More and more, those who believed in the restoration ideal found their voices muted in the agencies and convention controlled by the Disciple leadership. It was at the International Convention in Memphis, Tennessee, in 1926 that the conservative felt compelled to take a step they did not want to take. However, they had concluded that the International Convention, controlled by the liberal leaders, no longer offered an adequate platform from which the great restoration movement themes could be proclaimed. So, following the Memphis Convention, the conservative leadership set up a Committee on Future Action with P. H. Welshimer as chairman. It came forth with the recommendation for a "North American Christian Convention" to be held in Indianapolis, October 12-16, 1927. This initial gathering proved so successful that a continuation committee was appointed to plan the next Convention, and it produced a statement of purpose. The North American Convention was:

> To honor the Scriptures as the only ground for the unity of the followers of Christ.
>
> Disclaiming all affiliation with parties, factions, and special interests, to put forward the truths and objectives common to the whole brotherhood of believers.
>
> To provide opportunity for loyal followers of the cross to show their colors under the banner, "Where the Scriptures speak, we speak; where the Scriptures are silent, we are silent."

It was a minority group that formed the North American Christian Convention. Some believed that it was so small that it could not survive the blow it had received from modernism. However, the minority contained some persons of uncommon faith: P. H. Welshimer and W. R. Walker, who have been mentioned, were joined by such stalwarts as S. S. Lappin, James DeForest Murch, Ira Boswell, Will Sweeney, and others. This remnant used three new tools to re-dig those old wells in God's Word that would produce springs of living water and bring new life to the remnant.

The first of these tools was the Christian service camp movement. They began it to inspire young people and recruit a ministry loyal to the restoration ideal. It proved most successful. Then they started Bible colleges to train a ministry devoted to that ideal. Thirty-nine of them now operate in the United States and Canada. Some of these are quite large when one realizes that the vast majority of the young people there prepare for vocational church ministries. Ozark Christian College in Joplin, Missouri, has 481 students; The Cincinnati Bible Seminary has 634 enrolled in its undergraduate area and 303 in its seminary.[12] Others, however, are quite small. The third tool was a publishing company that would print literature true to the Bible.

This part of the restoration movement has experienced a renewal during the last sixty years that is little short of phenomenal. It has grown from a remnant to a large viable force within Christendom. It numbers 1,060,036 members in 5,674 autonomous interdependent congregations across the country.[13] They lay great emphasis upon the centrality of Christ in church life, follow the Bible as their only rule of faith and practice, and seek to be evangelistic both locally and in world missions. The movement has excelled in world missionary effort. From just a few missionary families in 1924, the number has grown to over six hundred foreign missionaries in 1982. Benevolent institutions have also proliferated.

The North American Christian Convention became the largest tent under which the people of this part of the movement stand. It is in no way a delegate convention, nor does it seek to speak for the movement. Its purpose is to provide inspiration and edification. It has done just that, and thousands gather for it each year.

Those churches and institutions within the movement whose leaders embraced modernism have become known as the Disciples of Christ. Their legal name is the Christian Church (Disciples of Christ). They number 794,326 in 4,386 congregations in the United States and Canada.[14] Their leadership is liberal, although many, perhaps most, in the churches remain conservative and have not embraced modernism. Their leaders have lost confidence in the restoration ideal and no longer hold it to be legitimate. They do not share the same emphasis on Bible authority with their forefathers in the movement and many of them believe that "the destiny of the Disciples is to lose their identity." They mean by this that they should cease to exist as a distinct people.

Most observers believe the Disciples' leaders have organized their part of the movement in such a way as to accomplish this extinction. They now have a "restructured church" with a delegate convention that can speak for the "denomination." This departs from local autonomy and gives the leadership the legal authority to speak for the whole group. Many see it as the means to merge in the near future with the liberal United Church of Christ. At that point, the Disciples will have ceased to exist and will have lost their identity.

Another area in which modernism has had an apparent impact on the Disciples is evangelism. Liberalism seems to carry a negative effect on this part of the church's mission. The Disciples have suffered serious losses in church membership in recent years. One of their leaders announced at their 1981 General Assembly that the large majority of Disciple congregations did not report one single baptism during the previous year.[15]

Some disenchantment in the Disciples' ecumenical approach to church union can be traced within their own ranks. This discontent gave birth to the "Continuing Christian Church Movement" (CCCM). It was begun by Disciples to give Disciples who will not merge with the United Church of Christ[16] a place to land when the merger occurs. Estimates vary as to how many this will be. Norman Conner, minister of First Christian Church, Santa Ana, California, and chairman of the CCCM, believes there will be a significant number within the Disciples—perhaps 2,000 congregations—who will want to continue in their restoration movement heritage.

There are many great saints within the Christian Church (Disciples of Christ) who love Christ and are devoted to His Word. They share much in their faith with those in the fellowship of Christian churches and churches of Christ that comes from their common heritage. It is hoped that when the Disciples denomination merges with the United Church of Christ, or some other group, those will continue to seek Christian unity on a Biblical basis. They would feel very much at home with a worldwide fellowship of autonomous, interdependent congregations who seek to be non-denominational and Biblical in their faith.

NOTES

[1]Norman F. Furniss, *The Fundamentalist Controversy,* 1918-1931 (New Haven: Yale University Press, 1954), p. 170.

[2]T. L. Jarman, *The Rise and Fall of Nazi Germany* (New York: New York University Press, 1956, pp. 17-19.

[3]Will Durant, "Brink of a New Age," *Look,* January 16, 1962, p. 91.

[4]"Fundamentalism" may have two meanings. It may represent those who hold to certain great doctrines of the faith, most of them defined by the Protestant reformers as being essential for true Christianity. It also refers to men who set themselves up to "defend the faith" but have done so intemperately upon occasion and have been given to excess in dogmatism. The "fundamentalist" here refers to those who hold the great doctrines who are sometimes called "evangelicals."

[5]James DeForest Murch, *Cooperation without Compromise* (Grand Rapids: Erdman's Publishing Co., 1956) p. 28.

[6]Ibid., p. 41.

[7]Ibid.

[8]Edwin A. Burtt, *Types of Religious Philosophy* (New York: Harper & Bros., 1951), p. 308.

[9]Stephen J. Corey, *Fifty Years of Attack and Controversy* (St. Louis: Christian Board of Publication, 1953), p. 55.

[10]Ibid.

[11]James DeForest Murch, *Christians Only* (Cincinnati: Standard Publishing Co., 1967) p. 257.

[12]*1986 Directory of the Ministry* (Springfield: Directory of the Ministry, 1986) pp. F-26, 27. Ozark lists 381 full-time students and 100 part-time. Cincinnati Bible College lists 508 full-time and 126 part-time. Cincinnati Christian Seminary lists 91 full-time and 212 part-time students.

[13]Ibid., p. F-41.

[14]Leroy Garrett, *The Stone-Campbell Movement* (Joplin: The College Press, 1981) p. 718.

[15]Ibid., p. 725.

[16]The United Church of Christ should not be confused with the a cappella Churches of Christ. The United Church of Christ came into being with the merger of the Congregational Christian Church and the Evangelical and Reformed Church. It is considered by many to be a most liberal denomination, while the a cappella churches are considered conservative.

25

THE CHARISMATICS

No contemporary attempt to restore the New Testament church can ignore two groups known as "Pentecostals" and "Neo-Pentecostals." The latter group is also known as the "Charismatics," which comes from the Greek term *charisma,* which means "gift of grace." Both of these together number in the millions in a worldwide fellowship and are characterized by their emphasis on sign gifts such as miracles, tongues, and healings, and their belief in the "baptism of the Holy Spirit" as an experience to be sought subsequent to one's becoming a Christian.

The Charismatics' emphasis on feeling or emotion has led some to excesses. John MacArthur, in his book concerning them, tells of testimonies on television talk shows about puppies raised miraculously from the dead, washing machines "healed," empty gasoline tanks miraculously filled, and one lady who reported receiving a new "belly button."[1] These may be unusual, and perhaps somewhat exaggerated, but much of the Neo-Pentecostals' appeal lies in their claim of signs, wonders, and miracles being worked in their midst.

The Pentecostals and Neo-Pentecostals are expanding rapidly, not just in the United States, but around the world. They have had an impact upon the traditional church that cannot be ignored, with virtually every denomination having many within their fellowship. It is important that the restoration movement, which seeks Christian unity on a Biblical basis, understand this large influential force on the contemporary religious scene.

The Pentecostals, as the name implies, is the older group, but it is not as old as one might think. It began at about the turn of the twentieth century and was characterized by glossalalia (speaking in tongues), alleged miraculous healings, and austerity of life. Members believed make-up, jewelry, tobacco, alcoholic beverages, and their like to be un-Christian. They traced their beginning to a woman named Agnes Ozman at Bethel Bible College, Topeka, Kansas. In 1901, she received what she called "the baptism of the Holy Spirit" and spoke in tongues. This began the Pentecostal Holiness movement, which has now come to rest in several denominations: The Pentecostal Holiness Church, The Assemblies of God, The Foursquare Gospel, and others.

The Neo-Pentecostals trace their history back only as far as 1960. The rector of St. Mark's Episcopal Church, Van Nuys, California, Dennis Bennett, had an experience similar to that of Agnes Ozman. He, too, received what he thought was the "baptism of the Holy Spirit" and spoke in tongues. Most people trace the modern-day Charismatic Movement to his experience, and it has proceeded to grow.

The Pentecostals and Neo-Pentecostals are similar and dissimilar. Both believe miracles today are signs of God's presence and favor, and both practice glossalalia. Old-line Pentecostals include snake-handlers who believe this is a sign of faith according to Jesus in Mark 16. While most Charismatics do not go that far, neither do they necessarily practice austere life-styles. Some of them see no contradictions, for example, between their faith and social drinking. While Pentecostals have congealed into identifiable denominations separate and apart from others, Neo-Pentecostals have risen from within the existing denominations and most remain within them. There are Charismatic Roman Catholics, Baptists, Methodists, Lutherans, and they are found in all mainline groups. They have become divisive in many, oftentimes causing separation of brethren.

Charismatics are persons with whom it is sometimes difficult to reason because of their emphasis on experience. "This is what I feel," they say. However, a Christian must never rely on feeling to guide him because our feelings fool us and emotions let us down. The Bible says, "The just shall live by faith" (Romans 1:17), and faith comes "by hearing, and hearing by the word of God" (Romans 10:17). Scriptural truths must always be the test of one's experience to determine whether he is in the right relationship with God. It can never be vice versa. As Thomas Campbell said, "The Bible is the only rule of faith and practice for Christians." All one counts as essential in his Christian experience must have either Scriptural command or approved precedent. Glossalalia and other claims of the Charismatic movement must fit into

God's revealed plan if they are to be legitimate practices for believers. Faith, not feeling, matters.

Let us consider one of the obvious characteristics of Pentecostals and Charismatics that most distinguishes them from other Christians. It is the practice of glossalalia. First, we will review two considerations outside the Bible and then proceed to study the Greek word *glossa,* which is in Scripture.

Glossalalia, or speaking with unintelligible ecstatic utterances, lacks historical continuity within the life of the church. You do not find it in the mainstream of the faithful. The post-apostolic fathers, such as Justin Martyr and Origen, looked upon it as a remote practice that occurred back in the earliest days of Christianity. The sixteenth-century reformers, Luther, Calvin, Knox, Zwingli, and the others never preached or practiced it. The Wesleys emphasized feeling in their faith, but glossalalia remained foreign to their tradition. A woman wrote Alexander Campbell, claiming that she had danced with the Holy Ghost and that the Holy Ghost burst through her fingers and toes. He responded by saying that the Holy Ghost works in creation and regeneration only through His Word. Glossalalia was unacceptable and irrelevant to the faith and life of the early leaders of the restoration movement.

There have been some prior to Agnes Ozman's twentieth-century experience who claimed to speak in "tongues." One was Montanus of the late second century, who claimed to talk directly to God through his own personal pipeline. Christians quickly branded him and his followers as heretics. Another was Mother Ann Lee, founder of Shakerism, whose followers Barton W. Stone called "worldly deceivers." She considered herself to be the female equivalent of Jesus Christ. The Irvingites of England claimed to speak in tongues, but they also set dates for the second coming of Christ and fell into disrepute when their prophecies failed. All of this indicates that Charismatics must align themselves with those of questionable faith to claim historical continuity for glossalalia. The practice is not found among the faithful in church history. Paul said in 1 Corinthians 13:8 that tongues "shall cease," and history shows that they did.

In the second place, ecstatic utterances exist in religions that have nothing to do with Christ. Indeed, they pre-date Him and go back to the Hittites (1400 B.C.), the Phoenecians (1100 B.C.), and to the ancient Greek worship of Apollo at Delphi. The pagan

Corinthians of Paul's day may have practiced it in their mystery religions, and it could have been brought into the church there by carnal Christians. However, ecstatic gibberish as religious expression is not just ancient. It exists even today among some tribes in Africa. Knofel Station points this out in his book, *Spiritual Gifts for Christians Today.* He writes, "Ecstatic utterances are still common among some pagan religions, and the experience is still attributed to the power of a deity taking control of the vocal cords."[1] The practice is also found among Muslims, Eskimos, and Tibetan monks. Ecstatic utterances could never be used to prove anything to be peculiarly Christian.

But the test to determine the legitimacy of glossalalia must come from Scripture because "the just shall live by faith." Have tongues ceased as Paul prophesied? Or do they continue as a tool to be used by Christians in evangelism and discipleship? The answer to these questions must come from God's Word.

The key to understanding the role of the gift of tongues in the New Testament is found in the etymology of the world *glossalalia.* The King James Version refers to an "*unknown* tongue" in Acts 2. This is misleading because the word "unknown" is absent from the original text. It should not be there, and this is the reason it is printed in italics in the King James Version and left out in the more contemporary versions.

The Greek word translated tongue in the New Testament is *glossa. Glossalalia* combines *glossa* with *lalia,* which means "speaking," to make "tongue speaking" out of it. *Glossa* is used over a hundred times in the Greek Old Testament, as well as in the New. It can be translated in either of two ways. It can be used as the organ within the mouth that enables a person to speak—the tongue. Or, it can mean "language"—a coherent, articulate, translatable language. It is most often used in the latter sense in the New Testament, but it can never be used to represent unintelligible ecstatic utterances or babbling. Spanish, French, Latin, and English are languages that *glossa* would represent.

John R. W. Stott, respected evangelical scholar, expressed it. He said, "The noun glossa has only two known meanings, namely the organ in the mouth and a language." Glossa as a language fits and makes sense everywhere it is used in Scripture.

The speaking in tongues is found only in three books in the New Testament. They are Mark 16; Acts 2, 10, and 19; and 1 Corinthians 12-14. The degree of their importance may be judged by the appearance just in these places compared, for example, to the repetition of the necessity of teaching.

Mark's version of the Great Commission has Jesus saying, "And these signs shall follow them that believe; In my name shall they cast out devils; they shall *speak with new tongues;* they shall take up serpents; and if they drink any deadly thing, it shall not hurt them; they shall lay hands on the sick, and they shall recover" (Mark 16:17, 18). The word he used in this passage is *glossa.* The prophecy came true when the apostles did speak in languages they had never learned, new to them, on the Day of Pentecost.

The speaking in *glossa* in Acts 2 is a most enlightening study. This is probably the most significant chapter in the Bible. The Holy Spirit came as Jesus had promised, the first gospel sermon was preached, the plan of salvation was defined, the church of Christ was established, the Christian era began, and an outline of church life was given, all in this one chapter. It says that the apostles "were all filled with the Holy Ghost, and began to speak with other tongues *(glossa),* as the Spirit gave them utterance" (Acts 2:4).

The word *glossa* would have to be translated tongues in the sense of other languages. Present was a great multitude who had come to Jerusalem for the feast of Pentecost. It says they came from every nation. The people were amazed because when the apostles spoke, each person heard in his native language, or dialect. Luke named the fifteen places from whence they came: Parthians, Medes, Elamites, dwellers in Mesapotamia, Judea, Cappadocia, Pontus, Asia, Phrygia, Pamphylia, Egypt, Libya, Romans, Cretes, and Arabians.

It is obvious that the apostles did not speak in ecstatic gibberish. The miracle was that each person present heard the message in his own peculiar, native language from Galileans who had never learned those languages. They said, "We do hear them speak in our tongues (languages) the wonderful works of God" (Acts 2:11). The Greek word, *dialektos* is used in verse eight where the people asked, "And how hear we every man in our own tongue *(dialektos),* wherein we were born?" Some heard in their language, others in their own dialect. The distinction between languages and dialects could never have been made if the apostles had merely used ecstatic utterances.

The household of Cornelius spoke in tongues in Acts 10. It was

* Could it have refered to hearing?
We don't know what was spoken, only heard.

209

a sign that God accepted Gentiles as well as Jews. It says, "And they of the circumcision [Jews] which believed were astonished, as many as came with Peter, because that on the Gentiles also was poured out the gift of the Holy Ghost" (Acts 10:45). Peter explained the experience to the Jerusalem Church in chapter 11. He said, "The Holy Ghost fell on them, as on us at the beginning. . . . Forasmuch then as God gave them the like gift as he did unto us" (Acts 11:15, 17). "The beginning" was the Day of Pentecost in chapter two, and "the gift" refers to the tongues, foreign languages, in which the apostles had spoken. Cornelius spoke in *glossa,* foreign languages he had never learned.

The nineteenth chapter of Acts tells of those in Ephesus who had merely received the baptism of John the Baptist. They had never received Christian baptism. Paul told them to believe in Christ and they were baptized. He laid his hands on them and "they spake with tongues [glossa] and prophesied" (Acts 19:6). They, too, spoke in foreign languages they had never learned.

The most exhaustive discussion of tongues is found in 1 Corinthians 12-14, and this is the only epistle in which the practice is mentioned. One should be aware that it was one of Paul's earliest epistles and was written to a church which he referred to as "carnal." The subject is never mentioned in any of his other epistles, nor in John's, nor Peter's, nor in Jude or James.

The Corinthian discussion uses the word *glossa* throughout. Its interpretation as a language fits here also, as it does everywhere it is used. It would seem that some of the carnal members of the church were pretending to have the gift to speak in foreign languages who had never received it. It had value to early Christians because it enabled a person to witness to one of another nationality without having to learn his language. It became a source of pride among the Corinthians. Some coveted it and faked possession of it. Paul wrote his first epistle to correct errors within the church there, one being the misuse of the gift of tongues.

He spoke of "divers kinds of tongues" in 1 Corinthians 12:10. Once again the word *language* fits and makes sense in this verse. There could not be different kinds of gibberish. Gibberish is gibberish. Then Paul spoke of the gift of "interpretation of tongues." The word is *hermeneuo,* from which comes the English word *hermeneutics.* It is used thirteen times in the New Testament and means to translate from one communicable language to another.

210

Paul proceeded to fence in this abuse of the gift to speak in other languages in 1 Corinthians 14. He said that the Christians should follow after love, for it is the superior, greatest way. Prophesying is also superior to tongues because it edifies the church. Those who would come into a church service where there is babbling would consider those present to be barbarians or even mad. One should never speak in a foreign language unless an interpreter is present, because its purpose is to lead the unbeliever to Christ rather than to edify those who already believe. It is for these reasons that the apostle said he would rather speak five words that people could understand than a thousand in a foreign language that would have no meaning to them. He uses the fourteenth chapter of 1 Corinthians to limit the abuse of tongues.

One would have to ask whether modern-day glossalalia fits into the New Testament description of tongues, *glossa*. Do persons today speak in foreign languages which they have never learned in order to communicate the gospel to those who have never accepted Christ? Or is it meaningless ecstatic utterances? At least one linguist testifies to its being incoherent babbling. William Sanarin, of the University of Toronto, wrote:

> Over a period of five years I have taken part in meetings in Italy, Holland, Jamaica, Canada, and the United States. I have observed old-fashioned Pentecostals and Neo-Pentecostals. I have been in small meetings in private homes as well as in mammoth public meetings. I have seen such different cultural settings as are found among Puerto Ricans of the Bronx, the snake handlers of the Appalachians and the Russian Molchans of Los Angeles. . . . I have interviewed tongue speakers, and tape recorded and analyzed countless samples of Tongues. In every case, glossalalia turns out to be linguistic nonsense. In spite of superficial similarities, glossalalia is fundamentally not language.[3]

Some try to justify modern-day tongues as a "prayer language." They say they use it to speak to God. However, this is an un-Scriptural usage. Paul explained that it was to be used to communicate to unbelievers (1 Corinthians 14:22). Its purpose in the Acts passages was to convince those outside of Christ to accept Him. It was a "sign" (Mark 16) to them that did not believe.

Tongues, the ability to speak in a language one had never learned in order to communicate the gospel, belongs to that group of gifts that were temporary in nature. They were peculiar to the first century church. Included in these were casting out demons (exorcism), healing the sick as a "sign," raising the dead, and speaking without error by direct inspiration. They were given to attest to the validity of the apostles' doctrine; to prove that what was spoken came from God. One should look upon them as *signs* pointing to something greater than themselves—the gospel and the plan of salvation. When both of these were understood perfectly, the signs were no longer necessary. The gospel would convict men of their sin and lead them to faith and obedience to Christ.

These temporary gifts could be compared to the scaffolding in the construction of a building. It is necessary in the beginning. The bricklayer could not ascend high enough to do his work without it. But, when the building is complete, the scaffolding is removed because it is no longer necessary and is unsightly.

The miracles, signs, wonders, and mighty acts of God were necessary in the beginning to establish the church and God's new covenant with man. They attracted attention and validated the authenticity of the disciples' message. But they ceased when their function was no longer needed. Their reappearance should not be sought by any contemporary generation because they are no longer needed and mar the beauty of that to which they pointed— the gospel of salvation. Jesus made it clear that it is "an evil and adulterous generation [that] seeketh after a sign" (Matthew 12:39).

Two other emphases of the Charismatics are a concern to Christians within the restoration movement. First is their claim that the Holy Spirit still directly and personally inspires people today to speak His Word, which is called "continuing revelation." One Charismatic leader expresses his delight when someone in his worship "speaks a 'Thus saith the Lord' and dares to address the fellowship in the first person—even going beyond the words of Scripture." One would infer from this statement that the Charismatic preacher is saying that the Bible is not the final, ultimate authority and source of God's revelation to man. "Continuing revelation" most certainly contradicts Thomas Campbell's observation that "The Bible is the only rule of faith and practice for Christians."

It also seems contradictory to several Scriptures. Jude wrote, "Beloved, when I gave all diligence to write unto you of the common salvation, it was needful for me to write unto you, and exhort you that ye should earnestly contend for the faith which was once delivered unto the saints" (Jude 3). The definite article *the* before *faith means that there was a body of God's truth given to the prophets and apostles once and for all. The Greek term used here is hapax,* which refers to that which is done for all time, with lasting results, and never needing repetition. Also, Jude 3 says "the faith . . . once delivered." The word *delivered* in the Greek is an aorist passive participle and can only mean an act completed in the past with no continuing element. Its being in the passive voice also means that it was received by the saints from God, and not conceived by them. Two other New Testament verses, Galatians 1:23 and 1 Timothy 4:1, use the term *the faith* and show the apostle Paul's knowledge of a body of divine truth given to man by God.

Those within the restoration movement could never accept anyone's claim to "continuing revelation." They hold the Scripture as the inspired, authoritative, written Word, once and for all given to the saints to reveal God, His will, and love for man.

A second emphasis of the Charismatics of great concern to Christians within the restoration movement is "subjectivism." It relies upon personal experience for assurance of salvation and knowledge of God. The Charismatic may express his subjectivism this way: "This is what happened to me, and the experience is the reason I believe." One should not doubt the sincerity of most of those who so testify, but he has the right, even obligation, to test both its validity and interpretation. There are those who testify that they walked the streets of Heaven in a vision, or took a picture of God with a *Kodak* camera, and some have even received the "instruction" to do something immoral. These are rare, but they show the danger of subjectivism.

Experience has its rightful place in the Christian life. Love, joy, and peace, for example, should be experienced by the Christian. But every experience must be examined in the searchlight of Scripture. Someone has used the illustration of the railroad train. The engine represents faith, which comes from hearing, reading, or being taught the Word of God. It contains the power to pull the entire train to its destination. The cars that follow are the experiences one has in Christ—the feelings of joy, forgiveness, brotherhood, cleansing—which are important. However, these feelings do not assure one of salvation, nor do they possess the power to carry him to Heaven. Faith must come first and guide one in the

Christian life. Then the experiences that follow will be real, legitimate, and edificatory.

The modern-day Charismatic movement is not harmless. It has split churches, ruined ministries, and caused deep disillusionment. It puts one on a roller-coaster of feeling, with highs and lows, which cannot edify or make one strong in Christ. John MacArthur, in his book, *The Charismatics,* quotes one who suffered this disappointment. George Gardener, a former Pentecostal, said:

> So the seeker of experience goes back through the ritual again and again, but begins to discover something; ecstatic experience, like drug addiction, requires larger and larger doses to satisfy. Sometimes the bizarre is introduced. I have seen people run around a room until they are exhausted, climb tent poles, laugh hysterically, go into trances for days and do other weird things as the "high" sought became more elusive. Eventually there is a crisis and a decision is made; he will sit on the back seat and be a spectator, "fake it," or go on in the hope that everything will eventually be as it was. The most tragic decision is to quit, and in the quitting abandon all things spiritual as fraudulent. The spectators are frustrated, the fakers suffer guilt, the hopeful are pitiful, and the quitters are a tragedy. No, such movements are not harmless.[4]

The restoration movement emphasizes rightly that it is the Word of God that edifies Christians and makes them strong in the Lord. The Scripture represents itself as milk, meat, and bread to nourish the soul. Feeling will not last and cannot satisfy very long. But the Word enables one to grow toward "the measure of the stature of the fulness of Christ" (Ephesians 4:13).

NOTES

[1]Knofel Staton, *Spiritual Gifts for Christians Today* (Cincinnati: Standard Publishing Co., 1976), p. 17.

[2]John R. W. Stott, *The Baptism and Fullness of the Spirit* (Downer's Grove, IL: Inter-Varsity Press, 1964), p. 112.

[3]John MacArthur, *The Charismatics* (Grand Rapids: Zondervan, 1978), p. 162.

[4]Ibid., p. 157.

26

THE FANTASTIC FUTURE FOR THE RESTORATION IDEAL

"... speaking the truth in love"
(Ephesians 4:15)

The admonition, "speaking the truth in love," was given to Ephesian Christians within the context of their growing toward maturity in Christ. It is one that the restoration movement must heed as it moves into the future. To teach the truth without love will accomplish little because the spirit is wrong. Conversely, however, to forsake truth in the attempt to be loving will mean to be unfaithful to the mission of God's people. The truth in Christ can be communicated by those within the restoration movement in a loving, winsome way. IT MUST BE!

With this in mind, the restoration ideal remains a viable option to guide those who believe in Christ. It calls for them to unite on the basis of the Bible. Those who have embraced this option believe that persons can be Christians only if they would but follow the Bible only, do Bible things in Bible ways, and call Bible things by Bible names. This ideal calls them to be both Biblical and undenominational. It is an honorable plea and a viable position.

Now, let us consider that which the restoration movement has to share in this modern age and that with which it must not be stingy.

First, it has the right **creed** to share with others in love. Peter first confessed it on the coast of Caesarea Phillipi. He said, "Thou art the Christ, the Son of the living God" (Matthew 16:16). Walter Scott called this truth "the Golden Oracle," the heart, center, and the core of the Christian faith, the foundation upon which Jesus would build His church. He said, "'Jesus is the Christ,' is the sun to which all other Christian truths are planets in the spiritual solar system."

Someone has observed that the liberal's faith is God-centered. He sees God in everything. He looks upon Him as the Heavenly clock-maker who wound up the universe, set it into motion, and now just lets it run. The charismatic's faith is Holy Spirit-centered. If you don't believe this, step into one of their meetings and mention the Holy Spirit, and you will receive a ripple of amens from them. The Roman Catholic's faith is church-centered. He wants to know what the hierarchy says on issues. The fundamentalist's faith is book-centered. But the restoration movement's faith remains Christ-centered; He is the fullness of deity in the flesh, the one to receive the pre-eminence. He is to be uplifted so all people can be attracted unto Him, for God said, "This is my beloved Son: hear him" (Mark 9:7). The truth that Jesus Christ is Lord must be shared with others. (See Philippians 2:9-11.) It is the creed to which all believers can subscribe.

Because the movement centers in the right creed, its constituency wears the best **name.** They are Christians. The apostle Peter said, "If man suffer as a Christian, let him not be ashamed; but let him glorify God in this name" (1 Peter 4:16, ASV). Barton Warren Stone believed that it had been both prophesied and oracularly given. He believed Isaiah referred to it when he said God's people would be called "by a new name, which the mouth of the Lord shall name, an everlasting name "better than of sons and of daughters . . . that shall not be cut off" (Isaiah 62:2 and 56:5). Therefore, he believed that when the disciples were first called Christians in Antioch in Acts 11, it was no accident or nickname, but that they were oracularly called Christians by God himself.

Stone believed that it was the one name around which all believers could unite. He said, in his discourse on Christian union, "To be united we must receive the one name given by divine appointment, which is the name Christian. Let all others be cast away and forgotten." He was convinced that every follower of Christ would be proud to honor God with that name. They could be Christians only. It was a divine name that could be shared with all in love.

The restoration movement looks to the right **Book.** Thomas Campbell was first to glimpse the vision of the unity of God's people on the basis of the Bible. He said that the Bible is the only rule of faith and practice for Christians; the one authoritative Word men have from God. It is true that the movement is Christ-centered, but no one can learn an authoritative truth about Jesus that does not come from the Bible. In fact, the whole book concerns Him. The restoration fathers pointed out correctly that the Old Testament is "the schoolmaster" (cf. Galatians 3:23-29) that prepared for the coming of Christ, and everything in the New Testament emanates from His person.

The movement remains a people of the Book. It seeks to speak where the Scripture speaks and remain silent where the Scripture is silent, as Thomas Campbell admonished. It believes that persons can be Christians only if they will but follow the Bible only, and commends this ideal to the religious world in love.

The restoration movement patterns after the right **church**. It seeks to restore the essential marks of the church as it was given to the apostles and is found in the New Testament. It is important for one to understand that the church belongs to Christ. He purchased it with His own blood and gave himself for it. Church members have no right to shape the church after their own intentions. To the contrary, they are to shape it according to Christ's plan that it might fulfill His purposes.

Alexander Campbell believed the essence of the church as Christ would have it can be found in the New Testament. He would ask, "Where else can it be found?" The ancient order of the church must be restored for it to be able to fulfill its mission. He believed that persons could be Christians only if they would but follow the Bible only and do Bible things in Bible ways and call Bible things by Bible names. This remains an exciting challenge to the restoration movement that it commends to others.

The movement has the most nearly explicit explanation of the **plan of salvation** to share in love. It begins with an explanation that everyone has sinned, is a sinner, and needs God's forgiveness, and goes on to explain how God's grace can be received by the sinner. No one can ever become a Christian until he recognizes this need. The gospel says, "Christ died for our sins" (1 Corinthians 15:3). This means that the one who knew no sin, but was prepared from the foundation of the world to be the Lamb of God to take away the sin of the world, went to the cross and paid the penalty for the Christian's sins there. *Faith* means to trust in Jesus alone for salvation—not one's own virtue, good works, or righteousness. It means for him to trust in Christ's atoning death on the cross to save him. "For by grace are ye saved" (Ephesians 2:8). When one wants Jesus to be his Savior, he must decide to become a Christian. The New Testament calls this *repentance*. It means to turn from sin to walk in righteousness; to give one's life to Christ, to belong to Him. Then, when a person wants Jesus to be his Savior and wants to be a Christian, Jesus tells him to take two steps. The first one is to *confess* his faith before men. Jesus said, "Whosoever therefore, shall confess me before men, him will I confess also before my Father which is in heaven" (Matthew 10:32). *Christian baptism* becomes the mark, seal, sign, climax, and culmination of one's acceptance of Christ in faith. And, with that faith and obedience, come at least four blessings from God: the remission of sins, the gift of the Holy Spirit, the promise of Heaven, and adoption into the family of God.

Walter Scott called this explanation of the plan of salvation "the gospel restored." Thousands have accepted Christ from this simple presentation, and many more thousands await its presentation to them. The movement must reach out in love to those who are lost outside of Christ with this simple, overt plan He has prescribed.

Finally, the restoration movement has the noblest **plea** to share with others in love. It calls for the unity of believers on the basis of the Bible in answer to Jesus' prayer. He asked in John 17, "Holy Father, keep through thine own name those whom thou hast given me, that they may be one, as we are. Neither pray I for these alone, but for them also which believe on me through their word; that they all may be one; as thou Father, art in me, and I in thee, that they may also be one in us: that the world may believe that thou hast sent me" (John 17:11, 20, 21). The movement earnestly seeks the realization of this prayer for unity by its Lord. The plea is for all to become Christians as they follow the Bible, striving to restore the church as it was given to the apostles and seeking the lost with the simple plan of salvation He has given. It is a noble plea, one that must be shared.

Never has the future looked brighter for the restoration movement. Many contemporary believers have experienced disillusionment in the attempt to effect church union by compromise. This has not worked, and, in some instances, has decimated every resemblance to a Biblical faith. These same people and others are disgusted by the cults that have arisen in the spiritual vacuum left by theological liberalism. They want to unite with other Christians in a faith centered in Christ and rooted in the Word of God.

The restoration ideal can lead these people to that which they seek. They have been searching for such a guide as it, and the movement that embodies the ideal must not be stingy with it. Instead, it must enter into the future with both vision and boldness to disseminate its blessings.

Attitude on the part of those who comprise the movement will determine much of how effectively Christ will be able to use it. A condemnatory view of others has often manifested itself among those who want to restore the New Testament church. It used to be called "skinning the sects." This attitude is both unwarranted and counterproductive, and it contradicts the Biblical principle of "speaking the truth in love." One does not have to condemn others in order to be faithful to the restoration ideal. A positive, warm presentation of it will accomplish much more.

An isolationist, exclusionist attitude will likewise be unproductive. The early leaders of the movement never considered themselves as the *only* Christians. That position would necessitate an unwarranted judgmental decision on the part of those who seek to be Christians only. Stone, the Campbells, and Scott looked upon themselves as a part of a movement within the church, calling all believers back to the church as it was given to the apostles. They did not want it to atrophy into a denomination, isolated from other believers by human creeds and traditions. The restoration movement must move into the future as a movement, not a sect, to be effective. It can respect the integrity of others and rejoice at their good works, as it calls them to unite on a Biblical basis. Once again, this is "speaking the truth in love."

The restoration movement must continue and quicken certain practices received from previous generations in order for it to be effective in the future. Foremost among these is *evangelism*. The gospel remains "the power of God unto salvation" (Romans 1:16). Jesus is still the only name under Heaven whereby persons can be saved (Acts 4:12). He instructed His church to go out and make believers. It was to bring people into such a proximity with the gospel that they could be saved by it. The congregations of the restoration movement must never leave this "first love" (Revelation 2:4). One that sits back comfortably, even though it might embody right doctrines, cannot be a church after the New Testament order. There must be a concerted effort to reach the lost. Walter Scott was deeply hurt when he found churches in his era that sought to be undenominational but had no passion to reach those outside of Christ. Jesus' parable of the wedding feast teaches that Christians must go out to invite people to their Father's feast until His house is filled (Luke 14:23). Someone has compared the church assembled on the Lord's Day to a "launching pad." The members meet for "refueling" and then are propelled out into their communities to witness. This most certainly follows the New Testament precedent, for Acts 8:4 says everywhere the early Christians went, they preached or witnessed. A church that wants to be Biblical must keep foremost in its purpose the reaching out to the lost with the news of salvation to be found in Christ.

Evangelism necessitates *discipling*. Evangelism brings one into Christ; discipling nurtures one in Him. The Biblical word *edification* best describes this necessity. It means "building up; making one strong; nourishing." Paul said to the Corinthians that they had to be fed "the milk of the word," and not "the meat," because they were carnal. His statement pictures one coming into the church as a "babe in Christ." He must be fed from the Word that which he can digest. Then, as he grows, he can ingest more profound truths.

Discipling requires that the congregation become both a family and a school. It is in a family that a child receives the love, support, and security he needs in order to grow. A babe in Christ will make mistakes, and his naivete will be evident. But a loving family will absorb these with understanding and support him in such a way as to enable him to grow in both grace and knowledge. A school teaches, and no one should ever doubt the church's responsibility in this effort. Jesus' Great Commission commands that those who have been made believers shall be taught "all things" that He commands (Matthew 28:20).

New Christians themselves must take their Christian education seriously. Paul said, "Study to show thyself approved unto God, a workman that needeth not to be ashamed, rightly dividing the word of truth" (2 Timothy 2:15).

A congregation must seek a balance between evangelism and discipling because the one depends upon the other. Someone observed that many churches are long on "obstetrics" and short on "pediatrics." He meant that they expend so much energy to bring people into Christ as "babes" that they have nothing left for their nurture. This happens sometimes. However, the opposite can be hurtful, also. A congregation may have an elaborate educational program, but, if it does not reach out to bring people into Christ, the program will do no one any good. An effective congregation will achieve a balance. It will be seen reaching out to bring people into Christ so that they can be fed the "milk" and "meat" of His word to enable them to grow in Him.

Christians within the restoration movement must continue a worldwide mission of evangelism and discipling. Many call this *missions,* or *world outreach.* They must seek to reach those both at home and away from home. Jesus told the disciples to go "into all the world" (Mark 16:15), and that they were to be His witnesses "both in Jerusalem, and in all Judea, and in Samaria, and unto the uttermost part of the earth" (Acts 1:8). The early Christians took the gospel around the world with great zeal, and that cause remains an essential mark of the New Testament church. Those of the restoration movement have sought to restore this mark. Missionary zeal surged within the movement at the end of the nineteenth century and in the early part of the twentieth. A renewal of that zeal has come in more recent years and must continue. Jesus ordained the church to be His agency of world evangelism and discipleship.

Christians should be encouraged by what has happened in missions. The secular world has held missionaries in disdain and even some liberal churches have called them meddlers. However, developments in recent years have more than justified their efforts. Indigenous churches in traditionally non-Christian countries are maturing. Some, such as China, have withstood brutal persecution and survived. Expulsion of missionaries in some places has even caused the church there to grow stronger. Lands where American missionaries went a generation ago now send out missionaries themselves, notably South Korea and the Philippines. One missiologist suggests that the great strength of Christianity by the turn of the twenty-first century will be in the third-world countries. "Christians only" have shared in the work that produced these victories and must continue in it with vigor to take the truth of Christ into all the world with love.

The restoration movement of this generation has received a heritage from its forefathers in *evangelism, discipling,* and *missions.* They may need refinement, but no remission. They remain an essential part of what must be restored in love.

Now the movement must look into the future. The Bible warns, "Where there is no vision, the people perish" (Proverbs 29:18), for no movement remains more than a generation away from extinction. If the baton of faith is not passed on to the new generation, it dies. The future looks bright for the restoration movement, and it may have more vitality now than ever before. It can move forward from a strong base. But it must *move* in order to remain a movement. If it merely takes pride in what its forefathers accomplished, it will shrivel up into just another denomination. The people who believe in the restoration ideal must take some bold steps into the future.

First, they must remember that Christian unity on a Biblical basis remains a primary goal. The future offers opportunity to reach out to others with the invitation to join them in that quest. History demands that rapprochement be made toward the a cappella Church of Christ. This constituency possesses so much in common, both historically and doctrinally, with all those who believe in the restoration ideal. Some within the a cappella fellowship earnestly desire this commonality, and it must be welcomed and encouraged. Nothing brings deeper fellowship than kinship. Those who choose to worship without the musical instrument possess a common heritage from the restoration movement that should make rapprochement possible.

Also, the hand of friendship should be extended to those within the Disciples of Christ churches who will not want to enter into a merger with the United Church of Christ. Many of these people believe in Biblical Christianity as sincerely as anyone, and they have a kinship with those in the restoration movement that is deep. Their faith would enable them to feel much more at home among those with whom they have that heritage.

"Evangelicals" comprise another group with whom conversation should be sought. These people believe without reservation in the deity of Christ, salvation through His blood, and the inspiration of Scripture. They, like the restoration movement, are both evangelistic and missionary-minded. Many of their churches have grown large in recent years. However, conversation with them may be difficult. They have traditionally held the churches of the restoration movement at arm's length because of the latter's association of Christian baptism with salvation (1 Peter 3:21; Acts 2:38, 41; 22:16; Mark 16:16; Romans 6:3). Most evangelicals teach salvation by "faith only." (See James 2:24.) This association also makes it difficult for the two of them to enter into evangelistic efforts together. But there remains the possibility of seeking conversation with these people in the interest of Christian unity on a Biblical basis without compromising one's faith. At least, there should be the attempt to discuss the truth in love with them.

Another opportunity, peculiar to this age, presents itself to the restoration movement. It lies in the area of communications.

The means of communicating have exploded in this present age. By satellite television, events can be seen in one's living room the instant they occur on the other side of the world. Someone pointed out that the prediction of every eye beholding Christ when He returns may now be possible through that means. Millions can hear a presentation of the gospel at one time through it. Radio is much older, but it remains a relatively new medium through which Bible lessons can be presented with broad dissemination. The printed word is another means "Christians only" have at their disposal, with new, inexpensive means of publication having come in recent years.

The restoration movement must enter into the new communications opportunities with greater vigor. Some denominational ministers preach to millions each week by means of them. Their message may not even be well presented, but they reach many people with it because of their utilization of television, radio, and the printed media. Few preachers in the restoration movement speak to more than hundreds each week. Means must be sought for wider dissemination of their plea with the knowledge that opportunities are available.

A bright future appears ahead for the restoration movement. It must remain faithful to the ideal that brought it into existence and move into the new era with optimism. It does not have so much of which to be ashamed as it has something to share. It may not have fully restored the New Testament church to its pristine purity, but many believe it is on the right track. It has the opportunity to move into the future to speak the truth in love.